Competition Policy in East Asia

Competition Policy in East Asia draws together a collection of papers on competition policy that were presented at the Twenty-Eighth Conference of the Pacific Area Forum on Trade and Development (PAFTAD), held in Manila on 16–18 September 2002. It seeks to clarify the issues and provide a framework for understanding competition policy, looking in depth at a number of regulated sectors for additional perspectives.

Until two or three decades ago, competition and consumer protection policies were the preserve of the major developed economies like the United States, the United Kingdom and some European countries. Now competition issues are at the top of the international agenda as globalisation spreads and as the operations of the World Trade Organisation, the World Bank, the Asia Pacific Economic Cooperation forum and other organisations have brought about a realisation that regulatory reform – and in many economies the creation for the first time of regulatory instruments for competition and consumer protection – is an imperative.

Erlinda M. Medalla is Senior Research Fellow at the Philippine Institute for Development Studies and Project Director of the Philippine APEC Study Center Network Secretariat.

Pacific Trade and Development Conference Series
Edited by Peter Drysdale, Australia–Japan Research Centre, The Australian National University

Titles published by Routledge in association with the PAFTAD International Secretariat and the Australia–Japan Research Centre, The Australian National University include:

Business, Markets and Government in the Asia Pacific
Edited by Rong-I Wu and Yun-Peng Chu

Asia Pacific Financial Deregulation
Edited by Gordon de Brouwer and Wisarn Pupphavesa

Asia Pacific Economic Cooperation/APEC: Challenges and Tasks for the 21st Century
Edited by Ippei Yamazawa

Globalization and the Asia Pacific Economy
Edited by Kyung Tae Lee

The New Economy in East Asia and the Pacific
Edited by Peter Drysdale

Competition Policy in East Asia
Edited by Erlinda M. Medalla

Competition Policy in East Asia

Edited by
Erlinda M. Medalla

LONDON AND NEW YORK

First published 2005 by Routledge
2 Park Square, Milton Park, Abingdon, Oxon OX14 4RN

Simultaneously published in the USA and Canada by Routledge
270 Madison Ave, New York, NY 10016

Routledge is an imprint of the Taylor & Francis Group

Transferred to Digital Printing 2007

© 2005 PAFTAD International Secretariat for selection and editorial matter; individual chapters, the contributors

All rights reserved. No part of this book may be reprinted or reproduced or utilised in any form or by any electronic, mechanical, or other means, now known or hereafter invented, including photocopying and recording, or in any information storage or retrieval system, without permission in writing from the publishers.

British Library Cataloguing in Publication Data
A catalogue record for this book is available from the British Library

Library of Congress Cataloging in Publication Data
A catalog record for this book has been requested.

Publishers note: This book has been prepared from camera-ready copy provided by PAFTAD International Secretariat.

ISBN10: 0–415–35075–1 (hbk)
ISBN10: 0–415–43599–4 (pbk)

ISBN13: 978–0–415–35075–4 (hbk)
ISBN13: 978–0–415–43599–4 (pbk)

Publisher's Note
The publisher has gone to great lengths to ensure the quality of this reprint but points out that some imperfections in the original may be apparent
Printed and bound by CPI Antony Rowe, Eastbourne

Contents

List of figures vii
List of tables viii
List of contributors xi
Preface xiii
Abbreviations xv

1 Perspectives on competition policy: an overview of
  the issues 1
  Erlinda M. Medalla

2 The evolution of competition law in East Asia 15
  Ping Lin

3 Implementing an effective competition policy: skills and
  synergies 41
  Rod Shogren

4 Competition policy, economic development and the possible
  role of a multilateral framework on competition policy:
  insights from the WTO working group on trade and
  competition policy 61
  Robert Anderson and Frédéric Jenny

5 Competition in electricity markets 86
  Maria Fe Villamejor-Mendoza

6 Telecommunications 111
  Christopher Findlay, Roy Chun Lee, Alexandra Sidorenko
  and Mari Pangestu

7 The airline industry 145
  Ralph Huenemann and Anming Zhang

vi Contents

8	The shipping industry *Deunden Nikomborirak*	170
9	The insurance industry *Melanie S. Milo*	186
10	The interaction between contract and competition law *Lewis Evans and Neil Quigley*	213
11	Regional cooperation in competition policy *David K. Round*	231
	Index	257

Figures

1.1	Assessing market power in an industry	7
1.2	Major functions of competition policy	9
3.1	A model for assessing economic objectives	47
5.1	Structure of the electricity industry under initial reforms	87
5.2	Structure of the electricity industry envisaged in Republic Act 9136	98
6.1	Index values in selected economies, 1998 and 2002	118
6.2	Policy changes in selected economies in absolute and percentage terms	118
6.3	The state of telecommunications policy liberalisation and the rate of liberalisation over 1998–2002	119
8.1	Top twenty liner operators (TEUs)	175
9.1	Insurance density: premiums per capita in the ASEAN5, 1994–2000	191
9.2	Insurance penetration: premiums as per cent of GDP in the ASEAN5, 1994–2000	192
9.3	Insurance density and insurance penetration in the United States and Asia, 2000	193
9.4	Life and nonlife insurance premium volumes in the ASEAN5, 1994–2000	193

Tables

1.1	Competition policy and law in APEC economies in 2002	10
2.1	Competition laws in selected East Asian countries	17
2.2	Main provisions of Japan's Antimonopoly Act	19
2.3	Court cases brought by the JFTC, 1995–2000	24
2.4	Competition cases concluded by China's State Administration for Industry and Commerce	29
2.5	Competition cases completed by the Hong Kong Telecommunications Authority	33
3.1	Comparing competition policy and economic regulation	57
3.2	Comparing the roles of competition agencies and economic regulators	58
B4.1	Relevant paragraphs of the Doha Ministerial Declaration	78
5.1	Major laws and regulations affecting the electricity industry	88
5.2	The number of IPP plants started up between 1986 and 1998	96
5.3	The national energy generation mix, 1990–2004	102
5.4	The age of NPC plants, 1992	103
5.5	Market share of private utilities, by number of customers, 2000–03	104

5.6	Average systems loss of electric cooperatives, 1997–2000	105
5.7	Average systems loss of private utilities, 1997–2000	106
5.8	Comparison of transmission and distribution losses in selected Asian countries, 1994	107
5.9	Average rates of Asian utilities, 1997	107
6.1	Individual components of the policy index, 1998–2002	117
6.2	Regression analysis of the influence of policy on penetration rates	121
6.3	Price and quantity impacts from market access policy in fixed telecommunications, index = MA/invest (fixed)	122
6.4	Price and quantity impacts from national treatment policy, index = NT/invest	123
6.5	Price and quantity impacts from market access policy in mobile telecommunications, index = MA/invest (mobile)	123
A6.1	Policy information by economy	131
7.1	Projected airfreight shipments in Asia Pacific, 2000	149
7.2	China's trade with Japan and South Korea	163
B8.1	Other forms of liner shipping arrangements	173
8.1	Tax exemptions offered to registered liner shipping companies in the ASEAN5	178
8.2	Conditions placed on foreign liners registering in the ASEAN5	179
B8.2	Doha Declaration	183
9.1	Number of insurance companies by type of business in the ASEAN5	187
9.2	Number of insurance companies by type of ownership in the ASEAN5	188

9.3	Foreign participation in the insurance industry in the ASEAN5, 1999	189
9.4	Degree of concentration in the insurance industry in the ASEAN5, 1999	189
9.5	Insurance sectors in the four incipient ASEAN markets, 1997	195
9.6	Size of the financial sector in the ASEAN5	195
9.7	Insurance regulation in the ASEAN5	208

Contributors

Robert Anderson, Counsellor, Intellectual Property Division, WTO Secretariat.

Lewis Evans, Professor of Economics, Victoria University of Wellington; Executive Director, New Zealand Institute for the Study of Competition and Regulation.

Christopher Findlay, Professor of Economics, Asia Pacific School of Economics and Government, The Australian National University.

Ralph Huenemann, Professor of International Business, University of Victoria; Founding Director, Centre for Asia-Pacific Initiatives.

Frédéric Jenny, Professor of Economics, ESSEC Business School, Paris; Vice-Chair, Conseil de la Concurrence, France; Chair, OECD Competition Committee; Chair, WTO Working Group on the Interaction between Trade and Competition Policy.

Roy Chun Lee, PhD Student, Asia Pacific School of Economics and Government, The Australian National University.

Ping Lin, Professor of Economics, Department of Economics, the Lingnan University, Hong Kong.

Erlinda M. Medalla, Senior Research Fellow, Philippine Institute for Development Studies (PIDS).

Maria Fe Villamejor-Mendoza, Assistant Professor for Public Policy and Public Enterprise, the National College of Public Administration and Governance (NCPAG), University of the Philippines.

Melanie S. Milo, Research Fellow, PIDS.

Deunden Nikomborirak, Research Director, the Economic Governance Section, the Thailand Development Research Institute (TDRI).

Mari Pangestu, Director, Board of the Centre for Strategic and International Studies, Jakarta.

Neil Quigley, Pro Vice-Chancellor (International) and Professor of Economics, Victoria University of Wellington; Adjunct Scholar, the C.D. Howe Institute, Toronto; Research Principal, ISCR.

David K. Round, Professor of Economics and Director, Centre for Applied Economics, University of South Australia.

Rod Shogren, Consultant, Access Economics Pty Limited, Australia.

Alexandra Sidorenko, Post-doctoral Fellow, Australia–Japan Research Centre, The Australian National University.

Anming Zhang, Associate Professor, YVR Professor in Air Transportation, University of British Columbia, Canada.

Preface

Although the justification for competition policy is well founded in the economic literature, in recent years there has been fresh discussion about the benefits of competition policy, largely because of the linkage identified with increased international trade. During the World Trade Organisation (WTO) ministerial meeting in December 1996 this linkage was highlighted as one of the four 'Singapore issues' that warranted further study by the WTO. More recently awareness has grown of the need to understand competition policy and its implications more fully in terms of a country's reform agenda and development objectives.

It is against this backdrop that the theme Competition Policy in the New Millennium was adopted for the twenty-eighth conference of the Pacific Area Forum on Trade and Development, held in Manila on 16–18 September 2002. The major aim of the PAFTAD conference, and this book, is to contribute to the debate and increase understanding of the issues surrounding competition policy.

This book contains eleven papers presented at the conference. The first four chapters provide a framework for understanding competition policy. The next five provide perspectives from selected sectors and draw some lessons about regulatory approaches. The last two chapters deal with the interaction between contract law and competition law, and regional cooperation on competition policy and enforcement in East Asia.

In this endeavour, profuse thanks are owed to the many individuals and institutions who provided their abiding and invaluable support for the project. PAFTAD twenty-eight received financial support from a number of institutions: the PAFTAD International Secretariat, which is the major sponsor of the annual conference; TAPS-PhilExport; USAID (Philippines); the Asia Foundation; and the Philippine Institute for Development Studies (PIDS), which hosted the conference during the institute's twenty-fifth anniversary. Among the key people responsible for the conceptualisation and planning of the conference were Hugh Patrick, Chairman of the International Steering Committee; Peter Drysdale, Director of the PAFTAD International Secretariat; and Mario Lamberte, President of PIDS and Chairman of the Local Steering Committee. They deserve special recognition for their steadfast support of PAFTAD. Thanks are also due to the then Philippine Secretary of Socio-Economic Planning, Dante Canlas, who delivered the opening address, and to the discussants, whose contributions made the conference lively and informative. Many PIDS staff helped ensure the success of the conference: thanks go to the teams led by Jennifer Liguton, Andrea Agcaoili and Mario Feranil. Finally, the publication of this book would not have been possible without the support of the Australia–Japan Research Centre, particularly Andrew Deane of the PAFTAD International Secretariat and Marilyn Popp. Finally, my appreciation to Sarah Leeming for her superb editing.

Erlinda M. Medalla
August 2003

Abbreviations

ACCC	Australian Competition and Consumer Commission
AFAS	ASEAN Framework Agreement on Services
AMPS	advanced mobile phone system
ANA	All Nippon Airways
APEC	Asia Pacific Economic Cooperation forum
ASA	air services agreement
ASEAN	Association for Southeast Asian Nations
BNM	Bank Negara Malaysia
BOT	build-operate-transfer
CAB	Civil Aeronautics Board
CAT	Communications Authority Thailand
CATV	cable television
CEO	chief executive officer
CERTA	Closer Economic Relations Trade Agreement
COMESA	Common Market for Eastern and Southern Africa
CPCN	certificate of public convenience and necessity
CRS	computer reservation system
DOE	Department of Energy
ECC	Energy Coordinating Council
ERB	Energy Regulatory Board
ERC	Energy Regulatory Commission
EU	European Union
FASC	Federation ASEAN Shippers Council
FCC	Federation Communications Commission
FMC	Federal Maritime Commission
FSA	Financial Services Agreement
GATS	General Agreement on Trade in Services
GATT	General Agreement on Tariffs and Trade
GDP	gross domestic product
GENCO	generating company
GPA	Government Procurement Agreement
GSM	global system for mobile telecommunications
HFC	hybrid fibre-coaxial

IATA	International Air Transport Association
ICAO	International Civil Aviation Organisation
IMF	International Monetary Fund
IPP	independent power producer
JAL	Japan Air Lines
JAS	Japan Air Systems
JFTC	Japan Fair Trade Commission
KAL	Korean Air
KDD	Kokusai Denshin Denwa
KGCL	Kapuni Gas Contracts Ltd
KT	Korea Telecom
KWH	kilowatt hour
LAN	local area networks
MAS	Malaysia Airlines
MAS	Monetary Authority of Singapore
METI	Ministry of Economy, Trade and Industry
MFN	most favoured nation
MHZ	megahertz
MITI	Ministry of International Trade and Industry
MOU	Memorandum of Understanding
MW	megawatts
NAFTA	North American Free Trade Agreement
NEA	National Electrification Administration
NMT	Nordic Mobile Telephones
NPC	National Power Corporation
NTT	Nippon Telegraph and Telephone
OEA	Office of Energy Affairs
OECD	Organisation for Economic Cooperation and Development
PAFTAD	Pacific Area Forum on Trade and Development
PAL	Philippine Airlines
PECC	Pacific Economic Cooperation Council
PIDS	Philippine Institute for Development Studies
PLDT	Philippine Long Distance Telephone Company
PPA	purchased power adjustment
PSALM	Power Sector Assets and Liaibilities Management Corporation
PSC	Public Service Commission
RBC	risk-based capital
REC	rural electric cooperative
RORB	return-on-rate-base
RTA	regional trade agreement
SAIC	State Administration for Industry and Commerce
SETC	State Economic and Trade Commission
SIA	Singapore International Airlines
SPUG	small power utilities group
TEU	twenty-foot equivalent unit

TMNC	Thai Maritime Navigation Company
TOT	Telephone Organisation of Thailand
TPT-WG	Transportation Working Group
TRANSCO	National Transmission Company
TRIPS	Trade-Related Aspects of Intellectual Property Rights
UK	United Kingdom
UNCTAD	United Nations Conference on Trade and Development
US	United States
USO	universal service obligation
VAT	value-added tax
VECO	Visayas Electric Company
VOIP	voice over internet protocol
WTO	World Trade Organisation

1 Perspectives on competition policy: an overview of the issues

Erlinda M. Medalla

INTRODUCTION

Competition policy has been the subject of debate at the international level for some time now, but especially since 1996, when it was included among a number of issues to be discussed by the World Trade Organisation (WTO). The early multilateral discussions dwelt on how domestic competition policies restrict market access. At the WTO ministerial conference in December 1996, the interaction between trade policy and competition policy was identified as one of the four 'Singapore issues' (so called after the host city) that warranted further study. In recent years the discussion has shifted somewhat to embrace a broader view of how competition policy can contribute to economic development. As barriers to trade have continued to fall, factors have become more mobile and technological change has increased, countries have been re-examining the place of competition policy in an overall national framework, often moving ahead of the policy agendas being shaped in international forums.

This book draws together a collection of papers on competition policy that were presented at the Twenty-Eighth Conference of the Pacific Area Forum on Trade and Development (PAFTAD), held in Manila on 16–18 September 2002. It seeks to clarify the issues and provide a framework for understanding competition policy, looking in depth at a number of regulated sectors for additional perspectives.

The book contains eleven chapters. The first four chapters outline a framework for competition policy, describe the work that has been undertaken in the WTO on the linkages between trade policy and competition policy, and discuss implementation issues. This introductory chapter, among others, suggests a broad framework for competition policy that would cover, in varying degrees depending on the objectives of different countries, four main areas: the antitrust or competition law at its core, consumer protection measures, the regulation of monopolies, and a review of other domestic policies and regulations that may affect competition.

Succeeding chapters build on this framework and discuss some of the major competition policy debates, including whether there is a need for a WTO agreement on competition policy and how competition policy is best implemented.

In Chapter 2 Ping Lin examines the evolution of competition law in East Asia, comparing the frameworks in place in Japan, China and Hong Kong, and evaluating each country's ability to deter violations of competition law. The chapter highlights some common difficulties that East Asian countries face in developing an effective competition policy.

The evolution of competition policy will differ across countries, depending on the overall policy environment and the influence of stakeholders, as Rod Shogren points out in Chapter 3. This chapter discusses a range of practical issues in implementing competition policy and describes the organisational skills and culture that are needed in a competition agency. Choices will need to be made in deciding whether competition policy and regulation should be carried out within a single agency or whether regulation is better undertaken by sector-specific agencies.

Chapter 4, by Robert Anderson and Frédéric Jenny, explains that current proposals for competition policy agreements do not explicitly link competition policy with market access concerns; rather they aim to ensure that all countries have national legislation in place to deal with anticompetitive practices. The authors predict that cooperation between member states on competition policy issues will most likely be voluntary and note that a commitment to competitive markets rather than regulatory approaches is more likely to increase economic welfare.

The next five chapters review regulatory approaches in the electricity, telecommunications, airline, shipping and insurance sectors. These chapters describe the intricacies in regulation, the difficulties in balancing objectives, and the need for clear principles and policies.

Chapter 5, by Maria Fe Villamejor-Mendoza, describes the evolution of the Philippine electricity sector, which has moved from being dominated by a public monopoly to gradual privatisation. The sector provides an example of the enormity of the task of transforming state-owned industries in developing countries. Reforms include the development of a wholesale spot market, the segregation of subsectors and the unbundling of tariffs. Although policy issues and legal challenges are still to be faced, these reforms are moving the sector in the right direction.

Telecommunications is another sector where regulatory reforms aimed at increasing competition have brought great benefits. Chapter 6, by Christopher Findlay, Roy Chun Lee, Alexandra Sidorenko and Mari Pangestu, reviews policy in a number of Asia Pacific economies. It provides information on their commitments under the General Agreement on Trade in Services (GATS) and on the extent of implementation. The policy environment in these countries is set against the performance of their telecommunications sector. Empirical work reported in the chapter shows that markets open to entry by both domestic and foreign suppliers are more competitive and should deliver better performance.

There has also been a strong trend toward deregulation and privatisation in the airline industry. In Chapter 7 Ralph Huenemann and Anming Zhang describe how substantial liberalisation in domestic and international routes over the past twenty years has improved efficiency in the industry. However, city pairs are not usually served by more than two or three carriers, so competition policy in air transport continues to confront oligopoly behaviour. The continuing resistance to cabotage and foreign ownership means that alliances between airlines will remain important. The implications for consumer welfare are ambiguous, and regulators will have difficulty in deciding which alliances to sanction.

Deunden Nikomborirak offers a further perspective from the shipping industry in Chapter 8. This chapter examines the problems governments and shippers face in countering the substantial market power of liner shipping operators that set up international cartels to set prices and allocate capacity. Blatant anticompetitive practices by liner conferences in developed countries have been sustained at the expense of shippers from developing countries with little bargaining strength. To counter this power governments should consider regulatory approaches and should push for having the issue addressed in the WTO.

In Chapter 9 Melanie Milo analyses how market structures and regulatory regimes affect competition in the insurance industry in five East Asian countries – Indonesia, Malaysia, the Philippines, Singapore and Thailand. The incipient insurance markets in the ASEAN5 continue to be highly regulated and protected. Reform of the insurance industry is still in the initial stages and more market-oriented reforms are needed.

In Chapter 10 Lewis Evans and Neil Quigley provide some perspectives on the interaction between contract law and competition law and suggest some lessons for the sequencing of reforms in developing countries. The chapter argues that priority should be given to promoting mechanisms that will reduce uncertainty about the enforceability of contracts. This means that the provisions of an existing contract could take precedence over competition law.

Finally, in Chapter 11, David Round looks at the progress being made in forging regional cooperation in East Asia on competition policy and its enforcement. The chapter suggests ways that national and regional cultures for competition can be developed. It considers how regional cooperation might be put into effect, and assesses how globalising companies might provide an added impetus to national and regional efforts to enhance domestic competitive mechanisms. The time is ripe for a leader – a particular government, or an individual, or a group – to take on the mantle of developing a truly regional approach to the promotion of competition and consumer protection.

In both developed and developing economics the role of competition is central to national goals of maximising economic benefits given scarce resources. This introductory chapter reviews the theory behind competition policy and suggests a framework that could be applicable to any market economy at any stage of development.[1] It discusses the primary objectives of competition policy, proposes an ideal framework for competition policy and looks at what will be needed to implement such a framework. It identifies the major areas of competition policy and briefly presents the current state of competition policy in the region. Then some of the issues that confront regional economies are examined.

COMPETITION POLICY OBJECTIVES

A market is perfectly competitive when there are many firms trying to outdo each other in the price and/or the quality of the product or service they offer, and when there is open entry and exit of firms. Most industries are not perfectly competitive. In reality, perfect competition is not necessary for the benefits to be realised, only effective competition – that is, the presence of an actual or potential rival that could viably contest the market. When there are no barriers to entry and the market is contestable, monopolists and oligopolists can behave like perfect competitors (Baumol and Willig 1981).

In a competitive setting, resources are allocated to where consumer welfare is optimised, led by the 'invisible hand' of market forces, in Adam Smith's words. If firms do not produce the best quality of products at the least cost, and sell at the price dictated by the market, market share will be lost to other firms. In such a setting, individual firms have no power to dictate the price or the quantity supplied in order to extract excess profits.[2] Competition, or the threat of competition, acts as an efficient market regulator that limits the market power of firms and induces production and consumption at optimal levels and costs. The result is lower prices, better quality products and wider consumer choice.

Competition also optimises efficiency by constraining firms to produce more with less (technical efficiency) and by inducing better resource allocation (allocative efficiency). Allocative efficiency is encouraged because investment is directed to where the highest returns exist. The dynamic gains from innovation that competition fosters and the flexibility that it develops enables the economy to cope better with change.

The welfare and efficiency impacts of competition are generally recognised as the main objectives of competition policy in most countries in the region. As the later chapters on selected sectors illustrate, even when regulatory objectives are entwined with social and other objectives, efficiency remains an avowed goal.

Aside from these direct benefits, another important and positive implication of competition is its effect on equity. By reducing, if not eliminating, the economic power of individual sectors and providing the best products for the best price, competition advances equity objectives.

Competition may not always be enough to ensure that the market performs its role of efficiently allocating resources. There may be genuine market failures that justify some limitation of competition – when more competition could cause inefficiencies. In such cases, rules may be needed to take the place of the competitive process that the market fails to bring about. The most notable example of a market failure is a natural monopoly, which occurs where a product or service is non-tradable and the market is too small to be optimally served by more than one firm. Allowing another firm to be established only creates duplication and wastes scarce resources. There will be a need to stipulate access rules if the monopoly provides a facility that is essential to the survival of rival firms. It can also be the case that anticompetitive conduct, such as high market concentration and mergers and acquisitions that reduce the number of firms in the market, can increase competition and efficiency by creating economies of scope or synergies between firms. Again, this would require some deviation from the general principle of discouraging market concentration.[3]

In short, competition is not an end in itself, and competition policy should promote competition as long as it encourages efficiency and growth. In addition, if possible, competition policy should be consistent with social objectives. These principles are, of course, more easily stated than applied in practice. Social objectives can conflict with competition objectives and the trade-offs are often difficult to resolve.

These considerations suggest that competition policy should primarily be about protecting and promoting competition and ensuring that the market is able to function effectively and efficiently. In many instances, this would simply entail making the market contestable by removing artificial barriers to entry, but there will be cases where the market fails and more will be required from competition policy. Additional rules will be needed to assist the market in bringing about the highest level of welfare.

In sum, competition policy has two main tasks: (1) to ensure that no entity can gain market power that it can abuse; and (2), where necessary, to implement rules that would make up for any failure of the market to perform its price-allocation function. In most instances, these rules may simply be about making the market more contestable and prohibiting and disciplining clear restraints of trade. Where market power is inherent in the structure of an industry, competition policy should strip the owner of the ability to use or abuse such power. This may require enforcing rules to guide the market and punish anticompetitive acts.

There are several steps involved in implementing competition policy. The first is to determine whether firms or groups of firms have market power. If they do, the next step is to find out how such power has been attained.

There are many factors that could affect the state of competition. Figure 1.1 describes a number of steps to be followed in determining the existence of market power in an industry and selecting a policy tool to promote greater competition. The first factor to consider is the presence of trade barriers. There is no question that the trade regime adopted by a country affects the state of competition. Simply by allowing imports to enter, some barriers to entry are broken down and the market becomes more contestable. Hence, because of its widespread impact on the economy, trade policy can be a major tool to promote competition and is usually the first to be implemented. If the good is tradable, and there are no significant barriers to trade, then it is likely that the market will be more or less contestable.

For goods that are non-tradable, perhaps because of transport costs or trade barriers, the geographic market will be limited to within local borders. In such cases there may be major barriers to entry that cannot be broken down by trade liberalisation. For instance, markets will be less contestable if domestic distribution channels are restricted to local producers through vertical integration or agreements on exclusive dealing. Such barriers will be a substantial deterrent to foreign producers, especially if there are substantial costs involved in setting up a separate distribution channel.

In determining what kind of barriers to entry are in place, it is important to ask whether the firm has deliberately erected these barriers. If barriers exist because the firm offers a superior product or is highly efficient, then this would not pose a problem. However, if the firm came about that market power through setting out to exclude other firms from the market, then it is committing an anticompetitive act that competition policy (through antitrust law) should disallow.

Two general types of anticompetitive behaviour are distinguished here. The first is deliberate efforts to exclude competitors from entering the market by means other than becoming more efficient. This is referred to as exclusionary abuse. Examples of exclusionary abuse include: predatory pricing, agreements to divide a market between firms, raising a rival's costs and unjustified refusal to deal with other firms. The second type of anticompetitive behaviour is exploitative abuse. This refers to the actual abuse of market power by setting prices above competitive levels or limiting supply. A prime example of exploitative abuse is a cartel agreement to fix prices or limit output.

Perhaps market power has resulted from structural factors or inherent market failures and rigidities that limit competition. Structural barriers to entry may not necessarily be bad for an economy if there are efficiency gains involved, for instance where there are economies of scope, synergies between firms and reductions in transaction costs. This is particularly true for natural monopolies, which have huge capital requirements that make duplication unviable and socially wasteful. These are cases where the market has failed and regulations are needed to make up for the market's inability to allocate resources efficiently.

Figure 1.1 Assessing market power in an industry

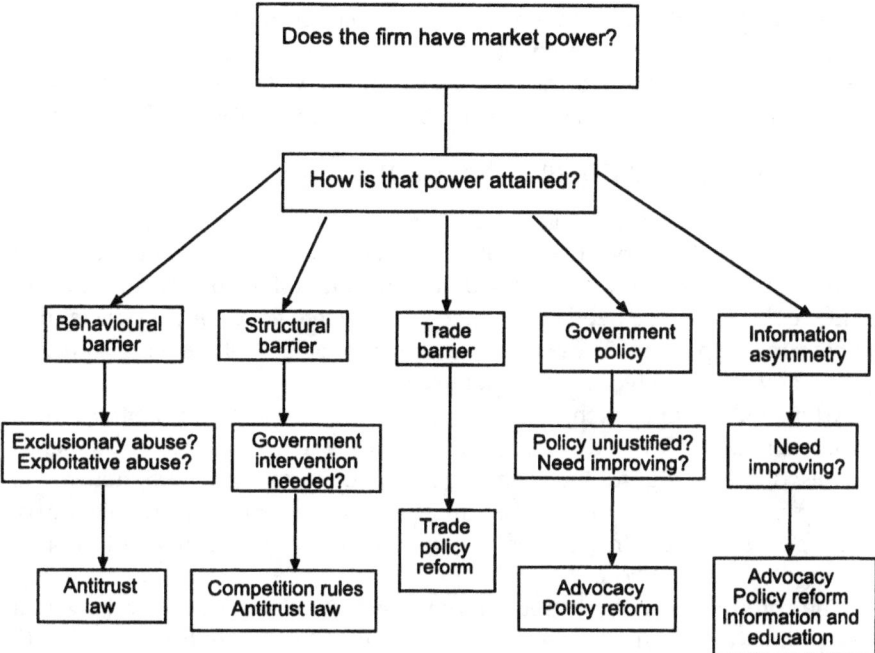

Although government policy or regulation is often needed to address structural barriers in an industry, the question of whether the rules are appropriate should still be raised. If a policy or regulation is not justified, reforms will be needed to let the market work more efficiently. The chapters on regulated sectors look more closely at the challenges governments face in attempting to address anticompetitive practices without excessively adding to administrative costs.

Aside from direct regulation of an industry, other government policies can also have an impact on competition. Even if the policy meets essential objectives, such as social or equity goals, there is reason to question whether national welfare is being served if there are serious conflicts with competition policy. This does not presume that competition policy objectives are always superior. Rather, it is wise to assess the possible trade-offs, weighing the benefits of the policy against any losses from reductions in competition. Among the various government policies and regulations, the most crucial to examine are those that directly intervene in the market, as this is where reforms are easier to isolate and the impact on competition is the most direct.

Imperfect information is another major barrier that can impede the competitive process. Where information asymmetry exists between consumers and producers, there is greater opportunity for producers to exercise market power. If consumers are not aware of the availability of other goods or the presence of competitors they cannot make informed choices, and consumer welfare is likely to be lower. In this case, the best form of consumer protection is the provision of information.

A FRAMEWORK FOR COMPETITION POLICY

The above discussion implies that there are two major requirements for competition policy to be able to fulfil its primary tasks. First, there is a need for an effective antitrust law to deal with the anticompetitive behaviour of firms. And second, there is a need to examine and evaluate government policies that impact on competition. These tasks are difficult to achieve if there is insufficient public advocacy in favour of competitive practices.

Whatever the approach of the particular country and the organisational structure in place, a working competition policy will have four main elements, as described in Figure 1.2. The suggested framework is designed to be comprehensive, covering not just antitrust law, but also the regulation of monopolies and the review of government policies and regulations that impinge on competition.

The core function of competition policy is the antitrust policy and law that deals directly with anticompetitive behaviour of firms. Antitrust law should be aimed primarily at preventing restrictive business practices and abuses of a dominant position. Considering the linkages between sectors, it should be applicable to all sectors and types of ownership. Thus, even firms under regulatory boards should be subject to the discipline of antitrust law. The objectives of the regulatory board need not be violated, as the law can allow for efficiency and public interest justifications.

A second area is the regulation of sectors where the market has completely failed and additional competition rules are needed – a prime example being the need to regulate access and pricing in the utilities sector.

Firms can also gain market power if information asymmetries exist between consumers and producers. This is why consumer protection is another inherent objective of competition policy, as it is about disciplining firm behaviour. Adequate consumer protection relies on public information and education, backed up by public advocacy for the enforcement of competition policy.

The fourth area of competition policy is the review of government policies and regulations that have an impact on competition. The most important policies and regulations to review are those that directly interfere in the market, as the impact on competition is the most direct and visible. This is a natural next step for countries that have implemented trade reforms but are not ready to fully implement an antitrust law. The review should include the regulatory framework covering natural monopolies and access to essential

Figure 1.2 Major functions of competition policy

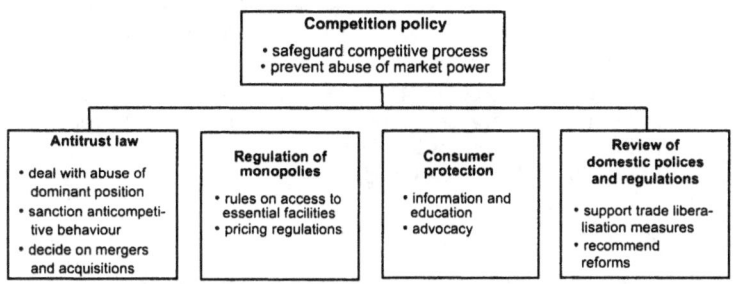

facilities. It should consider deregulating segments of the industry where greater competition may be introduced. Such a review is likely to result in strengthened competition rules, particularly on pricing and access to essential facilities. It could also examine ways to improve the administration and enforcement of the antitrust legislation.

Antitrust law, the regulation of monopolies and consumer protection are generally considered to be integral parts of competition policy. Although the review of domestic policies and regulations can involve more complex issues and is not always seen as a prime competition policy task, it should be an important part of a national competition policy as it has the ability to identify needed reforms.

It is important to emphasise that although many countries have established a central competition policy body, this need not be the case. The linkages between the four elements could be as close as feasible, or as loose as desired. For example, the task of reviewing government policies and regulations could be undertaken by the government agency involved, although this may not be as effective as where an independent body performs the review.[4] The final form the organisational structure takes should depend on what is most administratively feasible and efficient. Flexibility is the advantage of this framework, which has general applicability across countries.

SOME ISSUES

Table 1.1 provides an overview of competition policy and law in twenty-one economies in the Asia Pacific Economic Cooperation (APEC) forum. As of 2002 Brunei, Hong Kong, Malaysia, Papua New Guinea, the Philippines, Singapore, Thailand and Vietnam had no comprehensive competition law or specific institution to enforce competition policy, although some of these countries had some antitrust legislation in place. And, many of those with legislation in place had passed laws within the past decade.

Table 1.1 Competition policy and law in APEC economies in 2002

Country	Competition law	Enforcement agency
Australia	Trade Practices Act (1974) State and Territory Competition Policy Reform Application Acts Prices Surveillance Act (1983)	Australian Competition and Consumer Commission
Brunei	No specific competition law	
Canada	Competition Act (amended in 1986)	Competition Bureau of Industry Canada
Chile	Competition Law (1973)	National Economic Prosecutor's Office Antitrust Commission
China	Regulations on Development and Protection of Competition (1980) The Law of the People's Republic of China for Protecting Consumer's Rights and Interests (1993) Regulations on Anti-Dumping and Anti-Subsidisation (1997)	Industrial and Commercial Administration of China
Hong Kong	No comprehensive competition law	
Indonesia	Prohibition of Monopolistic Practices and Unfair Business Competition (1999)	Commission on Business Competition Supervision
Japan	Antimonopoly Act (1947) Act Against Unjustifiable Premiums and Misleading Representations (Premiums and Representations Act) Act Against Delay in Payment of Subcontract Proceeds	Japan Fair Trade Commission
Korea	Monopoly Regulation and Fair Trade Act (1980)	Korea Fair Trade Commission
Malaysia	No specific competition law	
Mexico	Federal Law on Economic Competition (1993)	Federal Competition Commission
New Zealand	Commerce Act (1986)	Commerce Commission
Papua New Guinea	No comprehensive competition law or specific institution to enforce competition policy	

Peru	Legislative Decree 701 (2000) Law 26876 Supreme Decree 017-98-ITINCI (2000)	INDECOPI, Commission on Free Competition
Philippines	Antitrust law and other legislation but no comprehensive competition law or specific institution to enforce competition policy	
Russia	RF Law on Competition and Limitation of Monopolistic Activity on Commodity Markets	
Singapore	No comprehensive competition law or specific institution to enforce competition policy	
Taiwan	Fair Trade Law (1991)	Fair Trade Commission
Thailand	Antitrust law but no comprehensive competition law or specific institution to enforce competition policy	
United States	Sherman Act (1880) Clayton Act (1914) Federal Trade Commission Act (1914) Robinson-Patman Act (1914) Hart-Scott-Rodino Antitrust Improvement Act (1976)	Antitrust Division, Department of Justice Federal Trade Commission
Vietnam	No specific competition law	

Note: Singapore passed competition laws with the conclusion of bilateral trade agreements with Japan and the United States.
Source: Abon (2002).

Despite the many differences in policy settings in the Asia Pacific region, there are also some notable common circumstances that could have important implications for the conduct of competition policy.

Government regulation exists in many sectors in varying degrees, for varying reasons, including industrial promotion, sector development, safety standards, and equity and access goals.

In general, governments have good reason to intervene in cases of market failure when there are public goods involved, equity and access objectives, problems with imperfect information or the presence of synergies between firms. Although in these cases, regulation is likely to be procompetitive, it is still important to examine how well it corrects market failures.

Other government regulations, such as those aiming to fulfil housing, education or health objectives, should be reviewed to assess their impact on competition policy. Education provides a good example of where equity and access objectives are indisputable, as education offers benefits not only to individuals but also to society as a whole. The question is whether government regulation, for instance of tuition fees, achieves these objectives or whether such intervention distorts the allocation of resources and lessens competition in the sector.

There is often a mix of objectives in regulating sectors such as power or telecommunications. There will be cases where conflicting objectives cannot be avoided; for example, where efficiency and equity are simultaneous goals. Regulating the prices of monopoly services is complex enough, but when equity objectives are also involved, regulation becomes even more complicated.

Ways need to be found to separate out social objectives in order to fully meet competition policy concerns, particularly in infrastructure projects with large capital requirements and long gestation periods. Competition policy objectives should be to the fore from the inception of the project, to its completion, to its operation. This suggests the need for competitive bidding processes like the Swiss challenge system, which requires firms calling for a limitation of competition to show that there will be gains from lower prices and better products, and for clear access policies.

One of the most effective ways of achieving these goals is separating out services that can be subjected to greater competition. Global studies of utilities suggest that they are not as 'natural' a monopoly as previously thought. Possibly the only segments of industries that are true natural monopolies are ports, the local loop in fixed-line telecommunications and electricity transmission. It is important to formulate a clear policy on access to such essential facilities (see Chapters 5 to 8 for more detailed discussion).

For regulators, price fixing appears to be a logical regulatory tool, since there is a presumption of market failure in the industry being regulated. Price fixing is also politically appealing. However, as many countries have experienced, price fixing, for instance through rate-of-return regulation, often creates more problems than it solves. Governments lack sufficient information on costs and find it difficult to price correctly to match demand and supply. Also, if they wish to increase investment, governments should not limit how much the firm can earn, certainly not at rates that are too low to cover interest costs. This creates regulatory risks for prospective investors on top of the commercial risks they already face (i.e., if the firm makes money, it runs the risk of losing it because of regulation). Moreover, regulation encourages cheating and can force honest players out of the market.

Another issue to consider is how privatisation is conducted. The transfer of ownership may not increase efficiency, and may only transfer rents, unless the conditions for a competitive market are in place. Indeed, the main problem may not be whether to transfer ownership, but rather how competition and discipline can be introduced. If a transfer of ownership is involved, any unfair advantages previously enjoyed by the firm should be removed and competitive neutrality should be ensured.

IMPLEMENTATION

A full national competition policy requires a great deal of technical expertise on the part of the competition authority. The authority needs competent and knowledgeable staff who are able to define markets, identify anticompetitive actions, and judiciously construct and administer tests for market concentration and the effects of mergers and acquisitions. This is perhaps the major reason why developing countries are reluctant to deal with this issue in the WTO's Doha Round. As newcomers to competition policy, they are likely to lack expertise and require assistance with building institutions and capabilities (Chapters 2 and 3 offer some insights into implementation issues).

What is the best way to develop such expertise and institutions? And, how should countries go about building public support for the reforms and overcoming political constraints?[5]

Countries are under different constraints in implementing a competition policy framework. Although a central authority is best able to accomplish this task, it may not be feasible to create one. However, one option may be to craft a competition law that would allow for the creation of a national competition authority in the future.

Whatever the approach, initial efforts should focus on developing physical and human capital, training judges, and educating consumers, the business community and government officials on the rationale for and the content of the antitrust law. The law should allow for the institutional foundations for competition policy to be put in place and for a system of enforcement to be established. However, the drafting of an antitrust law and the creation of a competition authority should follow efforts to identify the major sources of market failure and the institutional conditions that will allow for the correction of such failures.

In the long run, governments should work toward creating a competition authority that would be responsible not just for antitrust legislation and preventing anticompetitive behaviour, but also for the review of government policies and regulations affecting competition, and for information and education campaigns.

It is possible that competition policy will come into conflict with contract law, as Chapter 10 points out. Mechanisms will be needed to reduce uncertainty about contract enforceability and, in most cases, the provisions of an existing contract should take precedence over competition policy. Any uncertainty could derail growth and negate the benefits of even the best policies.

Finally, it is important to consider competition policy in the context of the international trading regime. For all countries the primary consideration will be national objectives, but it is crucial also to consider multilateral and regional perspectives, as Chapter 4 argues. Considering developments in other countries gives a wider perspective of the issues and helps governments decide on the most appropriate policies. And, as Chapter 11 points out, national and regional efforts to enhance competition can be mutually reinforcing and provide a further force to counter the interests of vested groups.

NOTES

1. This chapter draws heavily on Medalla (2002).
2. The market power of a monopoly firm, or how much it can increase prices, will depend on the elasticity of demand for the product. In a perfectly competitive market, firms face perfectly elastic demand and cannot influence prices. Limiting output simply allows other firms to produce more.
3. A market is defined as concentrated when only three or four firms dominate value-added (or another indicator of performance such as sales) in an industry.
4. An independent body is likely to be more objective and more likely to suggest reforms than the agency that needs reforming. However, an independent body may not have the resources to investigate all government measures and regulations.
5. There are valid fears that regulatory failures in competition authorities can result in serious errors in judgement, punishing those who should not be punished and leaving those who should be punished, unpunished.

REFERENCES

Abon, E.B. (2002) 'The need for a Philippine comprehensive competition policy and law', paper presented during a Competition Policy Seminar organised by the National Economic and Development Authority and the Korea Development Institute, Pasig City, June.

Baumol, W. and R. Willig (1981) 'Fixed cost, sunk cost, entry barriers and sustainability of monopoly', *Quarterly Journal of Economics* 96: 405–31.

Medalla, E.M. (2002) 'Overview and integrative report', in E.M. Medalla (ed.) *Toward a National Competition Policy for the Philippines*, Makati City: Philippine Institute for Development Studies.

2 The evolution of competition law in East Asia

Ping Lin

INTRODUCTION

Competition laws promote economic efficiency and social welfare by prohibiting restrictive business practices and creating a level playing field for firms. More than eighty countries now have competition laws (Pitofsky 1998). The Philippines was the first East Asian country to introduce a competition law, under American rule in 1925. Japan's Antimonopoly Law was passed in 1947, again under US occupation. It was not until the 1980s and 1990s that most other regional countries enacted competition laws. This chapter surveys the current state of competition policy in three East Asian economies – Japan, China and Hong Kong. It looks at the effectiveness of these policies and how well they are being enforced, and examines the lessons that can be learnt from the experiences of these countries.

The effective deterrence of competition law violations requires that the expected cost of violating the law be no lower than the illegal gain. The probability that a violator will be caught will depend on the effectiveness of the enforcement system, but will always be less than 1. This suggests that the penalty should exceed the illegal profit, thereby justifying a punitive (or multiple damages) system.

Japan made significant amendments to its 1947 Antimonopoly Law in the 1990s and is on the way to establishing a modern antitrust system. Although enforcement has improved, the administrative surcharge, which is the major mechanism for imposing sanctions, is still not consistent with the basic principle of deterrence. Like many other Asian countries, China and Hong Kong are in the early stages of developing an effective competition policy. China's 1993 Unfair Competition Law is enforced primarily by local administrative agencies, which are ineffective in combating violations by protected local interests. Hong Kong's laws are seemingly simpler, but its sectoral approach prevents enforcers from appearing impartial and independent.

Competition policy has not had a great deal of domestic support in many East Asian countries. Japan's antimonopoly law was imposed by the Allied Occupation after World War II, and it was pressure from the United States that drove the amendments of the 1990s. External factors played a similar role in the passage of competition laws in Taiwan and Indonesia. In many East Asian countries, competition policy will lose out if there is a conflict with other policy objectives. Governments frequently intervene to promote certain industries or firms (e.g., state-owned enterprises). It is difficult to establish a culture for fair competition in such an environment.

The experience of other countries demonstrates the importance of an independent enforcement agency. In East Asia this is easier said than done. In Japan, for instance, the conflict between the Japan Fair Trade Commission (JFTC), which administers competition policy, and the Ministry of International Trade and Industry (MITI), which implements industrial policy, has impeded the enforcement of competition law (Sanekata and Wilks 1996). The most challenging task for East Asian countries is to establish independent agencies that are able to enforce competition laws.

EVALUATING THE EFFECTIVENESS OF COMPETITION LAW

Competition law is defined as a set of rules that govern the way that businesses interact with each other in the marketplace. The Model Law on Competition put forward by the United Nations Conference on Trade and Development (UNCTAD) outlines the aim of competition policy:

> To control or eliminate restrictive agreements or arrangements among enterprises, or merger and acquisitions or abuse of dominant positions of market power, which limit access to markets or otherwise unduly restrain competition, adversely affecting domestic or international trade or economic development. (UNCTAD 2000)

The Pacific Economic Cooperation Council (PECC) has published a set of non-binding principles for guiding the development of a competition-driven framework for APEC's economies. These principles declare that:

> the ultimate goal of this competition framework is to promote the process of competition, as opposed to the welfare of individual competitors, in order to achieve greater overall economic efficiency and an increased average standard of living in domestic economies and the APEC region as a whole. (PECC 1999: 6)

In some countries, including Japan and China, competition laws also meet consumer protection objectives.

According to the Model Law on Competition, competition law covers three main areas: restrictive agreements or arrangements, the abuse of market power, and mergers and acquisitions. Unfair methods of competition are also prohibited in some countries, including the United States, Japan and China. Table 2.1 summarises the state of competition policy in East Asia.

Competition laws vary in terms of their coverage and content, reflecting differing social, political, cultural and legal contexts. Enforcement procedures

Table 2.1 Competition laws in selected East Asian countries

Country	Title of law	Date of enactment
China	Law of the People's Republic of China for Countering Unfair Competition (Unfair Competition Law)	1993
	Price Law	1998
Hong Kong	Competition policy statement/sector-based competition provisions	1998
India	Monopolies and Restrictive Trade Practices Act	1969
Indonesia	Law on the Prohibition of Monopolistic Practices and Unfair Business Competition	1999
Japan	Act concerning Prohibition of Private Monopolisation and Maintenance of Fair Trade (Antimonopoly Act)	1947
Philippines	Antimonopoly Law	1925
Republic of Korea	Monopoly Regulation and Fair Trade Act	1980
Taiwan	Fair Trade Law	1991
Thailand	Price-Fixing and Antimonopoly Act (renamed Trade Competition Act in 1999)	1979

also vary. To evaluate the effectiveness of competition law, it is useful to adopt a framework developed in the law and economics literature that has contributed significantly to the understanding of the economic incentives behind violations of competition laws (e.g., Posner 1977; Becker 1968).

Most laws rely on sanctions and penalties to prevent violations. The expected cost of violating the law is determined by the penalty imposed on those who are caught and by the probability that a violation will be uncovered and successively prosecuted: that is, the expected cost of violating the law = P (the probability of being caught) × L, will be specified in the national competition law. Different penalties can be imposed, the remedies can be criminal as well as civil, the size of the fine varies, and some countries allow multiple damages or punish repeated offenders more severely.[1] In the United States, for example, violations of the Sherman Act can result in a fine of up to US$350,000, imprisonment for up to three years, or both.

The probability of detecting a violation, P, depends on the administrative and legal power of the enforcement agency, the procedures it uses, the size of its budget, and the qualifications and experience of law enforcement agents. It also depends on the degree of independence the enforcement agency has to launch investigations and make decisions. Another factor affecting P is whether private cases can be brought before the court and how willing individuals and companies are to pursue such cases. In the United States, the 1914 Clayton Act allows anyone who has been injured by an antitrust violation to sue in a federal court and pursue treble damages plus the cost of the lawsuit.[2]

Another important factor concerns the burden of proof in a competition case. In the United States, the legality of a firm's conduct can be assessed under either the per se rule or the rule of reason, which are quite different principles. Clearly anticompetitive activities such as price fixing and certain types of vertical restrictions come under the per se rule and cannot be defended on other grounds (e.g., efficiency reasons). Illegality is not as easily defined under the rule of reason, which applies to horizontal mergers and monopolies, as the activity is assessed according to the effect on the marketplace. The distinction between the two rules lies principally in the burden of evidence each imposes on the parties to the litigation. Under the per se rule, the plaintiff need only demonstrate that the defendant engaged in proscribed conduct, whereas under the rule of reason, a further argument must be made that the conduct hurt the plaintiff or society.[3]

The effectiveness of enforcement also depends on the extent to which the enforcement agency is able to act without being constrained or unduly influenced by political forces that might have conflicting objectives. In the United States, for example, the Department of Justice was the only agency to enforce the Sherman Act until 1914, when the Federal Trade Commission Act stipulated that responsibility should be shared with the Federal Trade Commission. This was an attempt by Congress to reduce the influence of the president over the enforcement of laws. To cite another example, the conflict between Japan's Ministry of International Trade and Industry, now the Ministry of Economy, Trade and Industry (METI), and the Japan Fair Trade Commission has often been blamed for the weak enforcement of antimonopoly law in Japan up until the 1980s.

Given that corporate crimes are motivated by the desire for pecuniary gain, and that the probability of getting caught is less than complete, it is clear that the expected penalty must be greater than the illegal gains in order to deter crimes. Simply taking away the illegal profits gained will not deter future antitrust violations. The drafters of the US antitrust laws were aware of this simple principle, and instituted treble damages, where plaintiffs can be awarded three times the actual damages (plus legal fees).[4] China's Unfair Competition Law and Consumer Protection Law also allow multiple damages.

The differing experiences of Japan, China and Hong Kong are discussed below.

COMPETITION POLICY IN JAPAN

Powerful, family-owned industrial conglomerates dominated the Japanese economy up until the end of World War II, when the Allied Occupation forces undertook to break up Japanese industry in order to prevent the re-emergence of militarism. One of the key reforms was the introduction of a competition law.

The Antimonopoly Act

At the centre of Japanese competition policy is the 1947 Act concerning Prohibition of Private Monopolisation and Maintenance of Fair Trade, known as the Antimonopoly Act. The declared objective of the Act, which was modelled on US antitrust statutes, is 'to promote free and fair competition, to stimulate the creative initiative of entrepreneurs, to encourage business activities of enterprises, to heighten the level of employment and people's real income, and thereby to promote the democratic and wholesome development of the national economy as well as to assure the interests of consumers in general' (section 1). Table 2.2 lists the main provisions of the Antimonopoly Act.

Table 2.2 Main provisions of Japan's Antimonopoly Act

Section of the Act	Provision
Section 3	Prohibits 'unreasonable restraints of trade' (cartels)
Section 6	Prohibits international cooperation that results in unfair trade practices or unreasonable restraints on competition
Section 7(2)	Imposes surcharges on price cartels
Sections 8(1)–(3)	Prohibits collusion and conspiracy in trade associations
Section 8(4)	Prohibits the creation of 'monopolistic situations' in highly concentrated markets
Section 9	Limits cross-shareholdings and holding companies (revised in 1996)
Section 13	Limits interlocking directorates and the dispatch of directors to other companies
Section 15	Sets market concentration limits on mergers and acquisitions
Section 18(2)	Requires implicit collusion and parallel price increases be notified to the JFTC
Section 19	Prohibits 'unfair trade practices'; stipulates that these activities are to be further specified in 'JFTC Designations'
Sections 21–23	Defines exemptions for monopolies under intellectual property right laws, special cooperatives and natural monopolies (section 21 abolished in 2000)
Section 24	Defines exemptions for recession and rationalisation cartels (revised in 1999)

The Antimonopoly Act has three main pillars. First, it prohibits unreasonable restraints of trade; that is, collusive activities that restrain trade. Second, it prohibits the creation of monopolies through mergers, cross-shareholdings and interlocking directorships. The third pillar of the Act prohibits unfair business practices, including behaviour that closes competitors out of markets or rules that discriminate against other firms. Six practices are highlighted as particularly unfair business practices:[5]

1) unfairly discriminating against other firms;
2) dealing at unfair prices;
3) unfairly inducing or coercing customers away from a competitor;
4) dealing with another party on restrictive terms;
5) using bargaining power unreasonably when dealing with another party; and
6) unfairly interfering with competitors in their transactions with third parties or interfering in the internal affairs of a competitor.

The Japan Fair Trade Commission (JFTC) was created under the Act to implement competition law and was positioned as an extra-ministerial body of the Ministry of Public Management, Home Affairs, Posts and Telecommunications (the commission is now under the Cabinet Office). Although the JFTC is modelled on the US Federal Trade Commission, its commissioners are not independent, but are appointed by the prime minister from the ranks of retired bureaucrats. The key post of chairman is usually filled by the Ministry of Finance.[6] The four other posts are shared out among leading ministries: one from MITI, one from the Ministry of Justice, and two from the Ministry of Finance, the Ministry of Foreign Affairs or the JFTC itself. This opens up the possibility of conflicts of interest, as the commissioners might consider the interests of their parent ministries. It is widely believed that the relaxed application of antimonopoly law in the banking and securities sectors reflects the dominance of the Finance Ministry over the JFTC. Having said this, the commissioners are appointed for five-year, renewable terms and therefore enjoy substantial immunity from short-term political pressures. In addition, no more than three commissioners can be from the same political party. Independent administrative agencies of this kind were unknown before the creation of the JFTC.[7]

The JFTC can address anticompetitive business activities in four ways: through preventive consultations, informal measures such as cautions and warnings, formal recommendations and complaints, and criminal proceedings.[8] Although an investigation can be initiated by the JFTC, most investigations are held in response to a report from the public (Schaede 2000: 113). Of the 1,007 cases examined by the JFTC between 1947 and 1996, 78 per cent resulted in recommendations, and most of these were immediately accepted by the respondents (Schaede 2000: 117).

As originally enacted the Antimonopoly Act was quite stringent. The provision on monopolies in the original law (article 8) prohibits any 'undue imbalance in business powers'. An enterprise that has a market share exceeding a certain threshold may automatically be considered to exhibit undue business power. In contrast, US law has a greater focus on conduct, and companies that occupy a large market share do not necessarily violate the law.[9] The Antimonopoly Act prohibited the ownership of shares in a competitor and stipulated that mergers had to be approved by the JFTC.

The Antimonopoly Act has been amended several times, most substantially in 1953, 1977 and in the 1990s. The 1953 amendments relaxed some of the original restrictions, while later revisions generally strengthened the Act.

The first major revision in 1953 ended the prohibition of cartels and authorised two types of cartels – depression cartels and rationalisation cartels – both of which were subject to the approval of the JFTC. Depression cartels were temporary arrangements designed to alleviate economic hardship caused by a disequilibrium in supply and demand. Rationalisation cartels were deemed necessary 'for effecting an advancement of technology, an improvement in the quality of goods, a reduction in costs, an increase in efficiency or any other rationalisation of enterprises' (Kaserman and Mayo 1995: 403).

The 1953 amendments deleted article 8 of the Antimonopoly Act (the article was reinstated in a different form in 1977), made mergers and acquisitions unlawful only when they substantially restrain competition, and allowed an exemption for resale price maintenance of goods that fall under the category of intellectual property.[10]

One aspect of the Antimonopoly Act was strengthened by the 1953 amendments, namely the control of unfair trade practices. The original prohibition of 'unfair methods of competition' was widened to include 'unfair business practices' that lessen competition, including practices such as tying arrangements, exclusive dealing, price discrimination, resale price maintenance by enterprises that are not competitors (e.g., manufacturers and their suppliers or manufacturers and retailers). The aim was to control abuses of power by large enterprises able to place pressure on smaller firms (Matsushita 1993).

The next changes to the Antimonopoly Act in 1977 considerably strengthened Japan's antimonopoly law. First, the JFTC was allowed to levy an administrative surcharge on cartels of up to 1.5 per cent of their total sales during the period in which the cartel operated. The surcharge system was introduced after the first oil crisis as a response to consumer complaints about the number of cartels being formed (Matsushita 1993). Second, the JFTC was able to compel structural changes to correct a monopolistic situation and control an undue imbalance of business power. Third, a price reporting system was introduced to deter tacit collusion by businesses raising prices simultaneously.

Japan's enforcement of its antimonopoly law has been poor, particularly prior to the 1980s. According to *The Economist*, 'the law itself has teeth in plenty;

the problem is that its designated watchdog has been trained not to bite' (*The Economist*, 16 September 1989).[11] The lack of enforcement of antimonopoly law is often cited as one of the key traits of the Japanese government during the postwar period (Porter et al. 2000, Chapter 2).

Industry policy played a crucial role in achieving Japan's economic miracle during the 1960s and 1970s, and was the prime reason for the government's lack of interest in enforcing the Antimonopoly Act. To enhance the competitiveness of Japanese firms in international markets and catch up with the more advanced economies, Japanese ministries, particularly the Ministry of International Trade and Industry, encouraged measures that contradicted the principle of fair competition. As noted by Caves and Uekusa (1976: 149):

> The goals of the Ministry of International Trade and Industry have varied over time in weight and composition, but some have recurred regularly since the ministry's founding in 1949. One has been to promote the movement of resources to certain favoured industries ... Another goal has been to promote larger operations in certain industries – larger plants because of an abiding faith in economies of scale, and larger firms in the belief that ... Japanese firms should be as large as their American competitors in order to compete with them effectively. This goal has led at times to considerable enthusiasm for mergers and restriction of new entry into industries of interest to MITI.

The pursuit of industrial policy has affected both the content and enforcement of Japan's antimonopoly law. The introduction of depression and rationalisation cartels was a prime tool of industrial policy during the 1960s and 1970s.[12] According to Porter et al. (2000, Chapter 2), as many as 1,379 cartels were allowed between 1953 and 1994.[13] The extension of provisions governing 'unfair methods of competition' to cover 'unfair business practices' in the 1953 amendment was to a large extent intended to protect small suppliers (Matsushita 1993).

According to some scholars, 'the Japanese government takes a more pragmatic approach to antitrust enforcement, one that makes allowance for national goals such as industrial catch-up' (Okimoto 1989: 13). However, it is fair to say that the government has given more weight to industrial policy than to competition policy. Although the JFTC and MITI have negotiated over conflicts between the two policies, 'there are not many examples that can be cited in which the JFTC has ordered MITI to make major changes in industrial policy in order to conform to antitrust statutes' (Okimoto 1989: 14).

Recent changes to Japan's antitrust system

Japan's antitrust system has undergone substantial changes since the early 1990s, with the Antimonopoly Act being further strengthened and the power of the JFTC being greatly enhanced. The changes were driven by two factors: trade disputes between Japan and the United States, and the drive for economic reform through deregulation and increased competition in domestic markets.

In trade negotiations during the mid-1980s, the US government started to raise allegations of anticompetitive practices by Japanese firms and trade associations. The Structural Impediments Initiatives talks in 1989 resulted in several Japanese commitments on competition law and policy, including (Yamada 1997):

- increasing the number of JFTC investigators and boosting the commission's budget;
- having the JFTC take formal action against price-fixing cartels and bid rigging;
- having the JFTC increase transparency by disclosing detailed information on its cases;
- increasing the fines for violations; and
- having the JFTC publish a set of guidelines on prohibited distribution and trade practices.

In 1995 the Japanese government embarked on a comprehensive restructuring of the economy with the aim of ending the worst recession since World War II. Deregulation has been taking place in important sectors such as telecommunications, energy, transportation and financial services to boost domestic competitiveness.

In June 1990 the JFTC announced it would pursue criminal charges against cartels, bid rigging, boycotts and other serious violations likely to have a widespread influence on consumers. It would also come down hard on repeat offenders and firms or industries that did not abide by measures to eliminate violations. The penalty that could be imposed on individuals participating in an illegal cartel or a monopoly was set at up to three years in prison or a fine of up to 5 million yen.[14]

In 1991 the surcharge on cartels was quadrupled to 6 per cent for industries other than wholesale and retail businesses. In addition, the government has cut the range of cartels allowable under the Antimonopoly Act and other laws.[15] As a result, the number of cartels fell from a peak of 1,079 cases at the end of March 1966 to 15 cases under four laws at the end of April 2000.

In 2001 a system was introduced to allow those who have been injured by unfair trade practices to file a lawsuit seeking injunctive relief. This was a substantial improvement over the civil remedies allowed by the Antimonopoly Act.

Another recent development has been the decline in administrative guidance of firms' investment decisions that was so prevalent in government–business relations in Japan. Administrative guidance has been used by various ministries to accomplish policy objectives. Under the 1995 Deregulation Promotion Plan, ministries must consult with the JFTC in advance of issuing administrative guidance. In 1994 the JFTC made public its Antimonopoly Act Guidelines on Administrative Guidance, which identified instances where guidance could lead to anticompetitive activities.

During the 1990s, when many other ministries were being rationalised, the JFTC expanded in size. By 2000 the JFTC had a staff of 564, up from 484 in 1992.[16] Table 2.3 reviews the types of cases that the JFTC dealt with between 1995 and 2000, showing that its primary focus has been on bid rigging.

An evaluation of Japan's competition policy

Japan's competition law has been in place for over half a century. Prior to the 1990s, competition policy was subordinate to industrial policy. Cartels and administrative guidance contradicted the principles of competition policy. Since the early 1990s, Japan's antimonopoly law has been significantly strengthened and enforcement has improved. The law now has more clout and on the whole is as comprehensive as competition law in any other country. The JFTC is now more powerful, independent, visible and active.

However, there is an important aspect of the law that needs further revision. As mentioned earlier, the primary mechanism for imposing sanctions under the Antimonopoly Act is the surcharge system. Enterprises found to have engaged in major restraints of trade such as cartels and bid riggings are fined a fixed rate of 6 per cent of sales revenues for three years. The surcharge system was never intended to be punitive: 'it is regarded as a confiscation of excessive profits rather than as a fine' (Sanekata and Wilks 1996: 115). According to JFTC Commissioner Shogo Itoda, the surcharge system 'aims at forcing violators to fork out undue profit from cartels or bid riggings, and achieving social justice based on the crime-does-not-pay idea' (Itoda 2000).

Before the 1991 amendment, the fine had been 1.5 per cent of the long-term average profit across sectors, which was 3 per cent, because of an assumption that only half of an offending firm's profit would have come from

Table 2.3 Court cases brought by the JFTC, 1995–2000

Type of violation	1995	1996	1997	1998	1999	2000
Private monopolies	0	1	1	3	0	1
Bid rigging	14	15	13	15	22	9
Price cartels	5	7	4	3	3	2
Unfair trade practices	4	2	9	5	5	5
Other	2	8	0	1	2	1
Total	25	33	27	27	32	18

Source: JFTC annual reports, 1995–2000.

illegal cartel activities. The rate was raised to 6 per cent in 1991, following the finding that the actual profit was around 15–20 per cent of sales.[17]

The economic framework outlined earlier in this chapter illustrates that the fine is still too low to deter violations of the law. Given that the probability of detecting a violation, P, is less than 1, the fine should be greater (by a factor of 1/P) than the surplus profits accruing from illegal cartels. Anything less makes breaking the law profitable even when firms are caught. A move to a punitive system through an increase in the fine would make Japan's competition policy more consistent with this principle. If the profit rate of a cartel is in the range of 15–20 per cent against an average 3 per cent normal profit, then the fine should be at least 12 per cent.[18]

Much can be learned from the Japanese experience, for instance by looking at why enforcement has been ineffective. Before the 1990s the main problem was that the JFTC had little power, which meant that competition policy was placed behind national priorities such as industry policy. Today two main factors inhibit the power of the JFTC and the Antimonopoly Act (Schaede 2000). The first is a lack of public awareness of antitrust principles and of what the Antimonopoly Act permits or prohibits, which means there is little impetus for stricter enforcement. Second, in stark contrast to the United States, where the possibility of large private damages is a major deterrent to antitrust violations, private antitrust lawsuits are extremely rare in Japan. A total of 31,745 private antitrust suits were brought in the United States between 1945 and 1988, but only 18 such suits were filed in Japan in that period (Schaede 2000, Chapter 5). The discrepancy can be explained by the high cost and low probability of success of bringing such a lawsuit in Japan.[19] The effectiveness of Japan's competition policy would be enhanced if private parties had stronger incentives to report antitrust violations.[20] There are further lessons for East Asian countries from Japan's experience of building an independent enforcement agency.

COMPETITION POLICY IN CHINA

China did not have a competition policy until the early 1980s, when it started to move from central planning to a market economy. Under central planning there was no role for competition and therefore no need for competition policy.

The decision to permit the development of the private sector created the need for rules to govern competition between firms. Three main laws and regulations deal with competition issues: the 1980 Regulations on Development and Protection of Competition, the 1993 Unfair Competition Law and the 1998 Price Law. Other regulations exist at the sectoral and regional levels.

The State Council issued the Regulations on Development and Protection of Competition on 17 October 1980. The regulations stipulate that:

> in economic activities, with the exception of products managed exclusively by state-designated departments and organisations, monopolisation or sole proprietary management of other products are not allowed.

The regulations are brief. Article 6 provides that:

> Competition must be introduced by breaking down regional blockades and departmental barriers. No locality or department is allowed to block the market. No locality or department should impose any ban on the entry of goods made in other places. Localities should ensure that raw materials can be transferred out according to state plans and must not create any blockade. Departments in charge of industry, transport, finance and trade must revise any part or parts of their existing regulations and systems which impede competition so as to facilitate competition.

The Unfair Competition Law

The 1993 Unfair Competition Law was China's first competition law and was a significant step toward preventing anticompetitive practices and establishing a competition policy.[21] It states that the aim of competition policy in China is to 'safeguard the healthy development of the socialist market economy, encourage and protect fair competition, stop acts of unfair competition and defend the lawful rights and interests of operators and consumers' (article 1).

A total of eleven business practices are outlawed. Article 9 prohibits false or misleading advertising. It also extends liability for false advertising to advertising agencies that are aware or should be aware of a seller's misrepresentation. Article 13 limits the use of prizes as a marketing strategy and states that the drawing of prizes must be conducted honestly and that prizes must not exceed 5,000 yuan (about US$605). Article 8 prohibits the use of bribes, especially kickbacks to buyers, in money or materials. Article 14 outlaws the fabrication or spreading of false information intended to injure the reputation of a competitor.

Protection against trademark infringement is offered by article 5, which forbids the copying of trademarks and certificates of quality and origin, and also the use of similar brand identification, such as brand names, packaging or designs, that might confuse consumers. A fine of between 100 per cent and 300 per cent of the value of the illegal gains may be imposed. Criminal sanctions may be imposed under China's Trademark Law.

Article 10 protects trade secrets. Trade secrets refer to 'technical information and operational information not known to the public that is capable of bringing economic benefits to the owners of the rights, that has practical applicability and that the owners of the rights have taken measures to keep secret'. The law imposes a fine of between 10,000 yuan and 200,000 yuan on those who obtain such secrets illegally or who know or should know that trade secrets were obtained illegally but nevertheless distribute such knowledge to third parties.

The remaining five prohibited acts can be classified as antitrust provisions. Article 15 prohibits collusion in the tendering process (bid rigging).[22] Violators can be fined between 10,000 yuan and 200,000 yuan, depending on the seriousness of the offence (article 27).

Article 11 forbids predatory pricing. It provides that an operator should not sell a product at a below-cost price for the purpose of driving out a competitor.[23] The following circumstances do not represent unfair competition: (1) selling fresh products; (2) disposing of overstocked products or products that are at or past their expiry dates; (3) seasonal reductions of prices; and (4) selling products at reduced prices to pay off debts, when lines of production change or when a business closes.

Article 12 provides that 'In selling a product, a business operator shall not make a tie-in sale against the wish of the buyer or attach other unreasonable conditions'. And article 6 states that 'Public utility enterprises or other business operators that have a legal monopolistic status shall not force others to buy the goods or services of their designated business operators in order to exclude other operators from competing fairly'. A violation of article 6 may attract a fine of between 50,000 yuan and 200,000 yuan, as well as the confiscation of between 100 per cent and 300 per cent of the illegally acquired revenues (article 23).

Article 7 prohibits government officials from coercing people into buying products from designated suppliers, as well as blockades of regional competition. The article states:

> A local government and its subordinate departments shall not abuse their administrative power to force others to buy the goods of the operators designated by them so as to restrict the lawful business activities of other operators. A local government and its subordinate departments shall not abuse their administrative power to restrict the entry of goods from other parts of the country into the local market or the flow of local goods to markets in other parts of the country.

The Unfair Competition Law is enforced by the State Administration for Industry and Commerce (SAIC) and its branches at the provincial, city and county levels. All branches have investigative powers and can issue corrective instructions (including the suspension of business licences) and impose fines for violations of the law.[24] The law does not provide for criminal penalties except in cases of trademark infringements (article 21) and bribes (article 22). Even the extremely collusive behaviour of bid rigging does not trigger criminal penalties under the 1993 law, although it does under the Law of Public Tendering, which took effect in January 2000.

The Price Law

The main objective of the Price Law, enacted on 1 May 1998, is to curb price wars and predatory pricing in China's consumer goods markets. The law is enforced by the State Development and Reform Commission and local price administration agencies.

The law prohibits the following unfair pricing practices: price fixing (article 14), predatory pricing, discrimination against business operators, spreading rumours of price hikes, attracting business through deceptive pricing, among others. The Unfair Competition Law addressed predatory pricing but did not define costs. The Price Law suggests that costs include production and operation costs. The provision regarding discrimination against particular business operators was designed to prevent monopolies from applying a price squeeze to drive out competitors. The Unfair Competition Law contains similar provisions regarding discrimination against particular business operations. Criminal penalties cannot be imposed under the Price Law, but it allows for fines of up to five times the illegal gains.

Regional and sectoral regulations

In addition to the national Unfair Competition Law, various provinces and major cities have also passed laws and regulations to counter unfair competition. For example, price fixing was first prohibited under regulations passed by Guangdong province. Beijing enacted its own Unfair Competition Law in 1994, shortly after the promulgation of the national law. By 2000 more than twenty provinces and cities had enacted their own unfair competition laws or regulations (Kong 2001: 15). Some sectoral regulations, for instance the 2000 Telecommunications Ordinance, have also incorporated competition provisions.

An evaluation of China's competition policy

China's competition policy regime has two major weaknesses: the lack of a comprehensive antimonopoly law and pervasive regional protectionism resisting the enforcement of competition law. Although the fines specified by the existing laws are fairly steep, deterrence is hampered by the weak enforcement system. China also needs to extend the coverage of laws and increase the probability that violations will be detected and punished. Another problem is that public awareness of competition laws is poor.

Table 2.4 describes the activities of the State Administration for Industry and Commerce in enforcing the Unfair Competition Law during 1995–97. Although the majority of cases dealt with infringements of trademarks or trade secrets, SAIC has also been combating antitrust violations and bid rigging. A large number of the antitrust cases were against public utilities. Most of the cases were dealt with through administrative measures, with only a small number turned over to the judicial system. This reflects the fact that competition law enforcement in China is primarily carried out through administrative channels.

In 1994 Chinese officials announced their intention to supplement the Unfair Competition Law with an antimonopoly law. Officials from SAIC and the State Economic and Trade Commission (SETC) drafted the Antimonopoly Law Outline. The outline has been revised several times since, often after suggestions from organisations such as the OECD, the World Bank, UNCTAD and APEC, as well as from countries that have antimonopoly laws (e.g., Germany, the United States, Japan, South Korea and Australia). The 1999 version of the outline, for example, covers the standard categories of business conduct (price discrimination, tying

Table 2.4 Competition cases concluded by China's State Administration for Industry and Commerce

Type of case	1995	1996	1997
Consumer protection/business dishonesty	711	2,160	2,441
Infringement of trademarks/trade secrets	4,361	8,856	9,296
Abuses of administrative power	22	38	13
Restrictions by public utilities	55	102	94
Predatory pricing	10	59	32
Tie-in sales	91	42	85
Bid rigging	16	23	37
Removing/concealing/destroying illegal assets	24	108	46
Other	n.a.	n.a.	2,847
Number of cases	5,290	11,388	14,891
Value of cases (million yuan)	419.1	738.2	843.9
Penalty (million yuan)	36.8	85.8	107.9
Cases transferred to judicial system	35	104	5

Note: n.a. means not available.
Source: State Administration for Industry and Commerce, China.

arrangements, exclusive dealing, predatory pricing, market division, collusion, abuse of market power, etc.) and structural changes such as mergers and acquisitions that might lessen competition.[25] The outline also briefly spells out how an enforcement agency should be established.

Perhaps unique to China is the inclusion of administrative monopolies in the proposed law. Four types of administrative monopolies are defined: forced transactions, regional monopolies, sectoral monopolies and compulsory associations that restrict competition. Among them, regional and sectoral monopolies are the most prevalent.

Regional monopolies exist under the protection of trade barriers erected by provinces and regions. Local protectionism blocks the entry of goods and services into the local market, or prevents raw materials or technology from being exported to other regions. Sectoral monopolies are large, integrated enterprise groups that also assume a regulatory role over a sector. The groups usually have ties with government ministries or departments and receive preferential treatment. As natural monopolies, public utilities also have characteristics typical of administrative monopolies. Operators in sectors such as water, power, gas, postal services, telecommunications, civil aviation and rail transport are sheltered from competition laws and government regulations.

The outline has not yet come into law. The long delay has mainly been because views differ on the introduction of an antimonopoly law.

One view is that the government should promote the formation of large enterprise groups and focus on developing economies of scale, so as to enhance the international competitiveness of Chinese enterprises. The introduction of an antimonopoly law would work against these goals.[26]

Another view supports the introduction of an antimonopoly law after firms have attained greater economies of scale. For the immediate future it is more important to oppose unfair competition such as cheating and vicious competition, rather than control industrial structure. An antimonopoly law can be introduced later.

To complement the Unfair Competition Law, China needs to develop an antimonopoly law that broadly controls monopolistic behaviour and restraints of trade that lessen competition. It may take some time before a consensus is reached about the best time to introduce an antimonopoly law. As China starts to fulfil its WTO commitments, and the dominance of the state-owned enterprises in the economy declines, attitudes toward antitrust laws will change. The ongoing deregulation of important industries such as telecommunications, transportation and public utilities will speed up the process of building an effective competition law.

Within the existing legal framework of competition law, perhaps the biggest problem is that the current enforcement mechanism cannot effectively deal with sectoral and regional monopolies. First, the leading agency dealing with market power, SAIC, is an agency at the ministerial level directly under the State Council. It is one of many government departments and does not have the authority to monitor the anticompetitive acts of other ministries in the way that Japan's FTC oversees administrative guidance. In fact, several new laws in recent years have weakened the enforcement power of SAIC. The 2000 Telecommunications Ordinance, for example, specifies that anticompetitive acts within the telecommunications industry should be investigated by the Ministry of Information Industry, a task that had previously been under SAIC's jurisdiction. Similarly, the agency now no longer has the authority to fight bid rigging. Under the 1999 Public Tendering Law, various (unspecified) government agencies now have this responsibility. These developments underscore the need to set up a truly independent enforcement agency that has the power to implement existing laws in a consistent and effective way.

Second, enforcement currently relies almost solely on local administrations for industry and commerce at the provincial, city and county levels. However, the prevalence of regional protectionism makes it difficult for law enforcers to carry out their duties. Motivated by economic and political interests, local governments often protect enterprises by putting up trade barriers, tilting the playing field in favour of local firms, or putting pressure on law enforcers investigating local firms. Since local governments appoint the heads of local Administrations for Industry and Commerce, it is difficult for them to enforce competition law independently and fairly. The existing enforcement system is not well suited for combating regional monopolies.

Finally, a distinctive feature of Chinese law is the inclusion of strict penalties. Fines under the Unfair Competition Law and the Price Law can be up to five times the illegal gains for price fixing and three times the illegal gains for infringements of trademarks and refusals to follow instructions over other violations.[27] China has encouraged its citizens to report illegal acts. For example, the State Development and Reform Commission and the Ministry of Finance decided that individuals and groups reporting Price Law violations to the proper enforcement agency would receive a reward of 10 per cent of whatever fine is imposed. The reward can be higher for special cases but is generally no more than 2,000 yuan (*People's Daily*, 14 December 2001).

Although many in China are aware of the existence of competition laws, they are unsure what the laws prohibit. In one recent case in 2000, the managers of nine television manufacturing firms met to fix the prices of televisions.[28] They did not seem to be aware that this action would violate the 1998 Price Law. The meeting was held openly, with national media coverage, and the prices were announced to the public. The managers defended their action by saying that a collective decision was needed to end price wars in the industry. Officers from the State Development and Reform Commission had to state publicly that this was a breach of the Price Law.[29]

COMPETITION POLICY IN HONG KONG[30]

Hong Kong did not have a competition policy until 1998, when the government issued a policy statement based on a series of studies made by the Hong Kong Consumer Council (Consumer Council 1996).[31] The objective of its competition policy is 'to enhance economic efficiency and the free flow of trade, thereby also benefiting consumer welfare'.[32]

Instead of a competition law, the government has set up a sector-specific competition policy framework. Horizontal restraints of trade and abuses of market power that impair economic efficiency or free trade, or that are intended to distort the operation of the market, were included in the policy statement. For horizontal restraints, the following examples were given: price fixing; bid rigging, market allocation schemes, sales and production quotas; joint boycotts; and unfair or discriminatory standards among members of a trade or professional body that intend to prevent newcomers from entering or contesting the market. For abuses of market power, the following examples were listed: predatory pricing; setting price minimums for retail products or services for which there are no ready substitutes; and restricting the supply of products or services to the purchase of other products or services or to the acceptance of certain restrictions other than for the reasons of quality, safety, adequate service or other justifiable purposes.

The determination of whether a practice is restrictive 'must be made in the light of the actual situation. The intended purpose and the effects of the practice in question, and the relevant market or economic conditions, etc., must be all taken into account.'[33] Thus, the rule of reason, rather than the per se rule, would be followed even for practices involving price fixing and bid rigging, which are normally treated as per se illegal in most countries.[34]

The government also followed a sectoral approach in its policy statement, the essence of which is to identify anticompetitive behaviour and encourage competition through administrative or legislative measures in each sector. Instead of establishing an overall law for the entire economy, the government has proposed setting different rules to govern competition in different sectors, with the administration of these rules to be carried out by sector-specific agencies. For example, the Telecommunications Ordinance and the Broadcasting Authority Ordinance specify the principles to be followed in promoting competition in the telecommunications industry and the broadcasting industry, respectively. In addition, detailed competition provisions were incorporated in the contracts between the government and each licence holder. The Telecommunications Authority and the Broadcasting Authority enforce these provisions and issue warnings or instructions if violations occur.

For less severe violations, the authority concerned might require a licensee to cease the action prohibited by the rules, but serious violations may attract a fine. Up until 2000 the maximum fine that the Telecommunications Authority could impose for violations of competition provisions or breaches of a licence was HK$20,000 for the first offence (approximately US$2,600), HK$50,000 for the second offence and HK$100,000 for any subsequent offences. These fines were raised to HK$200,000, HK$500,000 and HK$1,000,000 in early 2000 when the Telecommunications Ordinance was amended. The Telecommunications Authority can request the court to impose a penalty not exceeding 10 per cent of the turnover of the licensee over the period of the breach, or HK$10 million, whichever is higher. For the broadcasting industry, the penalty is an amount not exceeding 10 per cent of the licensee's turnover over the period of the breach, or HK$2 million, whichever is higher. It is possible that the authorities may decide to suspend an operator's licence.

The Telecommunications (Competition Provisions) Appeal Board was established to hear appeals against the Telecommunications Authority's decisions. The appeal board's decisions are final. A board has not yet been set up for the broadcasting industry.

Table 2.5 lists the types of cases considered by the Telecommunications Authority during 1998–2001. Although over half of the cases related to advertising conduct, some important competition cases were considered over this period. Most cases were resolved without a fine, including a price-fixing case in January 2000 that involved all six mobile service providers.[35]

An evaluation of Hong Kong's competition policy

Hong Kong's current competition policy framework is transparent. During the three years since the establishment of its competition policy, the government, particularly the Telecommunications Authority, has handled competition cases in an open, transparent and timely manner.[36] Although there have been some controversies, the government seems to be satisfied with the current approach to competition policy.

Table 2.5 Competition cases completed by the Hong Kong Telecommunications Authority

	1997–98	1999	2000	2001 (Sept.)	Total
Price fixing	1	0			1
Predatory pricing	1	1	0	2	4
Mergers/acquisitions	3	0	1	0	4
Unauthorised discounting	8	1	0		9
Breach of advertising code	22	13	5		40
Exclusive dealing	2	0	0		2
Undue discrimination/unfair cross-subsidisation	3	0	0		3
Customer complaints	3	2	3		8
Operation without a licence	0	0	3		3
Other	6	0	0		6
Total	3	45	19	11	78

Source: Office of the Telecommunications Authority, Hong Kong.

Chen and Lin (2002) argue that there are two fundamental drawbacks with a sectoral approach.[37] First, a sectoral approach may hinder the efficient allocation of resources across the economy. In choosing where to invest, private agents not only follow price signals but also consider regulatory and institutional barriers. Under a sectoral approach, rules will be interpreted and enforced differently by different regulatory agencies. Varying institutional environments will therefore imply different rates of return on investment, and this will affect the decisions of private investors.

The second fundamental problem has to do with the dual roles performed by government regulatory agencies under a sectoral approach. On the one hand, as regulators of natural monopolies, they must fulfil their regulatory duties, such as issuing and administrating business licences, and reviewing and monitoring standards and prices. On the other hand, they hear complaints and judge the behaviour of the firms they regulate. When the same agency has dual responsibilities, it is difficult for outsiders to believe that decisions can be made independently.

Such a conflict occurred in a recent telecommunications acquisition case dealt with by the Telecommunications Authority. In 1997 Hong Kong Telecom CSL Ltd was unsuccessful in obtaining a mobile service licence through a bidding process, but was allowed to acquire the successful bidder, Pacific Link. The Telecommunications Authority was criticised for having compromised the regulatory environment by allowing the loser of the bidding process to buy back a licence. The Authority had difficulty defending its position because it was unable to convince critics that it had acted fairly in granting the licences and approving the acquisition. Similarly, it was not able to establish that its approval of the transaction was independent of its ongoing negotiations with Hong Kong Telecom (CSL's parent) on the termination of Hong Kong Telecom's exclusive licensing contract in the international calls market. Since the government had to compensate Hong Kong Telecom for early termination of its monopoly status, questions were raised as to whether the Telecommunications Authority's approval of the acquisition of Pacific Link was part of a compensation package for the early termination of the monopoly contract. Had an independent authority approved the acquisition and the Telecommunications Authority been responsible for making licence decisions only, this conflict would not have arisen.

The criticisms of the Telecommunications Authority's actions are not specific to individual cases. Rather, they reflect the problems of a sectoral approach that stems from the presence of asymmetric information, and will likely also arise in other sectors.

Chen and Lin (2002) further argue that a comprehensive competition law enforced by an independent competition authority would overcome these two fundamental drawbacks and better promote competition in Hong Kong.

LESSONS FROM EAST ASIA

In many Asian countries, external pressure or even direct intervention from foreign countries triggered the introduction of competition policy. Japan's 1947 Antimonopoly Act was imposed by the Allied Occupation forces, and the extensive changes of the 1990s were a response to pressure from the United States. In Taiwan the threat of trade retaliation from the United States played a decisive role in the passage of the Fair Trade Law in 1991 after nearly a decade of deliberation and revisions (Liu and Chu 2002). Indonesia's new competition laws were a direct consequence of an International Monetary Fund program designed to prevent the economy from falling into a financial crisis like the one in 1998 (Pangestu et al. 2002). As the world economy becomes more integrated, countries will be forced by both external and internal forces to establish rules for fair competition. Although economic integration has helped promote competition policy,[38] domestic demand is a key prerequisite for establishing a truly effective antitrust system. What are the main obstacles for developing an effective competition policy in Asian countries? What lessons can be drawn from the cases reviewed here for other countries in the region?

In East Asia competition policy is sometimes in conflict with other policy objectives. Asian economies have a long history of heavy government intervention through state enterprises or through administrative guidance of the flow of resources into selected industries. In Japan in the 1970s and 1980s, in the newly industrialised economies seeking to catch up with the industrialised world, as well as in other economies in the region, the state has played a crucial role in guiding development. The promotion of industrial policy has influenced industrial structures, increased concentration and market power, and helped create a culture of reliance on the government. It would be naive to expect to build an effective antitrust system in such an environment overnight.

Influences from government-supported enterprises may delay the introduction of competition policy or affect the scope and enforcement of such policy. This is illustrated by China's failure to enact an antimonopoly law. In Korea the state's desire to protect and promote the country's large conglomerates (*chaebols*) has meant that enforcement of the 1980 Monopoly Regulation and Fair Trade Act has focused on unfair practices rather than abuses of monopoly power (Shin 2002). It is reasonable to predict that there will be widespread resistance to the introduction of competition policy and to the development of a culture for fair competition in the region (Round 2002).

There has been a concern among developing countries that competition policy may adversely affect economic growth by imposing restrictions on the size of domestic industries and by depriving the government of its regulatory and discretionary power. Some hold the view that competition policy should be implemented only after economic growth is achieved through industrial policy.[39]

Japan's success in creating a 'miracle economy' in the 1960s and 1970s might lend support to the argument that industrial policy should come before competition policy. However, the increasing integration of the world economy has made it extremely difficult, if not impossible, for a country to grow without inflows of foreign capital and technology, and without liberalising its domestic industries and opening up to trade with the rest of the world. Adopting competition policy will help attract foreign investment, as well as promote trade and competition in domestic markets. It seems clear that the only way to achieve economic growth and the efficient allocation of resources is to utilise the market system and competition process. Competition law is an indispensable element of a modern market system, as it sets the rules of the game to create a level playing field for competition.

The passing of competition law does not guarantee an effective competition regime. A qualified, independent enforcement agency is crucial for the rigorous and effective enforcement of competition policy, as the drafters of America's 1914 Federal Trade Commission Act were aware.

The principle of independence has been emphasised repeatedly in East Asia, but experiences in the region suggest that the action does not match the rhetoric. In Japan the composition of the JFTC has been described as an impediment to the enforcement of antimonopoly law (Sanekata and Wilks 1996: 124).

Thailand's experience also underscores the importance of institution building. The Thai Competition Commission is chaired by the Ministry of Commerce. In two cases against large companies in 2000, the commission's poor institutional design was blamed for its inability to find the defendants guilty of violating the 1999 Trade Competition Act (Poapongsakorn 2002).[40]

Finally, acting independently is different from being seen to act independently. Hong Kong's experience with assigning dual roles to sectoral regulatory agencies indicates that problems with asymmetric information should be taken into account when designing the enforcement agency. This suggests that the principle of independence should be about building an enforcement agency that is willing, has the capacity, and can be seen to act independently.

CONCLUSION

This chapter has highlighted some common difficulties that many East Asian countries face in developing an effective competition policy. These include a lack of domestic support for competition policy, conflict with other national policies, particularly industry policy, the influence of state-supported companies, weak enforcement, and poor institutional design. Given the history of these countries, such obstacles are likely to continue to hinder the development of competition policy in the near future. However, Japan's achievements in strengthening antimonopoly rules in the 1990s suggest that competition policy can move at a much faster pace. As heavy government intervention becomes less popular and countries become more integrated with the world economy, they will find it in their best interests to set fair rules of the game for competition. This should not be surprising, as good competition laws are needed for the success of a market economy.

NOTES

The author thanks Gary Banks, Edward K.Y. Chen, Hugh Patrick, David Round, Frank Wiebe and other participants of the Twenty-Eighth PAFTAD Conference for their useful comments and suggestions.

1 Non-pecuniary penalties are not considered here.
2 For an analysis of the trends in private and public antitrust cases in the United States, see Lin et al. (2000).
3 Different countries may adopt different rules regarding the same conduct. For example, price fixing is considered per se illegal in the United States, and any effort by cartel members to set prices jointly is sufficient to prove that they have violated the law. This is so even when the cartel members did not implement the agreement or the agreement had no adverse effect on consumers. In Japan, however, the Japan Fair Trade Commission has to further prove that the cartel members followed the agreed plan and that the conduct affected competition.
4 This system has been criticised for encouraging too many lawsuits.
5 These activities were outlined in JFTC Notification 11 of 1953 and JFTC Notification 15 of 1982.
6 In August 1996 Yasuchika Negoro became the first JFTC chair in thirty-three years to come from outside the Ministry of Finance (MOF) or the Bank of Japan. Since his appointment, the JFTC has introduced greater transparency into its rules and systems.
7 The JFTC also implements the Act against Unjustifiable Premiums and Misleading Representations and the Act against Delays in Payment of Subcontract Proceeds, etc., to Subcontractors. These are special laws complementing the Antimonopoly Act.

8   A warning is a written guidance and is stronger than a caution. There does not need to be a legal case for a warning, and no penalty will be imposed. If the JFTC finds evidence of a substantial violation of the Antimonopoly Act, it can issue a recommendation, which is usually accompanied by a cease-and-desist order. The respondent must notify the JFTC within a certain period (usually ten days) whether it accepts the recommendation. If the JFTC receives an acceptance, it will close the case by issuing a final recommendation. There will be no further investigation or criminal proceedings. If, however, the respondent denies the alleged conduct and refuses to accept the recommendation, the case becomes a complaint and a trial hearing will be held. If the respondent rejects the decision of the hearing, he or she can appeal to the Tokyo High Court and, if necessary, to the Supreme Court.

9   Japanese businesses were highly critical of article 8 as they saw economies of scale as the way to revitalise the postwar economy.

10 Resale price maintenance occurs when upstream firms set vertical restrictions on retail prices.

11 Shogo Itoda, Commissioner of the JFTC, rejected this claim, saying that 'the JFTC barks loudly and bites violators hard' (Itoda 2000).

12 According to Iyori and Uesugi (1983: 19), 'the major exemption laws were enacted until 1952. The Stabilisation of Specific Small and Medium Enterprise Temporary Measures Act, which authorised depression cartels for specific small enterprises, and the Export Trading Act, which permitted export cartels, were both enacted in that year. Since that time, many exemption laws intended to prevent excessive competition between small enterprises or to promote rationalisation were enacted, revised or strengthened almost every year ... Many exemption laws opened the door for approval of cartels not by the JFTC but under the guidance of the ministries in charge of the industries. They also provided for restrictions on the activities of non-members of cartels in order to strengthen cartel activities.'

13 The Japanese government has not approved a recession cartel since 1989, despite Japan being in recession for the entire 1990s.

14 The amendment of the Antimonopoly Act in May 2000 set the maximum penalty that could be imposed on companies at 500 million yen, up from the previous maximum of 100 million yen. However, there are no criminal penalties for unfair trade practices.

15 About thirty-five exemptions under twenty laws other than the Antimonopoly Act and the Exemption Act were abolished or modified under the 1997 Omnibus Act. The 1999 Omnibus Act put in place measures to repeal the depression cartels and rationalisation cartels under the Antimonopoly Act, abolish the Exemption Act, and limit the scope or establish JFTC procedures concerning six exemptions under four other laws. Another amendment to the Antimonopoly Act took effect in June 2000, repealing section 21 and thereby eliminating the antimonopoly exemption for the electricity, gas and rail sectors, as well as other sectors that could be characterised as natural monopolies.

16 In 1999 the Antitrust Division in the US Department of Justice had 819 staff, the US Federal Trade Commission had 964 staff, and the Competition Directorate General of the European Union had 486 staff (JFTC web site: http://wwww2.jftc.go.jp/e-page/index.htm).

17 The US Trade Representative expected an increase to at least 10 per cent (Sanekata and Wilks 1996).

18 Under the treble damages system, the fine would be 36 per cent.

19 When bringing cases under the Antimonopoly Act, the full burden of proof is on the plaintiff, who must provide evidence of a causal relationship between

the cartel and the injury suffered, and of the extent of damages incurred. Moreover, with no allowance for double, treble or punitive damages, the incentive for bringing a private lawsuit is low. Class action suits are now allowed in Japan, but plaintiffs cannot pool litigation costs. In addition the likelihood of winning a private antitrust case is small, as courts side with the defendant in most instances.

20 Iyori (1986) argues that cultural differences lead Asian people to settle cases privately rather than through the courts.
21 A version of the law in English can be found at <http://www.apeccp.org.tw/doc/China.html>.
22 The Unfair Competition Law does not prohibit price cartels (price fixing), which are per se illegal in almost all competition laws in other countries. The omission was corrected in the 1998 Price Law.
23 The law, however, does not give a definition of costs.
24 No new agency was created to enforce the 1993 Unfair Competition Law. SAIC is under the State Council and has a long tradition of protecting market order. Its other duties include administration of business licences, registration of trademarks and the enforcement of other laws such as the Trademark Law and the Advertisement Law.
25 For a brief description of the outline, see Chen (2000).
26 For more on administrative monopolies, see Wang (1998) and Yang (2002).
27 The laws, however, do not provide for criminal penalties.
28 The nine producers (Konka, Skyworth, TCL, Rova, Hisense, Xoceco, Jinxing, Panda and Westlake) collectively had more than 80 per cent of the Chinese market. After several price wars, the manufacturers decided to fix television prices and agreed that televisions sold at lower prices would be considered poor quality. The alliance said that prices that were any lower would not allow manufacturers to recoup their production costs (*China Daily*, 25 June 2000 and 11 August 2000). The case has not yet been considered formally by the government.
29 In a similar case, the Chinese Automobile Industry Association stated in January 2000 that China's ten car manufacturers had decided not to fight a price war by lowering prices (*China Daily*, 3 August 2000).
30 This section is based on Chen and Lin (2002).
31 In October 1992 the Hong Kong Consumer Council launched a series of studies on market competition in sectors such as banking, retailing, gas supply, telecommunications, radio broadcasting and real estate. Low levels of competition were found in most sectors. The November 1996 report on competition policy in Hong Kong strongly recommended the adoption of a comprehensive competition law and the establishment of an independent competition authority (Consumer Council 1996).
32 See <http://www.info.gov.hk/tib/roles/psoc.htm>.
33 See <http://www.info.gov.hk/tib/roles/psoc.htm>.
34 According to the Secretary for Trade and Industry, Denise Yue Chung-yee, firms can achieve economies of scale and provide better service under many 'apparently collusive agreements' and it 'would not be proper to rule these out indiscriminately' (*South China Morning Post*, 4 November 1997).
35 This price cartel lasted for two weeks and the companies rescinded the simultaneous price increases after receiving warning letters from the Telecommunications Authority. In another incident, the dominant operator in the international calls market was fined HK$50,000 for having repeatedly violated the terms of its contract that prohibited it from offering unauthorised discounts

to its customers. This is probably the heaviest fine levied so far in a competition case in Hong Kong.
36 Since 1997 the Telecommunications Authority has handled over eighty-one competition cases. For details, see Chen and Lin (2002).
37 The Consumer Council pointed out that the sectoral approach is piecemeal and fails to provide consistent, comprehensive guidelines. It also stated that competition provisions in different sectors may be subject to different interpretations and carry different penalties, and that a sectoral approach may be prone to the capture of regulators by interest groups. The government, on the other hand, stated that it did not see the need to introduce a broad competition law and that a sectoral approach is less expensive, less intrusive and can take into account industry conditions and provide greater certainty to the business community.
38 For a detailed discussion of the link between trade policy and competition policy, see Wu and Chu (1998).
39 The promotion of economic development is one of the objectives of the UNCTAD Model Law.
40 One of the companies serviced cable televisions and the other was in beer manufacturing.

REFERENCES

Becker, G.S. (1968) 'Crime and punishment: an economic analysis', *Journal of Political Economy* 76: 169–217.
Chen, K.Y. Edward and P. Lin (2002) 'Competition policy under laissez faireism: market power and its treatment in Hong Kong', *Review of Industrial Organization* 21: 145–66.
Chen, Lijie (2000) 'Some issues on the Antimonopoly Law of China', in Ji Xiaonan (ed.) *On Antimonopoly Law in China* (in Chinese), Beijing: Publishing House of the People's Court.
Consumer Council (1996) 'Competition policy: the key to Hong Kong's future success', Hong Kong: Consumer Council.
Itoda, Shogo (2000) 'Japan Fair Trade Commission barks – yesterday, today and tomorrow: competition policy of Japan', paper presented at Chatham House, London, 22 February.
Iyori, Hiroshi (1986) 'Antitrust and industrial policy in Japan: competition and cooperation', in Gary Saxonhouse and Kozo Yamamura (eds) *Law and Trade Issues of the Japanese Economy: American and Japanese Perspectives*, Seattle and London: University of Washington Press.
Iyori, Hiroshi and Akinori Uesugi (1983) *The Antimonopoly Laws of Japan*, New York: Federal Legal Publications.
Kaserman, D. and J. Mayo (1995) *Government and Business: The Economics of Antitrust and Regulation*, Orlando: The Dryden Press.
Kong, Xiangjun (2001) *Interpretation and Application of the Antimonopoly Laws in China* (in Chinese), Beijing: Publishing House of the People's Court.
Lin, P., B. Raj, M. Sanfort and D. Slottje (2000) 'The US antitrust system and recent trends in antitrust enforcement', *Journal of Economic Surveys* 14: 255–306.
Liu, K.C. and Y.P. Chu (2002) 'Market power in Chinese Taipei: laws, politics and treatments', *Review of Industrial Organization* 21: 129–43.
Matsushita, Mitsuo (1993) *International Trade and Competition Law in Japan*, New York: Oxford University Press.

Okimoto, Daniel I. (1989) *Between MITI and the Market: Japanese Industrial Policy for High Technology*, Stanford: Stanford University Press.

Pangestu, M., H. Aswicahyono, T. Anas and D. Ardyanto (2002) 'The evolution of competition policy in Indonesia', *Review of Industrial Organization* 21: 205–24.

PECC (1999) *PECC Competition Principles*, Singapore: PECC.

Pitofsky, Robert (1998) 'Competition policy in a global economy – today and tomorrow', speech at the European Institute Eighth Annual Transatlantic Seminar on Trade and Investment, Washington DC, 4 November.

Poapongsakorn, Nipon (2002) 'The new competition law in Thailand: lessons for institution building', *Review of Industrial Organization* 21: 185–204.

Porter, M., H. Takeuchi and M. Sakakibara (2000) *Can Japan Compete?*, London: Palgrave Macmillan.

Posner, R. (1977) *Economic Analysis of Law*, Boston: Little, Brown and Company.

Round, D. (2002) 'Editorial introduction: market power in East Asian economies', *Review of Industrial Organization* 21: 107–12.

Sanekata, K. and S. Wilks (1996) 'The Fair Trade Commission and the enforcement of competition policy in Japan', in G.B. Doern and S. Wilks (eds) *Comparative Competition Policy*, Oxford: Clarendon Press.

Schaede, Ulrike (2000) *Cooperative Capitalism: Self-Regulation, Trade Associations, and the Antimonopoly Law in Japan*, New York: Oxford University Press.

Shin, Kwang-Shik (2002) 'The treatment of market power in Korea', *Review of Industrial Organization* 21(2): 113–28.

United Nations Conference on Trade and Development (UNCTAD) (2000) 'Model Law on Competition', TD/RBP/CONF.5/7, Geneva: UNCTAD.

Wang, X.Y. (1998) 'Establishing antimonopoly laws in China', in X.Y. Wang (ed.) *Antimonopoly Law and Market Economy* (in Chinese), Beijing: The Law Press.

Wu, Rong-I and Yun-Peng Chu (1998) 'Trade and competition policy', in Rong-I Wu and Yun-Peng Chu (eds) *Business Markets and Government in the Asia Pacific*, London and New York: Routledge.

Yamada, Akinori (1997) 'Competition law and policy in Japan', paper presented at the Global Economic Development and Competition Policy Conference, 17 March, New Delhi, India.

Yang, Jijian (2002) 'Market power in China, manifestations, effects and legislation', *Review of Industrial Organization* 21: 167–83.

3 Implementing an effective competition policy: skills and synergies

Rod Shogren

INTRODUCTION

This chapter discusses a range of practical issues in implementing competition policy. Although the treatment is intended to be down to earth, it will turn out that many of the issues are dealt with in terms of principles, and the hope is to provide a framework for thinking about these matters rather than have the last word on the details.

My perspective necessarily reflects my own background, most recently as a commissioner on the Australian Competition and Consumer Commission (ACCC) and before that as a policy advisor to government. The ACCC has a unique role among competition agencies. It combines the function of antitrust regulator with that of a utility regulator in areas such as telecommunications and energy, and in addition has responsibilities for consumer protection. Thus its responsibilities include those that are more usually carried out by industry-specific regulators. In US terms it has the functions of the Federal Trade Commission, the Antitrust Division of the Department of Justice, and some of the functions of the Federal Communications Commission, the Federal Energy Regulatory Commission and state public utilities commissions.

This Australian model has been both commented on and commended in forums like the Organisation for Economic Cooperation and Development (OECD), but will not be assumed in this chapter to be a clearly superior way of doing things.

DEFINING TERMS

Competition policy and economic regulation

It has been traditional to separate the activities involved in controlling anticompetitive business conduct and mergers, on the one hand – this being the field of competition policy – and regulating monopolies and/or network industries and/or essential infrastructure, on the other. There has been debate about whether controlling anticompetitive structures and behaviour through so-called general competition policy is all that is necessary across the economy, even public utilities. It is not a debate this chapter will enter into. Rather, it will take as given that such an approach is not enough and that some more direct forms of economic regulation are needed. (Even New Zealand, which was once something of a bastion of the idea that general competition policy is sufficient, has substantially moved away from that stance in recent times.)

As to what economic regulation entails, the objective of pure monopoly regulation is to limit the impact – both on income distribution and on efficiency – of monopoly pricing and associated output restrictions. In essential facilities, particularly network industries, the objective of access regulation is to prevent the foreclosure of competition in markets upstream and downstream of a bottleneck facility[1] and to facilitate efficient investment in and use of the infrastructure.

Although a salient feature of both forms of regulation is the existence of strong market power,[2] some would see a clear distinction between the two (OECD 1999). That distinction is not critical here. What does matter is that the key characteristic that distinguishes both forms of regulation from general competition policy is that regulation ultimately involves intervention in a firm's setting of prices, whether they be prices to users in general or access prices in particular.

In practice, general competition policy is usually put into place through legal prohibitions on specified conduct, including anticompetitive mergers. Such mergers, along with anticompetitive agreements and the misuse of market power, are against the law of the land, and the law provides penalties and other remedies against those who break it. Regulation is different. There the regulator usually gets involved in the prices a firm can charge, for example by setting the price, putting a cap on the price, setting a path for the price over time, or a combination of all those actions.

Regulation often involves much more than prices. For example, non-price terms and conditions of access can be important. However, the proposition advanced here is that pricing decisions lie at the heart of economic regulation (which concerns only a few industries in the economy) but are not necessarily a part of controlling anticompetitive conduct across the economy as a whole. (Indeed, pricing becomes an issue only in the particular form of misuse of market power known as predatory pricing.)

Implementing

When speaking of implementing change, the term carries connotations of influencing and persuading (Leavitt 1985). When talking about implementing policy, the sense is of making something happen, getting it into place. When the context is implementing the law, it almost means 'enforcing'.

Although the topic of this chapter is implementing competition policy – putting it in place – all the above-mentioned aspects of implementation are relevant. Indeed, implementing may best be seen in a framework of managing change, where it is only one part of the process. A useful framework has three elements: path finding, problem solving and implementation (Leavitt 1981).

Path finding is the visionary step of deciding what the question is – discovering the problem to be solved, setting out a mission or purpose, proposing the change. This requires creativity, imagination, perhaps even dreams of what might be. It is not an entirely rational process but has an aesthetic aspect as well.

Problem solving is a familiar term. Particularly for public servants and academics, analysis is a daily staple. It is the height of rationality and may be associated with systems and planning, whiteboards and hard thinking. What does the change involve? What will the consequences be? What are the costs and benefits?

Implementing – in this framework where it is (somewhat artificially) placed at the end of the process of managing change – is about action rather than deep thought. It involves influencing, persuading and commanding. It is about people – individuals and groups – and involves emotions, values and commitments.

Of course, these aspects of managing change are all interrelated. Moreover, there is not a simple sequence from path finding to problem solving to implementation. Rather, there are feedback loops and linkages between them. For example, in a competition agency, enforcement of the law requires problem-solving skills combined with gritty determination to carry through to a good result. The leadership role ideally combines the visionary ability to propose new approaches with the political skills to get them accepted. Imagination is needed not just in seeing what needs to be done but also in coming up with workable solutions.

Thus, path finding, problem solving and implementation should not be put into separate boxes. In addition, the question of who is responsible for this overall process of managing change needs to be considered. In practice, responsibility is shared, for example between the political level of government and the competition agency itself. Many of the big decisions about the nature of competition policy must of their nature be decisions of government, but even in highly specified competition policy frameworks, there is discretion for the agency and its head to determine approaches to governance and principles.

CHARACTERISTICS OF EFFECTIVE COMPETITION POLICY AND REGULATION

The above discussion gives a framework for thinking in more detail about what it is that needs to be implemented. What is meant by effective competition policy? In trying to answer that question, as mentioned earlier, the topic will be expanded beyond narrow competition policy – in the sense of general controls on anticompetitive conduct and mergers – to also include economic regulation involving intervention in firms' price setting (e.g., for access).

The topics covered are the environment in which competition policy is being implemented, its objectives and some suggested principles and practices of effective competition policy and regulation.

The policy environment

It is not possible to implement any policy properly without taking account of the political, economic and social environment. In some circumstances and countries, the environment for implementing competition policy is ripe, and of course some already have competition agencies. It is hoped that this discussion of objectives, principles and practices will be just as relevant to them as to countries that are still wrestling with the question of whether they should establish a competition agency and, if so, in what form.

What is the starting point? In Australia the environment when competition policy was introduced several decades ago was quite different from what it had become by 1995 when the competition agency took on broader responsibilities for regulation of utility industries. Back in the 1970s there was still a concern that Australia was too small an economy to be concerned with restricting monopolisation. Anticompetitive agreements were widespread and widely regarded as a natural feature of a small country with little in the way of economies of scale. High levels of industry concentration were seen as inevitable and vigorous competition as hardly feasible and not necessarily desirable.

By 1995 all this had changed. The antitrust laws were largely considered to have been successful in facilitating more competitive behaviour and industry structures. Attention had turned to two related issues: restructuring and introducing competition into the state-owned and generally vertically integrated public utilities; and dealing with the especially high degree of market power held by bottleneck facilities. In the event, the general competition agency was given new powers to deal with access to essential facilities and became, in addition, a regulator of utilities.

This historical background in Australia is mentioned only to make the point that the way competition policy and regulation are handled in Australia has been an evolving process. The current legislation and organisational arrangements have been built up over time and may have been quite different in other circumstances. If, for example, the development of antitrust legislation had been delayed or regulation of utilities had occurred earlier, it is quite possible that Australia would not have ended up with an Australian Competition and Consumer Commission with such a broad role. It is likely that separate regulatory agencies for telecommunications, energy, transport, and so forth, would have been established.

All sorts of thinking and events influence the way in which each country decides these matters. Australia came to utility regulation very late because its utilities were almost exclusively state owned. At least, it came late to regulation in the US sense, where independent regulatory agencies have oversight of retail pricing of telecommunications and electricity, for example. In Australia these prices were entirely in the control of government. On the other hand, corporatisation and privatisation of these utilities in Australia were more or less contemporaneous with splitting them up (in the case of electricity supply and rail transport) or at least opening them up to competition (in the case of telecommunications).

The circumstances that affect the implementation of competition policy include:

- The existence and nature of property rights and the means of enforcing them, for example civil law and court processes.
- General macroeconomic conditions and the health of individual industry sectors. For example, it was easier to open the telecommunications industry up to competition a few years ago when there were plenty of new entrants than now, when telcos are in a generally poor state.
- The level of political and economic uncertainty. Sovereign risk and doubts about due process undermine trust and make it more difficult to build credibility.
- Other regulatory frameworks outside the competition/regulatory agency's responsibilities, for example accounting standards and the regulation of corporations. These can affect the general standards of corporate behaviour, including with respect to competition, and conduct such as rent seeking and regulatory gaming (i.e., the practice of manipulating the regulatory framework to achieve higher profits, impede competitors, etc.).

Little more is said in this chapter about the historical context, beyond the fact that it needs to be understood in each country's individual circumstances. But while each country's circumstances are unique, there are some general frameworks for thinking about what effective competition policy and economic regulation mean.

Generally, policy objectives are set by governments and handed down to executive agencies. Nevertheless, agencies have the discretion and the need to set objectives for themselves as well. This brings us back to the external environment. One part of setting objectives is finding out what stakeholders expect. How will they measure the agency's – and competition policy's – success? Of course, an agency will also seek to influence stakeholders' expectations and criteria for success rather than accept them passively.

How long does the agency have before it will be judged? Again, the agency should seek to stake out its own timeframe, especially if expectations of early results are unrealistic, as is often the case with the development of competition in industries previously closed to it.

Up until now the question of who the stakeholders are has been set aside. Generally, the key groups will be the government; in particular, the minister and ministry responsible for competition policy; the industries and firms subject to the agency's powers; and users/consumers. But there may be others and there will certainly be subgroups within the major categories, for example small business and big business, city and rural consumers, access providers and access seekers, established firms and new entrants. These groups are likely to form moving alliances on issues with which the competition agency deals. It can be very much in the agency's interests to try to ensure it does not get too many groups offside at once. Support from interest groups – or at least an absence of concerted opposition – is vital to an agency's success, and even its survival over the long term.

On the other hand, clearly the agency should not consistently seek to curry favour with any one group. Even consumers are likely to oppose some of the agency's positions, for example if it seeks to make cross-subsidies – where one group of users is required to pay higher prices so that another group can be charged lower prices for the same service – more transparent or reduce them. It may even be a measure of success that the agency upsets every interest group at some time, but not always in the same way and not always the same groupings. This is not a matter of adjusting decisions to make them more acceptable to particular groups, but rather of trying to control the agenda – the subject matter and timing of decisions – so that no group is consistently on the wrong end of the agency's decisions and no group is seen to be unduly favoured.

Even the government comes into these calculations. Any active, effective and assertive competition agency will incur the wrath of government officials and ministers sooner or later. At that time, it can be helpful if the government can also recall occasions when the agency has been of assistance to it, for example by taking the heat out of some consumer issue or supporting the government when it makes necessary but unpopular reforms.

Objectives of competitive policy and economic regulation

Objectives come in several forms. In the first place there are those related to market and industry outcomes, such as changes in industry structure, reductions in anticompetitive behaviour, and so on. There are also objectives related to the agency, such as the number and quality of its decisions, and issues like transparency and consistency. This framework is set out in Figure 3.1.

To expand on this, it is clear that the objectives of competition policy and economic regulation relate to market outcomes. In terms of *market structure*, one of the aims of general competition policy is not allowing monopolisation of industries and, more broadly, not allowing anticompetitive mergers. While the existence of a monopoly or of a substantial degree of market power is not usually against the law, mergers that substantially lessen competition are prohibited. In regulated industries the aim may be more specifically to disaggregate vertically a dominant incumbent firm and to foster the development of competition, including facilitating new entry into the industry.

Turning to *market conduct*, the competition policy objective is to prevent anticompetitive agreements and the misuse of market power. Economic regulation is likely to aim for non-discriminatory access to the services provided

Figure 3.1 A model for assessing economic objectives

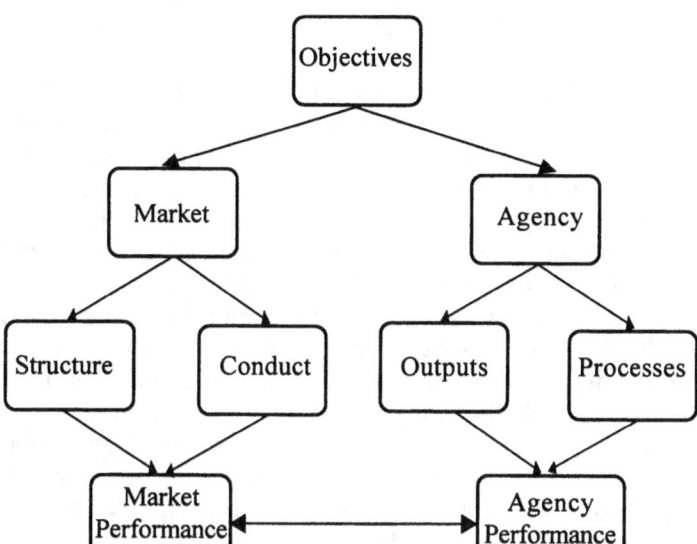

by firms that control bottleneck facilities, including by controlling the access prices they charge. Economic regulation may also seek to reduce the prices paid by end users for services such as electricity and telecommunications below what a monopoly supplier would charge. In addition, the market conduct of regulated firms is often constrained in other ways, such as by requirements to provide universal access to their services and to cross-subsidies between customers.

It can be seen that these market objectives are largely the matters that were mentioned earlier in the initial brief discussion of what competition and economic regulation consist of. However, some elements of regulatory objectives, such as universal service obligations (USOs) and cross-subsidies, are new. In any case, these market structure and conduct objectives are largely given to the competition or regulatory agency by government; they may well be set in legislation or flow directly from the prohibitions provided for in general competition policy and the powers and obligations provided for in regulatory frameworks. In the case of legislative prohibitions, market objectives may be summarised as good compliance with the law.

However, market structure and conduct are of interest because they influence what really matters, in terms of how firms and industries service their customers and in terms of market performance.[3] Compliance with the law is of interest only because of the underlying purposes of the law, which go to how well markets perform. Generally, such performance is best understood in terms of economic efficiency, in all its forms. Thus, the legal and administrative manifestations of competition policy need to be related back to the idea that social welfare is improved by greater economic efficiency. Incorporated in this framework is the idea that competition is the best driver of greater efficiency.

In the area of economic regulation, it is a bit more complicated. Often, more specific objectives are set in terms, for example, of promoting competition, as opposed to protecting it or trying to ensure it is not deterred. This is an important distinction and can lead to the mistake of seeing competition as an objective in its own right, which can have undesirable consequences if it translates into a desire to promote the interests of competitors and increase the number of firms in an industry, even at the expense of economic efficiency.

In regulated industries there are often issues of sunk and stranded costs, natural monopoly and whether firms are able to recover their total costs. One quite specific formulation of the market performance objective in regulated industries is 'to achieve the lowest possible prices for consumers (on, say, an annual average basis) consistent with a financially viable industry' (Wolak 2002). In more formal terms this is expressed as maximising consumer surplus subject to the marginal firm in the industry earning zero economic profit.

This formulation is not inconsistent with others such as 'promoting the long-term interests of end-users', which is the statutory objective of telecommunications regulation in Australia. They have in common the idea that consumer welfare cannot be maximised over anything but the short term without regard to producer welfare. Thus efficient investment in and use of infrastructure are brought into the picture. Notions of innovation and choice are also seen as part of the objective. Thus, even for economic regulation, it is appropriate to see the ultimate market performance objective in terms of economic efficiency, including dynamic efficiency. However, it must be conceded that USOs and cross-subsidies do not sit easily with efficiency, so trade-offs are required.

These market-related objectives, which are the ultimate ends of competition policy and economic regulation, are also objectives of the competition or regulatory agency. But the agency should also have objectives that go to the means of achieving those ends. Whether these are called sub-objectives or something else does not matter; but an agency needs to have ways of measuring its internal performance as well as market outcomes, not least because market outcomes are influenced by many things in addition to the agency's performance.

One way of categorising these *internal agency objectives* is in terms of outputs and processes. *Outputs* include matters such as the quantity and quality of decisions, guidelines for firms on the agency's approaches to its functions, and success in court proceedings. *Processes* include such things as the timeliness of decisions, the effectiveness of consultations, and compliance with the requirements of administrative law, including procedural fairness or natural justice.

These categories overlap. For example, the quality of decisions depends partly on the effectiveness of consultation processes. Nevertheless, it is useful for an agency to set itself objectives that try to capture its essential outputs and important aspects of its processes and to monitor its performance against both sorts of objectives. How it should report externally against those objectives – and indeed against market performance objectives – is perhaps best left to a separate debate. Processes will be discussed in more detail shortly.

The *agency's performance* against both output and process objectives will be reflected in its reputation, and the agency should also have aims that relate directly to that reputation. Is the agency seen as credible in the sense that its announced intentions and forecasts are believed? Is it trustworthy in the sense that firms can rely on advice it gives them about its approaches being adhered to? Is it seen to have integrity? Does it have a reputation for not shirking difficult issues? Is it considered fair? Is it respected? Is it feared, and, if so, by wrongdoers or by all who have dealings with it?

Perhaps most tellingly, is the agency seen to be successful? Does it take on and win hard cases? The reason this is important – beyond its impact on agency morale – is that such a reputation aids in future performance. It helps in getting compliance with legislation and in achieving good market outcomes.

Principles

Some of the principles for effective competition policy have already been mentioned in the discussion on objectives. This chapter takes the view that economic efficiency is a key principle of both competition policy and economic regulation. However, there is more to be said about principles.

One of the most difficult issues – it might even be called a dilemma – in competition policy is how to prevent anticompetitive conduct without hampering desirable competitive conduct. The reason this is difficult is that there is sometimes a narrow line between competitive conduct and anticompetitive conduct. Behaviour that is unexceptionable when carried out by a firm that does not have market power can be damaging to competition when undertaken by a firm that does have a substantial degree of market power.

The competitive process is vigorous and combative. Firms can be destroyed by healthy competition. The process by which businesses jockey for position and seek to obtain market power is socially desirable. What is not desirable is if they succeed in obtaining market power and keeping it for sustained periods. But damage to competitors must not be mistaken for damage to the competitive process, even though damage to the competitive process usually involves damage to individual firms. The principle, therefore, is that prohibitions on anticompetitive conduct should be neither too inclusive nor too exclusive.

Another way of saying this is that antitrust action may sometimes err in penalising behaviour that is in fact desirable. At other times it may err in allowing behaviour that is harmful. Clearly both types of errors are to be avoided as far as possible. This requires careful drafting of legislation, sensible interpretation by the courts and responsible administration by the competition agency.

It is not unusual for an agency to be over-zealous in attacking borderline anticompetitive conduct. For example, behaviour by a firm clearly designed to damage a competitor and successful in doing so may be subject to action, even if barriers to entry in the industry are low. Delicate issues of judgement are involved in deciding whether a firm's substantial market power is of major concern or whether that power is only transitory. These are matters of considerable debate between economists, even now. In some ways they appear to revolve around differences of time horizon: how long must power be exercised before it is considered sustained and dangerous to competition? How far are governments prepared to go in deterring attempts to increase market power, even if such attempts would turn out to be unsuccessful in the long run?

One of the things that makes economic regulation different from general competition policy is the timeframe concerned. Competition policy is an ongoing activity. There is no reason to think that a time will come when anticompetitive agreements and mergers will no longer be a concern, or when the misuse of market power will fade away. Antitrust activity is always in season. Some forms of economic regulation, however, may have a limited life. Indeed, it is generally hoped when access regimes are set up that their need will diminish over time as competition develops.

Some suggested principles for economic regulation therefore include:

- that regulation should be restricted to the smallest possible portion of an industry (with only general competition policy applying elsewhere);
- that regulation focus on areas of strong market power and opportunities to leverage that market power; and
- that the need for and scope of regulation be reviewed from time to time, and not just by the regulator.

A very useful framework for access regulation proposes the idea of an indifference test: competitive neutrality is achieved when a firm's ability to compete successfully on the basis of efficiency advantages and to recover total costs is invariant to the identity of the firm that provides access. The access price will have been set at the right level by the regulator if a firm is indifferent whether it sells access or purchases access (Tye 2002).

Another principle worth remembering is that incentives are stronger in their impact on behaviour, and are probably more enduring, than attempts at external control. Although it is not always easy, it is well worthwhile to look for ways of encouraging corporate conduct that is desirable from a community perspective (e.g., cost minimisation) and rewarding to the corporation. Perhaps finding disincentives to undesirable conduct is less difficult.

As to institutional matters, perhaps the most obvious and widely acknowledged principle is that regulatory decision making should be free of undue influences.

Effective regulation requires the ability to make decisions that are unpopular in some quarters, to stand up to powerful interests and to take a measured view. This cannot be done consistently without *independence* from government. Moreover, despite their not infrequent desire to become involved in the day-to-day work of regulators, governments just as frequently find it advantageous to be at arm's length from regulatory action.

There is a continuing debate over the desirability of separating policy formulation from policy administration. In areas other than competition policy and economic regulation (e.g., health and welfare policy, program administration), views differ about separation. In some countries and at certain times, such programs are run by the same ministries that advise the government on policy. Experience with running programs provides very useful insights into needed policy changes. On the other hand, sometimes programs are administered by separate agencies with varying degrees of independence from the policy-advising ministry. This provides the opportunity to ensure that program administration is closely in accordance with the law and less susceptible to political influence.

It might be thought to follow from the desirability of the independence of the competition/regulatory agency from government that the agency should not have a role in formulating competition or regulatory policy. However, it is not uncommon for such agencies to advocate changes that they see as desirable, whether they be fine-tuning of legislation or fundamental shifts in a regulatory regime.

Again, the agency with experience in administering legislation invariably has valuable knowledge of the legislation's shortcomings and is well placed to suggest improvements. Nevertheless, a good principle is to ensure that the agency is not the sole or even the pre-eminent source of advice to the government on its own functions. It is a rare agency that will not succumb to the temptation to seek greater and greater powers.

A further but related form of separation concerns decisions about what should be regulated vis-à-vis actual day-to-day regulation. Generally speaking, it seems desirable that decisions about whether a service (e.g., one provided by particular infrastructure) is to be regulated should be made by someone other than the access regulator. However, it is difficult to be confidently dogmatic, because the regulator may well have a deeper understanding of the relevant market dynamics and appear to be better placed than other parts of government to make the decision.

This raises the issue of the degree of finality of regulatory decisions. A key tension is between timeliness of regulatory action and rights of appeal against regulatory decisions. (This applies to both general competition policy decisions and to economic regulation.) This chapter will not discuss in any detail the various types of appeal that may exist against the decisions of a regulator or competition agency, for example appeals against administrative errors and appeals on the merits of a case. However, it would seem sensible that where a regulator is given the power to decide what services or parts of an industry fall within the regulatory net, those decisions should be able to be appealed on the merits of each case.

Rights of appeal may be seen as part of the wider issue of *accountability*. An agency may have many different types of accountability, for example to Parliament, to the courts and to the general public through the media. The greater the powers of the agency, the greater should be its accountability and the more external scrutiny it should be subjected to. Similarly, the greater its discretion, the more carefully the way in which that discretion is exercised should be monitored.

Building a robust but fair and effective regulatory framework, including in relation to general competition policy, requires all sorts of balances to be established. Not least is the need to ensure that the regulatory agency is not too powerful or too unconstrained in its actions. Nevertheless, care must be taken so that appropriate checks and balances on the regulator do not so circumscribe its effectiveness that the result is the 'Enronisation' of an industry, where a powerful firm is allowed a key role in writing the rules of the game, is able to limit the umpire's role, plays the game hard, and is then the one to report the score to stakeholders.

Processes[4]

As with principles, some of the processes associated with effective competition policy, such as consultation with stakeholders, have been discussed above in the context of objectives. Moreover, issues such as accountability may be seen as matters of process. However, accountability is ultimately imposed on the agency from outside. Under the heading of processes will be discussed areas over which the agency itself has substantial control.

An example is *transparency*. The agency should strive to make its objectives, administrative procedures, approaches to issues and decision-making principles as widely known and easily understood as possible. In addition, it should clearly explain the reasons for its decisions. Of course, various requirements for achieving transparency may be imposed on the agency through its legislation. Thus, transparency is an essential part of being accountable. However, the agency should seek to establish high standards of transparency beyond what is formally required of it. An agency may be tempted to hide behind weasel words such as 'decisions are matters of judgement' and not release the calculations behind decisions for fear that their spurious precision makes them difficult to defend. This temptation must be resisted. The reason is partly that transparency is necessary to ensure fairness, but most importantly because it improves decision making and hence the quality of decisions.

A wise agency will facilitate scrutiny of its decisions; in the long run that is the best safeguard against sloppy thinking and eventual embarrassment.

At times, however, transparency has to be balanced against other requirements, such as reasonable rights to privacy and the protection of commercially or otherwise sensitive information.

Balance is even more an issue in dealing with some other administrative processes, especially consistency, predictability and flexibility. *Consistency* is highly desirable, but can be a debilitating constraint if taken too far. Consistency in decision making applies across industries, firms and time. It is obviously necessary to achieve fairness, although, paradoxically, in extreme circumstances breaking with consistency may be fairer if an approach is shown to have become so outmoded and inappropriate that it would create injustice to persist with it.

The adage goes: there is no virtue in consistency if you are consistently wrong. But in many decisions, the difference between right and wrong is one of fine judgement, for example in the interpretation of provisions in legislation or in setting a price. Views can change over what was right and what was wrong. An agency might with full justification make a decision that 'x' is right, but on re-examining the matter a year later, might decide that a better view is that 'y' is right. Sometimes it is better to stick with the earlier decision rather than overturn one's prior thinking, for the reason set out by Justice Brandeis in relation to the law: 'in most matters it is more important that the applicable rule of law be settled than that it be settled right'.[5]

Predictability is related to consistency. As far as possible, businesses should not be subjected to unexpected changes in the policy and regulatory environment. The competition agency should not signal that it will act in one way and then act in another way. Similar conduct should be treated in a similar manner. Business should be able to plan and act in accordance with the agency's past decisions. More than that, the agency should try to foreshadow how it will act in the future, given particular circumstances, and then stick to its promises.

The tendency is always for an agency to keep its options open: to be afraid to say what it would do in hypothetical circumstances in case it wishes to act differently when a real case comes along. This is another temptation that, while natural, should be resisted. The agency should of course be careful in circumscribing its discretion and freedom to act in the future, but it should positively seek to do so nonetheless. Again, so long as reckless promises are not made, signalling future approaches leads to better decision making. This can be done by publishing decision-making criteria, timetables, and so on.

Flexibility in decision making is often regarded as a virtue. Certainly an agency needs to be able to respond appropriately as circumstances change. In addition, a mix of regulatory tools may be available, to some extent alternative approaches can be experimented with, and major changes in the regulatory environment need to be acknowledged. However, in practice, flexibility is much easier to achieve than consistency and predictability. This is because consistency and predictability reduce discretion and require greater forward thinking if they are to be exercised sensibly. Flexibility can degenerate into indecisive and capricious decision making. It is a question of balance, but courage and skill are required to get the right level of consistency and predictability.

Other elements of best-practice processes include administrative efficiency, timeliness and good communication. These are all well understood and do not raise difficult issues about how to get the balance right.

ORGANISATIONAL SKILLS AND CULTURE

If the objectives, principles and processes associated with effective competition policy and economic regulation are largely accepted, the next question is how to build an agency with all these attributes.

Skills

Some things have already been said in passing about the skills needed in a competition/regulatory agency. Obviously an agency needs staff with legal and economic skills, and a smattering of other disciplines such as accounting is also useful.

A challenge is to bring economic and legal approaches together productively. Especially in competition policy, when dealing with legal prohibitions, the law is in some ways paramount. However, the law is trying to express economic concepts and to deal with economic behaviour. As mentioned above, understanding the difference between anticompetitive conduct and healthy, vigorous competition in which some firms get hurt is not always straightforward. Economic analysis is needed to ensure that the underlying objectives – efficiency and the competitive process – are kept in mind when considering whether the black-letter requirements for finding a breach of the law are being met.

Another difficult task requiring economic expertise – more commonly confronted in the regulatory role – is the process of market design. Often deregulation is a process of removing outmoded government intervention that prevents competition from taking place. Once the impediments are removed, it is only a matter of time before new entrants get a foothold in the industry.

However, in some areas it is not as simple as this. In electricity market reform, the actual design of the market – how participants transact with each other, rules about settlement, the introduction of new instruments to manage risk – is very much a matter of regulatory policy choice. Similarly, designing means of selling electromagnetic spectrum so as to achieve efficient outcomes raises complex economic issues. Indeed, in both these areas new property rights are being created. However, processes, rules and rights ultimately have to be expressed in legally enforceable terms.

A separate question is the types of personal styles and approaches that are needed in a successful agency.

If the agency has the task of taking cases to court, skills in litigation management are needed. This is a function that cannot be delegated to outside lawyers. Rather, agency staff with tenacity, drive and even cunning are required if cases are to be pursued expeditiously in the face of the multiple opportunities that all legal systems provide for slowing litigation down. Cases have to be fought from time to time against large corporations with huge resources and lawyers who can resort to all sorts of tricks and stratagems to delay and frustrate the course of justice. Only concerted efforts can overcome such opposition.

Thus it is not just a matter of an agency needing lawyers on its staff. It needs the right sort of lawyers to get the job done. Another use of lawyers is in interpreting legislation, advising on the scope and limits of the agency's powers, and designing and maintaining oversight over processes to ensure, for example, that procedural fairness is provided. On the one hand, an agency needs lawyers who can give careful and cautious advice that will keep it out of trouble. On the other hand, there are times when a lawyer is needed whose approach is – rather than advising against a proposed course of action because of all the difficulties – to come up with ways of making the approach work.

This need for complementary skills – thinkers, doers and even dreamers, those who are cautious and those who crash through, introverts and extroverts, reactive people and proactive people – extends beyond lawyers across all subject matters and disciplines. One of the major tasks of the agency head is to seek out people with these complementary approaches and skills and, in particular, to find people whose skills are complementary to his or her own.

Culture

The balance between these different sorts of skills partly determines the agency's organisational culture. Are thinkers or doers in the ascendant? Is the general approach cautious and risk averse or does the agency stick its neck out and seek to open new frontiers, to push the envelope? Moderation in all things is probably a sensible approach, but culture often follows from a leadership style. The example and personal approach of the agency head are critical.

In its early days, an agency may be well advised to get some quick runs on the board. One or two early successes can generate long-term goodwill and keep critics at bay. This is a matter of carefully picking marks and throwing all necessary resources into the task. Developing a reputation for overcaution will severely hamper an agency's effectiveness, but the other extreme – where the typical command to the troops is 'Ready! Fire! Aim!' – is not to be encouraged.

As suggested earlier, a useful aspect of organisational culture – which like other aspects must be reinforced by the leader's example – is a welcoming of scrutiny. Secretiveness breeds trouble, for eventually secrets tend to be revealed.

Although a strong culture – one in which staff share values – is usually a strength, it can be dangerous if it leads to groupthink, where everyone in the organisation approaches issues in such a similar manner that changes in the external environment, and new and better ways of doing things, are ignored. Again, awareness of this risk needs to be imbued in the top leadership of the organisation without disturbing the commitment of the staff more generally.

For example, it is useful for agency staff to believe strongly in the rightness of what they do, to be determined to stamp out anticompetitive behaviour and to pursue wrongdoers vigorously. This can often lead to a sceptical and aggressive approach to businesses being investigated for breaching the competition laws. This is all right if not taken to extremes, manifesting itself in gratuitous rudeness or even bullying of firms. It is up to the agency's senior management to encourage such determination and commitment while maintaining their own open-mindedness and being receptive to other points of view than those commonly expressed internally.

There are some differences in the nature of regulatory activities and the enforcement of competition policy that lead to differences in organisational culture. A competition agency that operates by taking cases to court necessarily adopts an adversarial attitude to firms that it investigates. Moreover, the relationship between the agency and such a firm is likely to be tense, but to last only for the period of the particular case.

A regulatory agency, on the other hand, necessarily deals with the same firms more or less daily, year after year. While a similar adversarial relationship may develop, both sides also need cooperation as there are likely to be ongoing information flows in both directions.

Moreover, a regulated industry often involves a series of bilateral relationships between a dominant firm such as an access provider and a series of smaller access seekers-cum-competitors. The regulator may be required to intervene in these bilateral relationships. In competition policy, by contrast, the focus is more squarely on the process of competition rather than individual competitors. This difference also leads to different agency approaches and even outlooks. It also suggests the need to examine how well competition policy and regulatory functions fit together in a single agency.

SYNERGIES[6]

'Synergy' comes from a Greek word meaning 'working together', so it is highly relevant to competition policy and economic regulation.

Although there are important differences between competition policy and economic regulation roles, the similarities are also great. Both fundamentally involve dealing with market power. Both seek to have competition work in the interests of community welfare through greater economic efficiency. Consequently, synergies exist between competition policy and economic regulation, largely because the same staff expertise can be applied and because combining several possible approaches in a single agency through its range of powers increases the chance that they will be used in a co-coordinated manner.

Nevertheless, it is worth examining the differences, or what are said by some commentators to be differences. The OECD identifies five, paraphrased in Table 3.1.

There is a lot of truth in this exposition of typical differences, but some of these characteristics that make for differences are within the control of the agency and can be changed. For example, it may be of benefit (there may be a further synergy) when exercising the regulatory role to have regard to the

Table 3.1 Comparing competition policy and economic regulation

Competition policy	Economic regulation
Reducing market power.	Attenuating the effects of market power.
Prefer structural remedies.	Impose behavioural conditions.
Ex post enforcement (except for mergers).	Ex ante prescriptive approach.
Rely on complaints; gather information only when necessary in relation to particular enforcement action.	Intervene frequently; require continual flow of information from regulated firms.
Relatively narrow range of goals that do not substantially conflict with each other.	Broader range of goals requiring adeptness at making trade-offs.

Source: OECD (1999).

desirability of employing structural remedies wherever possible. This is more likely to happen where one agency exercises both competition policy and regulatory roles.

The OECD goes on to suggest differences between the approaches of competition agencies and economic regulators, which the list in Table 3.2 expands a little.

This list suggests some further synergies as well as tensions. For example, when regulation is carried out within the general competition agency, problems of jurisdictional boundaries are lessened, if not removed, and regulation is likely to be more consistent across sectors. Similarly, the risks of regulatory capture and the tendency to hold onto powers no longer needed as competition develops may be reduced.

Indeed, this whole list may be thought to support a case for bringing competition policy and economic regulation under one roof. Why should the benefits of regulation be offset by any significant lessening of the effectiveness of competition policy?

However, this conclusion rests on an assumption that the desirable characteristics of a competition policy approach would beneficially influence modes of regulation; that the organisational culture of a competition agency would apply in a combined agency. The assumption may be wrong.

What if the agency gets to like exercising the greater, more intrusive and more detailed powers of a regulator and opts to apply them more broadly – beyond the network/utility industries for which they are designed? What if the general competition agency loses its aversion to setting prices? Suppose the competition agency clings to its broader powers and becomes less objective

Table 3.2 Comparing the roles of competition agencies and economic regulators

Competition policy agency	Economic regulatory agency
Believes in the benefits of competition and motivated to demonstrate them across many sectors.	Resigned to the existence of market failure and sustained market power, and ready to impose regulation indefinitely as a result.
Sees static and dynamic efficiency as the ultimate goal.	Sees efficiency as desirable but unachievable; may also have distributional goals.
Familiar with market analysis and identifying market power and anti-competitive conduct.	Works within a predetermined market definition.
Recognises similarities and differences between industries.	Sees regulated industries as unique; oriented toward particular firms.
Willing to wind down economic regulation as competition becomes strong enough.	Would lose raison d'être if regulation ceased, or staff and influence if wound back.
Less subject to regulatory capture since there is less interdependence between agency and industry/firms; staff skills and experience less sought by firms.	May come to share regulated firms' perspectives, scepticism about competition, need for cross-subsidies. Future of agency intertwined with that of regulated firms.
Dislikes the idea of setting prices.	Setting prices is a routine activity.
Not subject to much political involvement.	Utility prices and performance are quintessentially political.

Source: OECD (1999).

about opportunities for winding back regulation. Perhaps the competition policy role will become more politicised rather than the economic regulation role less so.

All this is without even discussing the fact that network/utility industries generally require technical regulation as well as economic regulation. Technical regulation typically involves the setting and policing of standards so as to ensure compatibility and allow interconnection between networks, as well as matters such as safety and environmental protection. The skills required are partly of an engineering nature, but clearly standards also have economic dimensions and impacts.

It would be impractical to give these technical regulation functions to a combined competition policy and economic regulator. The agency would become too large, as technical expertise is largely specialised to each industry, whereas the competition policy and economic regulation issues are largely generic, although they have to be applied in the particular circumstances of individual industries. But there are also synergies between technical regulation and economic regulation through familiarity with the industry and depth of knowledge of its peculiarities. These would be forgone if economic regulation were combined with competition policy rather than with technical regulation. Indeed, sector-specific combined technical and economic regulators are the norm rather than the exception.

It is not possible to have everything. On balance, genuine synergies do potentially seem to exist between competition policy and economic regulation, but perhaps safeguards are needed – at least in the form of constant vigilance – to see that they are exploited and that the downside risks are minimised. After all, the experience in the private sector is that potential synergies of merging activities are often identified, but actually achieving them is very hard work.

It can surely be said with some certainty, however, that general competition policy should not be restricted in its application. It should apply to regulated industries as well as to the general economy.

CONCLUSION

Implementing any policy effectively involves a vast number of processes and skills as well as strong leadership and good management. This chapter proposes a few simple frameworks for thinking about the issues.

First, it is useful to think about implementation in terms of a series of leadership and management tasks, each requiring distinctive skills.

Second, the policy environment and of course the specifics of what constitutes competition policy in a given country need to be taken into account. Competition policy is broadened out to consider economic regulation in the same context. Given individual circumstances, setting the objectives of effective policy can be structured in terms of separate market and agency goals, going to market structure and conduct on the one hand, and agency outputs and processes on the other. Market objectives can be drawn together through their impact on overall market performance, while agency goals combine to determine agency performance, which affects the agency's reputation (which can itself be seen as a matter of agency choice).

Third, it is useful to explore the principles and processes of effective competition policy and economic regulation in the light of market and agency objectives. Transparency and accountability are argued to be essential for good decision making, which manifests consistency and predictability over flexibility.

Fourth, consideration of skills and organisational culture throws up not only requirements for effective implementation but also choices.

Finally, choices are also apparent in thinking through the question of whether competition policy and regulation are best carried out together in a single agency, or in the more traditional manner where regulation is undertaken by sector-specific agencies. Potential synergies certainly exist, but there are also risks.

As in other areas of public administration and law enforcement, many balances need to be achieved if competition policy and economic regulation are to be effective. While some of these choices are within the control of those charged with administering policy (e.g., in a competition and/or regulatory agency), others involve decisions about the way the agency is established and the relationships between it and other parts of government.

NOTES

1. Access regulation typically applies where downstream competitors (e.g., train operators) require access to an upstream bottleneck facility (e.g., railway track) that exhibits natural monopoly characteristics. Other examples of bottleneck facilities are the local loop in telecommunications (i.e., the set of wires connecting subscribers to their local exchanges) and electricity and gas distribution networks.
2. Some forms of anticompetitive conduct proscribed by general competition law, such as price fixing and market sharing, may not require the existence of market power. Nevertheless, for the remainder of the discussion in this chapter, market power is a common element between general competition policy and economic regulation.
3. Note that despite the use of the terms structure, conduct and performance, the familiar structure–conduct–performance paradigm is not being used here. In particular, no causal link is being postulated (or denied) between structure and conduct. Rather, all that is being suggested is that if high-level objectives are set for market performance, sub-objectives in terms of market structure and conduct may also be useful; that is, that structure and conduct separately and perhaps together influence performance.
4. The following discussion owes something to Office of Water Regulation (1999).
5. See Burnet vs Coronado Oil and Gas Co., 285 US 393, 406 (1932) (Justice Louis Brandeis, dissenting).
6. This discussion draws on OECD (1999), but takes some liberties in expressing the very useful ideas therein and does not necessarily agree with all of them.

REFERENCES

Leavitt, Harold J. (1985) *Corporate Pathfinders: Building Vision and Value into Organizations*, August, New York: McGraw Hill.

Office of Water Regulation (1999) 'Best practice utility regulation', discussion paper prepared for the Utility Regulators Forum, Perth, Western Australia, July.

Organisation for Economic Cooperation and Development (OECD) (1999) 'Relationship between regulators and competition authorities', proceedings of a roundtable held by the Committee on Competition Law and Policy, DAFFE/CLP(99)8, June, Paris: OECD.

Tye, William B. (2002) 'Competitive neutrality: regulating interconnection disputes in the transition to competition', paper presented to the ACCC Regulation and Competition Conference, Sydney, July.

Wolak, Frank A. (2002) 'Market-based regulatory mechanisms in re-structured network industries', presentation to the ACCC Regulation and Competition Conference, Sydney, July.

4 Competition policy, economic development and the possible role of a multilateral framework on competition policy: insights from the WTO working group on trade and competition policy

Robert Anderson and Frédéric Jenny

INTRODUCTION

The relationship between competition policy and economic development has been a central theme in the work of the World Trade Organisation's Working Group on the Interaction between Trade and Competition Policy and of related technical assistance activities undertaken by the WTO Secretariat over the past several years. This work has identified a number of ways in which anticompetitive practices of firms can impede economic development, and in which national competition policies that are appropriately adapted to the circumstances of developing countries can support development. These findings are independent of questions regarding the pros and cons of a possible WTO agreement on competition policy, which has also been extensively discussed in the working group but on which a consensus has been lacking.

This chapter examines the links between competition policy, development and trade liberalisation. It begins with a review of the role and importance of competition policy and its relationship to economic reform in developing countries. Account is also taken of the role of such policy in addressing international anticompetitive practices. The chapter outlines some of the arguments that have been put forward in the WTO working group regarding the potential benefits for developing countries of a WTO framework on competition policy. It also outlines the principal elements that have been proposed for inclusion should negotiations on such a framework be launched, which has now been ruled out for the duration of the Doha Round (see discussion below). The purpose is not to defend or advocate a particular approach toward future WTO work (if any) on trade and competition policy, but to facilitate informed discussion in the international community.

The central theme of this chapter is the fundamental complementarity of competition policy, trade liberalisation and domestic economic reform, and their importance for development. In debates on development, poverty alleviation and the WTO, it is sometimes argued that a WTO initiative on competition policy would deplete scarce human and institutional resources that would be better applied in the pursuit of external liberalisation (see, e.g., Winters 2002). This reflects a false dichotomy. As important as external liberalisation is, it is unlikely to achieve its objectives absent internal market reforms to facilitate an appropriate supply-side response. Furthermore, absent effective competition policies, the economic welfare gains expected to materialise from the reduction of government-imposed barriers to trade can be undercut by the operation of international anticompetitive practices such as cartels. Ample evidence now exists that such cartels are a recurring feature of markets that lack effective competition rules and institutions, and that appropriate enforcement actions by developed countries, while of vital importance, do not adequately protect the interests of developing countries in this area.

In addition to addressing the above concerns, competition policy can itself contribute to continuing external liberalisation, through the advocacy activities of competition agencies. In particular, competition agencies can become an important source of analytical support for continuing market-oriented reforms, both internal and external. For these reasons, appropriate investments in national competition policies are more likely to contribute to than detract from external liberalisation efforts. Nonetheless, in order to be effective, it is important that competition law and institutions are adapted to national economic circumstances and institutional constraints.

The possible role and content of a WTO agreement in this area has been widely misunderstood, including in learned journals and by otherwise well-informed authors. For example, in the run-up to the 2004 Cancun Ministerial, an article in *Foreign Affairs* (Evans 2002) reiterated the concern that WTO rules on competition policy 'could be administered through a supranational agency', notwithstanding that this possibility figured nowhere in any of the recent or earlier proposals that have been made in the context of the WTO and has been explicitly disavowed by the proponents of WTO negotiations on various occasions (see, e.g., Garcia-Bercero and Amarasinha 2001). Also, extensive references were made to the possibility of a WTO antitrust code – implying a comprehensive set of substantive rules. As elaborated below, the proposals for a WTO agreement in this area indicate that any such agreement (if negotiations were eventually to be launched) is likely to be a good deal more modest in its content and aspirations. In particular, such an agreement would likely focus on the promotion of voluntary cooperation and technical assistance, in addition to modest commitments to action against hardcore cartels and to adherence to core principles of transparency, non-discrimination and procedural fairness that are widely recognised as being central to the effective implementation of competition policy.[1] It would not involve the harmonisation of competition laws, where this term is understood as implying the enforcement of uniform approaches to competition policy at the national level (Garcia-Bercero and Amarasinha 2001).

This chapter discusses the role of competition policy in developing countries, drawing on, among other sources, work completed in the WTO Working Group on the Interaction between Trade and Competition Policy, and considers the domestic and international applications of competition law in addition to the advocacy function of competition institutions. Some of the arguments that have been made in favour of action on competition policy in the framework of the WTO are discussed, in addition to the major reservation that has been voiced by developing countries with regard to a possible WTO agreement in this area – namely, the concern that such an agreement would limit their policy options and development strategies. To carry the discussion forward, some key aspects of the recent proposals for a multilateral framework on competition policy are outlined.

THE RELEVANCE OF COMPETITION POLICY FOR DEVELOPING ECONOMIES

Competition law and/or policy[2] is important to protect consumers and industrial users from anticompetitive practices that raise prices and reduce output. This is no less true in developing countries than in developed ones. In fact, there are reasons for believing that less mature markets tend to be more, rather than less, vulnerable to anticompetitive practices. The reasons include: (a) high 'natural' entry barriers due to inadequate business infrastructure, including distribution channels, and (sometimes) intrusive regulatory regimes; (b) asymmetries of information in both product and credit markets; and (c) a greater proportion of local (non-tradable) markets. For these reasons, consumers in developing countries are more vulnerable to anticompetitive practices and have a particularly compelling need to be protected against cartels, monopoly abuses and the creation of new monopolies through mergers. The competition agency can also play a useful role in making the case for related policy and legal reforms (e.g., property rights, contract enforcement and corporate governance) that are necessary to create a healthy market economy (see, for useful elaboration, Dutz 2002).

A specific role of competition policy which may be of particular importance in developing countries (although it is important in all economies) relates to the prevention of bid rigging in public procurement processes. Empirical evidence suggests that the costs of bid rigging to public treasuries substantially exceed the costs of establishing a competition office to investigate and deter such activities (see discussion and references cited below). The possibility of rigged bids cannot be prevented merely by opening procurement processes to foreign competitors, since the latter may be party to any bid-rigging conspiracies (see, e.g., US Department of Justice 2000).

The argument is sometimes made that competition policy is irrelevant in circumstances of extreme poverty. However, where incomes are severely limited, it would seem even more important than otherwise that the purchasing power of consumers not be further diminished through anticompetitive practices. There is growing evidence that anticompetitive practices are particularly prevalent in regard to goods for which there are limited substitutes available in developing country markets, for example foodstuffs. Many of the major international cartels disclosed in the mid- to late 1990s were believed to have been active in developing country markets, for example those relating to the sale of vitamins, lysine and citric acid, all important inputs to agrifood production (Levenstein and Suslow 2001; Evenett et al. 2001; Jenny 2001; Anderson and Holmes 2002). Similarly, the effective prevention of bid rigging would seem to be particularly important where, as in many developing countries, governments are subject to severe fiscal constraints.

Fortunately, the evidence is also growing that, with appropriate resources and training, developing countries can take steps to deal effectively with anticompetitive practices that affect their consumers. A recent comparative study of the role of competition policy in Africa and South Asia initiated by the Consumer Unity and Trust Society with participation from numerous outside researchers found important parallels between the experiences of developing and transition economies (Consumer Unity and Trust Society 2003). The countries studied were India, Sri Lanka, Pakistan, Zambia, Kenya, Tanzania and South Africa, all of which have taken steps to reduce protectionism, reliance on state-owned enterprises and bureaucratic control of the private sector, and have seen fit to implement competition laws in one form or another. In addition, in a few cases, advanced developing countries such as Mexico, Brazil and Korea have initiated successful enforcement actions in relation to international cartels (Working Group on the Interaction between Trade and Competition Policy 2003a; Hur 2002; Mexico 2002). Moreover, evidence regarding the implementation of competition policy as tool of economic transformation in Central and Eastern Europe suggests that in the majority of countries in that region competition law provisions (in particular, provisions relating to abuses of a dominant position) have not, contrary to concerns expressed by some Western analysts at the time the laws were enacted, been overused or used in ways that are counterproductive (see Pittman 2004).

Work in the WTO working group in addition to other venues has highlighted the need for a pragmatic approach to the introduction of competition policies in developing countries, focusing on the most blatantly harmful practices and avoiding overly elaborate institutional structures. The inappropriateness of a one-size-fits-all approach and the necessity of adapting competition policy to the economic circumstances and institutional endowments of individual countries have been repeatedly stressed, including by the proponents of a WTO agreement in this area (WTO Working Group on the Interaction between Trade and Competition Policy 2001, paragraph 15; WTO Working Group on the Interaction between Trade and Competition Policy 2003b, paragraph 16). Under one possible approach discussed in the working group, a national competition authority would first focus on the suppression of horizontal cartels (the most unambiguously harmful type of enterprise practice) and on basic competition advocacy activities relating to essential market reforms. After gaining adequate experience in these areas, it would then take on additional responsibilities for matters such as merger review and anticompetitive vertical restraints. In the last stage, it would take on more sweeping responsibilities for competition advocacy activities relating to all aspects of the interplay between competition policy and regulation (WTO Working Group on the Interaction between Trade and Competition Policy 1998, paragraph 51). Noteworthy here are both the non-insistence on immediate adoption of comprehensive competition laws and the emphasis placed on the advocacy function (for elaboration, see below).

Facilitating a supply-side response to trade liberalisation and reinforcing domestic reforms

As Osakwe (2001) emphasises, in many cases failures of trade liberalisation to generate sustained development and growth can be traced to a failure to introduce complementary domestic policy reforms. In most cases, countries will not be well poised to take advantage of the potential benefits of trade liberalisation unless they simultaneously take steps to reduce costs and enhance the efficiency of infrastructure sectors such as telecommunications and transportation; to promote flexibility by eliminating artificial restrictions on entry, exit and pricing in manufacturing and other industries; and to establish and strengthen incentives for investment, innovation, the creation of efficient management structures and productivity improvement. Competition policy has a role to play in all of these areas. A failure to implement competition policy and related reforms will prevent countries from realising the potential gains from external liberalisation, by inhibiting an appropriate supply response (see also Krueger 1984).

The point has also been made in the WTO Working Group on the Interaction between Trade and Competition Policy that the implementation of a transparent and effective competition policy can be an important factor both in enhancing the attractiveness of an economy to foreign investment and in maximising the benefits of such investment. Competition policy can make an economy attractive to foreign investors by providing a transparent dispute-settlement mechanism that is consistent with international norms. Vigorous competition in markets, reinforced by competition policy, encourages foreign firms to construct state-of-the-art production facilities in host countries, transfer modern technology and undertake training programs, and also prevents the exploitation of consumers. These effects may be particularly important in developing countries, in view of the crucial importance of technology transfer to economic development (WTO Working Group on the Interaction between Trade and Competition Policy 1998).

In the WTO working group, the point has also been stressed that competition policy can reinforce, and may be essential to realising, the potential benefits of privatisation programs and initiatives. The argument here is that, unless appropriate measures are taken to prevent the continuation and/or re-establishment of monopolistic market structures, privatisation will not result in any fundamental change in the incentives facing firms that will improve their behaviour and performance. Supporting the importance of this concern, there has been a frank acknowledgement in the working group that, in many cases, privatisation and deregulation in the developing world have failed to deliver their vaunted benefits owing precisely to a failure to engage in procompetitive restructuring and related market reforms (WTO Working Group on the Interaction between Trade and Competition Policy 1998).

The advocacy function of competition agencies

Apart from the potential benefits for developing countries of appropriate competition law enforcement activities, discussions in the WTO Working Group on the Interaction between Trade and Competition Policy and other relevant forums such as the OECD Global Forum on Competition Policy and the UNCTAD Expert Group on Competition Law and Policy have also called attention to the importance of the advocacy activities of competition agencies, particularly in regard to the implementation of procompetitive regulatory reforms. Such activities may include public education activities, studies and research undertaken to document the need for market-opening measures, formal appearances before legislative committees or other government bodies in public proceedings, or behind-the-scenes lobbying within government. These, it has been suggested in the working group, may be among the most useful and high-payoff activities undertaken by competition agencies (WTO Working Group on the Interaction between Trade and Competition Policy 1998, paragraphs 34 and 229).

A particularly important focus of competition advocacy activities is in relation to regulation. To be sure, in both developed and developing economies, regulation can serve valid efficiency-related public purposes. For example, it is well established that regulation can be an efficient response to market failures such as imperfect information, the existence of a natural monopoly (a situation in which a market is most efficiently supplied by a single firm) and other such problems. Nonetheless, it is important to recognise that, notwithstanding its avowed aims, regulation often thwarts rather than promotes efficiency and economic welfare. This is likely to be the case, for example, where it imposes restrictions on entry, exit and/or pricing in non-natural monopoly industries. Experience in both developed and developing countries shows that, in many cases, rather than having regulation imposed on them for the public benefit, incumbent firms have sought regulation for their own benefit, for the purpose of limiting entry into the industry and helping them to enjoy higher prices for their products (the classic diagnoses of this problem are presented in Stigler 1971 and Jordan 1972). Recognition of the significance of such conduct as a barrier to economic development dates back at least to Krueger (1974), and is affirmed in recent analyses by the World Bank and other development-related agencies (see, e.g., World Bank 1997; UNCTAD 1998). In the light of this, efforts to remove inefficient regulatory restrictions and related interventions are central to the establishment of healthy market economies in developing and transition economies (World Bank 1997; World Bank 2000; Frischtak 1995).

In the discussion in the WTO Working Group on the Interaction between Trade and Competition Policy, important links have been made between competition advocacy, successful efforts at regulatory reform and external trade liberalisation. The following examples of regulatory situations having adverse effects on competition and trade have been noted: outmoded or unnecessary regulations; a failure by countries to recognise each others' technical standards; state zoning laws or sanitary and phytosanitary requirements that limit entry unnecessarily or serve as disguised tools for excluding competing suppliers; legal systems that facilitate strategic use of courts by firms to harass competitors; and discriminatory research and development funding. The following additional categories of regulation have been mentioned as warranting appropriate reforms: regulations that openly discriminate in favour of domestic suppliers; regulations that are non-discriminatory on the surface but subtly discriminatory in their substantive requirements; regulations that simply are no longer needed; and poorly designed regulations that are desirable in principle but unnecessarily intrusive. The potential contribution of competition advocacy in addressing these measures has been emphasised (WTO Working Group on the Interaction between Trade and Competition Policy 1998, paragraphs 110 and 111).

The foregoing clearly points to the important contribution that competition advocacy activities can make to both the internal efficiency of markets and to trade liberalisation. As noted, competition agencies in both the developed and (in some cases) the developing world attach high priority to such activities which aim at minimising unnecessary regulatory intervention and ensuring that, where it is used, regulation serves genuinely procompetitive purposes (for the experience of Canada, see Anderson et al. 1998). In doing so, the agencies advance goals that are closely related to those of international trade liberalisation – a further and little-noted but important example of why the proliferation of strong competition agencies is in the broad interest of the multilateral trading system (see also Anderson and Holmes 2002).

THE ROLE OF COMPETITION POLICY IN ADDRESSING INTERNATIONAL ANTICOMPETITIVE PRACTICES

In the 1990s, extensive evidence surfaced that international cartels are alive and flourishing in the 'globalising' economic environment. Investigations conducted by the US Department of Justice, the European Commission, the Canadian Competition Bureau and authorities in other jurisdictions revealed the existence of major cartels in (to cite but a few of many examples) the following industries: graphite electrodes (an essential input to steel mini-mill production); bromine (a flame retardant and fumigant); citric acid (a major industrial food additive); lysine (an agricultural feed additive); seamless steel pipes (an input to oil production); and vitamins (for details, see Levenstein and Suslow 2001). In many such cases, the cartels are known to have operated extensively throughout the developing world, substantially raising the costs of developing countries' imports of the affected products (Levenstein and Suslow 2001; Evenett et al. 2001; Anderson and Holmes 2002; Jenny 2003).

The costs imposed by such cartels on the world economy, and specifically on developing countries, have been shown to be in the multi-billions of dollars annually. Levenstein and Suslow (2001) note that many examples of international cartels involve firms headquartered in the developed world with substantial exports to developing countries. Looking at sixteen 'cartelised' products, they note that:

> Examining these sixteen products – which were cartelised at some point during the 1990s and for which we were able to obtain reasonably reliable trade data – the total value of such 'cartel-affected' imports to developing countries was $81.1 billion. This made up 6.7% of all imports to developing countries. It is equal to 1.2% of their combined GDP.

The price impact of cartels supplying these products appears to have been in the range of 20–30 per cent on average – implying a total overpayment by developing countries for their imports of something in the order of US$10–24 billion annually in respect of these cases alone. It is also noteworthy that in many or perhaps most cases, the immediate impact of cartels is on other firms using the products as industrial inputs. This underscores the detrimental impact of cartels on the development prospects of poor countries.

The available evidence suggests that the benefits for developing countries of the implementation of effective measures to tackle international hardcore cartels may exceed the welfare gains for these countries from agricultural liberalisation. An article in the September 2002 edition of the IMF's *World Economic Outlook* suggests that the increase in the welfare of developing countries that would result from a 50 per cent liberalisation of the agricultural policies of industrialised economies would be approximately US$8 billion per annum (International Monetary Fund 2002). While this is unquestionably a significant gain, it is less than the above-noted costs imposed on developing economies by international cartels – implying that the gains from the implementation of effective competition regimes and related cooperation arrangements to tackle the operations of such cartels in developing countries could be even greater (see, for related discussion and additional supporting references, WTO Working Group on the Interaction between Trade and Competition Policy 2003a).

International cartels are not only more numerous and durable, but also impair the process of development in developing countries more significantly than has previously been thought. This is true for at least three reasons (Jenny 2001):

1) In the early stages of their industrialisation, and given their narrow domestic industrial base, developing countries have to rely on imports. To the extent that such imports are subject to anticompetitive practices either by domestic

firms (e.g., an import cartel) or by foreign suppliers of these imports (e.g., an export or international cartel), the importing country will be penalised by higher-than-necessary import prices.
2) To achieve economic development, and in view of the fact that narrowly based domestic markets lead them to rely on export markets, developing countries will be penalised by international cartels, or by import cartels, and by abuses of dominant positions in the countries of export.
3) Foreign firms are more likely to engage in across-the-border anticompetitive behaviour when the countries to which they export do not have a domestic competition law and can neither individually nor through cooperation with foreign competition authorities challenge the firms' market behaviour. Thus, countries that do not have a domestic competition law will be the prime victims of transnational anticompetitive practices.

The implications of international cartels for the gains from trade are also clear: to the extent that they raise prices and reduce output in transnational markets and, in some cases, limit cross-trading by one country's suppliers into markets assigned to other countries' suppliers, they directly inhibit realisation of the gains that should accrue to participating countries. This is not to suggest that the international trading system should itself carry the primary responsibility for investigating and prosecuting cartels – clearly, this will continue to be done primarily at the national level and through the work of specialised agencies – but that ensuring that measures are in place to deal appropriately with such arrangements is a legitimate concern of the system (Anderson and Holmes 2002). Over time a failure to respond adequately to the costs imposed by international cartels on developing countries is likely to subvert confidence in the market economy on the part of the citizens of such countries (Jenny 2003).

To be sure, international cartels are not the only example of anticompetitive practices with an international dimension that can have an impact on trade and development. Access to markets by foreign suppliers can be directly undermined by exclusionary vertical market restraints (contractual linkages between manufacturers and their suppliers or distributors), import cartels and other forms of anticompetitive conduct (Wolff 1994). The empirical significance of such practices and the appropriate policy response have been much debated in relevant literature and official proceedings. In its comprehensive 2000 assessment of the available evidence and commentaries on this issue, the US International Competition Policy Advisory Committee concluded that, although uneven, the record is sufficient to show that private, governmental and mixed public–private restraints that inhibit market access are a problem worthy of the attention of policymakers in both national and international contexts (US International Competition Policy Advisory Committee 2000; see also Marsden 2003 for useful commentary on this issue).[3]

Competition policy, dynamic efficiency and the 'policy space' available to developing countries

An important consideration in discussions on the importance of competition policy for economic development in the WTO working group has been the implications of such policy for dynamic as opposed to static efficiency. The point has been made that dynamic efficiency gains are likely to be even more important for development than static efficiency considerations. Developing country representatives have expressed concerns that conventional approaches to competition policy may undervalue or possibly even represent an obstacle to the realisation of dynamic efficiency gains (WTO Working Group on the Interaction between Trade and Competition Policy 2001, 2002b; Singh 1999, 2002).

In response, the point has been made that modern approaches to competition policy are by no means concerned only with the achievement of static efficiency; rather, dynamic efficiency is increasingly an explicit goal of such policy.[4] Indeed, much attention has been given in recent years to appropriate ways of supporting and factoring dynamic efficiency gains into competition policy analysis (see, e.g., Gilbert and Sunshine 1995; Gilbert and Tom 2001; Anderson and Gallini 1998). The consensus among scholars is that this has not involved a radical realignment of competition policy principles; rather, it has been a question of adapting well-founded principles to the subject matter of the 'new economy' (see, e.g., Posner 2001). On the whole, competition and competition policy are more likely to contribute to than detract from the attainment of dynamic efficiency gains and other developmental objectives, in that inter-firm rivalry provides a key incentive for firms to lower their costs; to provide better service and expanded choices for consumers; and to innovate and/or adopt the best available technologies (WTO Working Group on the Interaction between Trade and Competition Policy 2003b, paragraph 67). As one particular dimension of its role in promoting dynamic efficiency, competition policy in many jurisdictions is employed to ensure that intellectual property rights are used in ways that support rather than restrict innovation and technology transfer (US Federal Trade Commission 2003; Anderson and Gallini 1998; Anderson 2002).

A closely related argument has been that, even recognising that competition is one important determinant of dynamic efficiency, it is by no means the only determinant, perhaps particularly in the context of developing countries (Singh 1999, 2002). In pursuing development, developing countries may need to have access to a range of tools, possibly including sectoral initiatives and forms of intervention that are at variance with competition policy tools and objectives. In this regard, it is important that their 'policy space' not be unduly restricted (WTO Working Group on the Interaction between Trade and Competition Policy 2001, 2002b).

In responding to this concern, the point has been made that the efficacy of sectoral initiatives and interventions such as the promotion of national champions is a matter of debate. Interventions by relevant WTO members in the working group and related scholarly analyses suggest that, at least to an extent, the success of the various East Asian economies which have undergone periods of rapid growth and development in recent decades has been despite, rather than because of, efforts to promote national champions and other forms of industrial policy intervention (see WTO Working Group on the Interaction between Trade and Competition Policy 2003a and other studies referenced therein). Nonetheless, it has been acknowledged that all governments have employed such measures from time to time and it is understandable that developing countries would not wish their recourse to such tools to be restricted. In this regard, a study prepared for the WTO working group in 2003 identified five ways in which potential conflicts between competition policy and national industrial policy have historically been managed, and the policy space of countries thereby preserved. These are: (1) the use of industrial policy instruments which, even where they tended to restrict competition in markets, are not actionable under the competition laws of most countries (e.g., tariffs, subsidies, training programs and public ownership); (2) the explicit incorporation of goals such as dynamic efficiency gains in national competition laws; (3) the explicit taking into account, by responsible officials, of dynamic as well as static efficiency considerations in the application of national laws; (4) where necessary, the provision for exemptions, exceptions and exclusions from competition law; and (5) allowing for a governmental body to overrule a decision made by the competition enforcement agency in the event that national development priorities might be compromised (WTO Working Group on the Interaction between Trade and Competition Policy 2003a).

The study also found that, by and large, the adoption of a multilateral framework on competition policy along the lines that have been proposed by some WTO members is consistent with and would not jeopardise the ability of members to continue to use these five tools (WTO Working Group on the Interaction between Trade and Competition Policy 2003a, 2003b, paragraph 67). This is not to suggest that such derogations necessarily constitute good policy in all cases, but only that they have been widely used and would continue to be available under the terms of a multilateral framework on competition policy as they have been put forward by the proponents.

Beyond the perceived potential for intrusion on the domestic policy space, developing countries expressed a further concern about the cost of setting up and operating a national competition agency. The 2003 study prepared for the working group suggested, however, that the direct operating costs of national competition agencies in developing countries may be smaller than has been feared and, in any case, pale in comparison to the potential benefits. For example, data assembled by the Consumer Unity and Trust Society indicate that the annual budget of competition enforcement agencies in seven countries, namely India, Kenya, Pakistan, South Africa, Sri Lanka, Tanzania and Zambia, in 2000 was in all cases less than 0.06 per cent of the total budget for the central government – that is, less than one-thousandth of the total government budget (in several cases, much less) (Consumer Unity and Trust Society 2003: 54; reprinted in WTO Working Group on the Interaction between Trade and Competition Policy 2003a: 64).[5] Clarke and Evenett (2003:127) estimate that the resource saving that would be generated by only a 1 per cent reduction of bid rigging on government contracts would be greater than the operating budget of the competition agency in these countries, in most cases by a factor of several times over.

Summary: why external liberalisation is not, by itself, sufficient to ensure the efficient functioning of markets

A strong case can be made that the implementation of well-adapted competition policies in developing countries will help to advance development-related goals, both by contributing to and complementing domestic reform processes and by tackling domestic and transnational anticompetitive practices that reduce the welfare of consumers and raise business input costs. With appropriate care, such policies need not restrict countries' access to other tools through which they can promote their development.

In debates on the role of competition policy in the WTO, the argument is sometimes made that competition policy, and especially competition law, may be an inferior instrument for achieving satisfactory economic performance – rather, competition may be more efficiently induced through external market-opening measures such as the reduction of tariffs (Winters 2002; see also Blackhurst 1991). Indeed, the elimination of barriers to international trade and investment can be a powerful instrument in promoting competition and the efficient functioning of markets – there is no disagreement on this point. However, it is a fallacy to conclude from this that competition policy itself is unimportant. The reasons for this follow directly from the foregoing description of the role of competition policy and competition authorities in developing countries.

First, depending on the natural configuration of industries as well as a variety of policy-related factors, markets for many goods and services (particularly the latter) may be largely insulated from external sources of competition. This problem is likely to be particularly prevalent in developing or least-developed countries, due for example to inefficient infrastructure sectors that can impede trade and investment flows.

Second, in many cases, the potential benefits of market-opening measures will not be realised unless countries simultaneously take steps to address anticompetitive practices/structural barriers to development such as private and public monopolies in infrastructure sectors, domestic and international cartels that raise business input costs, and restrictions on entry, exit and pricing in manufacturing and other industries.

Third, experience shows clearly that certain manifestly harmful anticompetitive practices (e.g., international cartels) cannot be remedied by external (or internal) liberalisation alone, where the relevant arrangements cover the main foreign firms in addition to any domestic firms operating in the relevant market(s). Similarly, the possibility of rigged bids cannot be prevented merely by opening procurement processes to foreign competitors (since such competitors may also be party to bid-rigging conspiracies).

Competition law can be important for other reasons as well. For example, in many jurisdictions it is recognised that competition law has a role to play in preventing abusive practices relating to intellectual property rights in the domestic economy. It is unlikely that the mere absence of tariffs, quotas or other traditional trade barriers can suffice to prevent such practices – particularly since patents or copyrights can themselves affect the ability to supply domestic markets through imports.

Finally, the existence of vibrant competition agencies in developing countries can itself be an important factor contributing to the adoption of external and internal market-opening policies, through the agencies' advocacy function. Numerous interventions in the WTO Working Group on the Interaction between Trade and Competition Policy, including by developing country representatives, have stressed the importance of such activities and their contribution to the process of economic reform and development (WTO Working Group on the Interaction between Trade and Competition Policy 1998, paragraphs 36, 45, 51, 53 and 109).

POSSIBLE RATIONALES FOR INTERNATIONAL COMMITMENTS ON COMPETITION POLICY

The subject of international cooperation in the field of competition law and policy is not new. A number of developed countries and a few developing countries are party to bilateral cooperation agreements regarding competition law enforcement. Such agreements have been a key factor in the progressive strengthening of competition law enforcement in various countries over the past two decades, particularly in developed countries (Evenett et al. 2000). Limited cooperation arrangements also feature in a large and growing number of regional trade agreements (World Trade Organisation 1997). The benefits of such arrangements include not only the obtaining of information and sharing of insights relevant to specific investigations but also the resulting learning process for the participating officials (WTO Working Group on the Interaction between Trade and Competition Policy 2002a).

Nonetheless, much evidence suggests that the actual extent of international cooperation in competition law enforcement is less than is optimal in light of what is known about the extent and frequency of anticompetitive practices with an international dimension (see, e.g., Jenny 2002). In this context, a key focus of the exploratory work of the WTO Working Group on the Interaction between Trade and Competition Policy has been on the scope for and potential benefits of new approaches to cooperation in the field of competition law enforcement, particularly at the multilateral level.

A number of rationales for international collective action on competition policy, including at the multilateral level, have been put forward in the economic literature and by delegates in the WTO working group. Clarke and Evenett (2003) postulate two sources of positive spillovers that provide rationales for international action in this area. First, public announcements of cartel enforcement actions in one country tend to stimulate enforcement efforts in other countries, particularly where there is an established relationship between the relevant enforcement authorities. In this way, trading partners benefit from active enforcement abroad. Second, the investigation and prosecution of arrangements such as international cartels can be greatly facilitated by accessing information about the nature and organisation of the arrangement from another jurisdiction that has successfully completed such an investigation. Conversely, a failure to take action against cartels headquartered in a particular jurisdiction may create 'safe havens' that make it more difficult for other affected jurisdictions to take such action. These considerations point to the potential benefits of some form of international accord committing the participating countries to take action in this area (Clarke and Evenett 2003: 117–18).

An important related argument is that the field of competition policy may be subject to 'political market failures' that result in systematic under-investment in related institutions in many countries, owing to the diffuse nature of the interests whose welfare is promoted by such institutions (i.e., consumers). In the work of the WTO Working Group on the Interaction between Trade and Competition Policy, the view has been expressed that cooperation at the multilateral level could be particularly helpful in generating political support for the implementation of effective competition policies at the national level; in ensuring that such policies are applied in a non-discriminatory and transparent manner; in promoting common approaches to particular practices where this seems feasible and warranted; and in promoting educational exchanges regarding the content and sound application of competition policy.

In a recent contribution to the theory of international economic policymaking, Birdsall and Lawrence (1999) state that a principal benefit of trade agreements aimed at measures beyond the border can be to facilitate domestic policy reforms, by providing a tool for overcoming domestic constituencies that could otherwise block the reform process. They refer specifically to the case of competition policy, observing that:

> When developing countries enter into modern trade agreements, they often make certain commitments to particular domestic policies – for example, to antitrust or other competition policy. Agreeing to such policies can be in the interests of developing countries (beyond the trade benefits directly obtained) because the commitment can reinforce the internal reform process. Indeed, participation in an international agreement can make feasible internal reforms that are beneficial for the country as a whole that might otherwise be successfully resisted by interest groups. (Birdsall and Lawrence 1999: 136)

The foregoing are by no means the only rationales that have been advanced by proponents of a multilateral framework on competition policy. Specific objectives that have been advanced include promoting the growth of strong competition agencies in developing countries to protect them from anticompetitive practices that impact on their consumers and businesses; promoting (voluntary) cooperation between the competition agencies of participating countries to assist them in investigating particular cases; and contributing to a greater degree of 'balance' in the WTO system between the rights of producers and the protection provided for consumers and other members of society.

The argument has also been made in the WTO working group that a multilateral framework could reinforce the effectiveness of institution-building programs in the area of competition policy by providing hands-on exposure to best practices in dealing with cross-border cases. Within such a framework, technical assistance programs could receive higher priority and be better focused on the needs of recipient countries (WTO Working Group on the Interaction between Trade and Competition Policy 2001, paragraph 57). A cooperation framework might also contribute to the promotion of a culture of competition (WTO Working Group on the Interaction between Trade and Competition Policy 1999, paragraph 61).

The view has also been expressed that the introduction of appropriate peer review mechanisms could reinforce and enhance the effectiveness of capacity building through technical assistance (WTO Working Group on the Interaction between Trade and Competition Policy 2000, paragraph 61). Peer reviews, which would be voluntary in nature, would be an instrument through which enforcement issues could be discussed in an open and constructive manner. For example, in the case of developing countries, peer review could identify capacity constraints as well as examine enforcement policies being followed in individual countries. Peer review provides an opportunity for countries to learn from others with similar experiences or similar problems. If done well, it promotes convergence and builds confidence among agencies as well as credibility and support. It has been suggested that a peer review process would help to establish benchmarks or guidelines to evaluate the implementation process. However, peer review needs to exist side-by-side with capacity building since they both have a role to play (WTO Working Group on the Interaction between Trade and Competition Policy 1999, paragraph 43; WTO Working Group on the Interaction between Trade and Competition Policy 2000, paragraphs 23 and 47).

The foregoing is not intended to resolve the debate as to whether there is a need for a multilateral framework on competition policy in the WTO and, if so, what would be the appropriate content of such a framework. A range of concerns have been advanced about the implications of such a framework, including that it might not yield sufficient benefits for developing countries. As already mentioned, a key related concern of developing countries relates to the perceived potential for a multilateral framework on competition policy to intrude on their 'policy space'. Clearly, much would depend on the terms of such a framework. As an initial step toward further evaluation of this question, some aspects of the past proposals for a multilateral framework for competition policy are discussed below.

A MULTILATERAL FRAMEWORK FOR COMPETITION POLICY?

At the WTO Ministerial Conference in Cancun, Mexico, in September 2003, the majority of developing countries rejected the launching of negotiations on a multilateral framework on competition policy as had been proposed by the European Union and various other countries in the lead-up to the conference. This seemingly reflected a range of tactical and more fundamental concerns, including concerns about a perceived lack of negotiating capacity in this area, the costs that might be involved in setting up a national competition authority, the perceived risk that a multilateral framework in this area might intrude on industrial policy goals, and other considerations. Subsequently, the General Council of the WTO decided, as part of the 'July Package' of 2004, that no further work would be undertaken toward negotiations on competition policy (or on the separate issues of investment and transparency of government procurement) as part of the Doha Round. Still, it is useful to review the nature and content of recent proposals for such a framework to the extent that a number of WTO members remain committed to the long-run goal of developing an agreement to integrate better the implementation of competition policy with the goals and instruments of the multilateral trading system (see, e.g., Lamy 2004a).

As noted in the introduction to this chapter, there have been extensive misconceptions regarding the nature and scope of a possible WTO agreement on competition policy. Such misconceptions may, in some cases, have reflected a confusion between the proposals that were put forward in the WTO and the considerably more far-reaching proposal that was put forward by the Munich Group in the early 1990s (Draft International Antitrust Code 1993).[6] In addition, they may reflect the continuing influence of commentaries made by leading representatives of the antitrust community during the early stages of the WTO's exploratory work in this area, before the likely parameters of a possible agreement became clear. These commentaries (perhaps motivated, in part, by the excesses of the Munich Group proposal) called attention to certain risks posed by the prospect of WTO negotiations in this area, including: (1) a suppression of the scope for innovation in national competition policies, owing to the premature locking in of detailed substantive standards; and (2) an undermining of the scope for the exercise of prosecutorial discretion in antitrust enforcement, which of course is central to current approaches to competition law enforcement in the United States and other common law countries (see, in particular, Klein 1996; Melamed 1997; Tarullo 2000). Furthermore, the concern was voiced that a WTO agreement on competition policy would likely have an undue focus on market access objectives and that this would inevitably distort

Competition policy, economic development 77

the principles of competition policy and/or be inimical to the interests of developing countries in this area (Tarullo 2000; Hoekman and Holmes 1999).

These commentaries served a useful purpose in highlighting the potential downsides of an overly rigid or sweeping approach to the implementation of international norms in this area. What is perhaps less well known is the extent to which the early commentaries influenced the debate in the WTO and were even taken on board in the proposals put forward in the run-up to Cancun. This is not to imply that the approach proposed by the proponents of a multilateral framework was necessarily 'right' but only that it was a good deal more modest than has sometimes been pictured and that it deliberately sought to avoid some of the pitfalls identified in the early commentaries.

The main elements of the proposal for a multilateral framework on competition policy are described in the relevant paragraphs of the Doha Ministerial Declaration (see Box 4.1, especially paragraph 25).[7]

Further insights are provided in relevant submissions to the WTO working group by members favouring the development of such a framework. Broadly speaking, these sources indicate that, in the view of those members, a multilateral framework on competition policy would embody the following five elements:

1) A commitment by WTO members to a set of core principles relating to the application of competition law and policy, including transparency, non-discrimination and procedural fairness.
2) A parallel commitment by member governments to the taking of measures against hardcore cartels.
3) The development of modalities for cooperation between member states on competition policy issues. These would be of a voluntary nature, and could encompass cooperation on national legislation, the exchange of national experience by competition authorities and aspects of enforcement.
4) A commitment to ongoing support for the introduction and strengthening of competition institutions in developing countries through technical assistance and capacity building, in the framework of the WTO but in cooperation with other interested organisations and national governments.
5) The establishment of a WTO standing committee on competition policy that would administer the agreement and act as a forum for the ongoing exchange of national experiences, the identification of technical assistance needs and sources for such assistance, and so on. The committee could also provide a forum for discussion of policy issues such as market access barriers arising out of a combination of government policies (or tolerance of anticompetitive conduct) and private actions.

Without attempting a comprehensive assessment of these proposals, the following observations are offered for reflection.[8] First, as already noted, the recent proposals had little in common with earlier calls for a detailed multilateral

> *Box 4.1* Relevant paragraphs of the Doha Ministerial Declaration
>
> *Interaction between trade and competition policy*
>
> 23. Recognizing the case for a multilateral framework to enhance the contribution of competition policy to international trade and development, and the need for enhanced technical assistance and capacity-building in this area as referred to in paragraph 24, we agree that negotiations will take place after the Fifth Session of the Ministerial Conference on the basis of a decision to be taken, by explicit consensus, at that Session on modalities of negotiations.
>
> 24. We recognize the needs of developing and least-developed countries for enhanced support for technical assistance and capacity-building in this area, including policy analysis and development so that they may better evaluate the implications of closer multilateral cooperation for their development policies and objectives, and human and institutional development. To this end, we shall work in cooperation with other relevant intergovernmental organizations, including UNCTAD, and through appropriate regional and bilateral channels, to provide strengthened and adequately resourced assistance to respond to these needs.
>
> 25. In the period until the Fifth Session, further work in the Working Group on the Interaction between Trade and Competition Policy will focus on the clarification of: core principles, including transparency, non-discrimination and procedural fairness, and provisions on hardcore cartels; modalities for voluntary cooperation; and support for progressive reinforcement of competition institutions in developing countries through capacity-building. Full account shall be taken of the needs of developing and least-developed country participants and appropriate flexibility provided to address them.
>
> *Source*: World Trade Organisation, Ministerial Declaration, Fourth Session of the Ministerial Conference, Doha, WT/MIN(01)/DEC/1, 9–14 November 2001.

code on competition policy as proposed by the Munich Group. Certainly, the idea of establishing an international competition law enforcement agency figured nowhere in the proposals. Clearly, the proposals also did not aim at a comprehensive harmonisation of competition law (Garcia-Bercero and Amarasinha 2001). Rather, they were framed in terms of adherence to certain core principles and other elements that embody fundamental values of both competition policy and the multilateral trading system (i.e., non-discrimination, transparency and the suppression of hardcore cartels). As such, these approaches seem unlikely to undermine the scope for continuing adaptation of national approaches to competition policy in response to economic learning and national circumstances (one of the concerns raised in the early commentaries); arguably, they might encourage accelerated learning in this area.[9]

Second, the approaches to hardcore cartels and modalities for cooperation that were called for under the recent proposals were extensively informed by cooperative approaches favoured in other forums, for example the OECD Recommendations on Hardcore Cartels and Cooperation, and were less ambitious than elements that were proposed in the past. For example, an early proposal for the introduction of 'compulsory positive comity' (i.e., a legal obligation for national authorities to undertake investigations into activities allegedly affecting other countries' national interests, when requested to do so by such countries) was dropped some time ago. The proponents of negotiations also made it clear that, as they envisaged it, a WTO framework would not require the exchange of confidential information (WTO Working Group on the Interaction between Trade and Competition Policy 2002b, paragraph 76) – although it also would not preclude individual countries from exchanging such information to the extent it is provided for in relevant bilateral arrangements. Much emphasis would be placed on voluntary cooperation in the development of national legislation and the exchange of national experience, in addition to the enforcement process.

Third, the proposals (and the Doha Ministerial Declaration) placed considerable emphasis on support for technical assistance and capacity building in this area, responding to a key concern of developing countries. This represented a clear recognition that simply mandating the adoption of relevant laws without long-term support for institution building is unlikely to yield satisfactory or appropriate results. Moreover, the expectation was that the required capacity-building activities would be undertaken not principally by the WTO itself; rather, it would be a cooperative effort in which the support and cooperation of other organisations would be essential (although the WTO would play a catalytic role).[10]

Fourth, by relying on broad principles, measures to strengthen cooperation and support for institution building, rather than on detailed legal prescriptions, the recent proposals sought to avoid problems that would have been inherent in a more detailed, intrusive approach. For the most part (and contrary to the way in which the proposals were sometimes characterised in academic commentaries), it would have been left for individual countries to define the details of their national legislation.

Fifth, and notwithstanding concerns expressed previously by some commentators, the recent proposals were not geared inordinately toward market access objectives. Rather, the focus of the proposals was on promoting the development of effective national competition institutions and expanded international cooperation to address anticompetitive practices as they are generally recognised in the competition policy community. In the work of the WTO working group, the value of competition advocacy activities has also been stressed. This approach would undoubtedly yield significant benefits for market access, in that robust competition policies and institutions are supportive of market access objectives in various ways (including through both advocacy and enforcement activities).

Notwithstanding any of the foregoing, this chapter is not suggesting that the case for a multilateral agreement on competition policy is or was self-evident. As noted, at Cancun the initiation of negotiations leading to the development of such a framework was rejected by the majority of developing countries. In addition to possible tactical considerations, the reasons underlying this rejection included the above-noted concern regarding a perceived intrusion on developing countries' 'policy space', concerns about a lack of negotiating capacity in this area and, for some, a sense that the proponents' proposals were unbalanced and might not, in the end, yield tangible benefits in the form of cooperation for developing countries.[11] It remains to be seen if these concerns can be resolved through some combination of: (a) further educational work and capacity-building activities, particularly to address the perceived deficit in negotiating capacity;[12] and (b) clarification or possible adjustments to the proponents' proposals.[13]

Much is at stake for developing countries and for the success of the multilateral trading system. The empirical record shows clearly that anticompetitive practices impose heavy costs on developing countries. Furthermore, where present, practices such as international cartels directly undermine the goals that the system is intended to serve – including not only access to markets but the continual improvement of living standards and the optimal use of the world's resources in accordance with the objective of sustainable development (as set out in the Marrakesh Agreement Establishing the World Trade Organisation). Unless measures are put in place to counteract such practices (whether at the multilateral or some other level), the realisation of these benefits will continue to be impeded. This, in turn, may contribute to an erosion of confidence in the benefits of the market economy and a liberalised trading order.[14]

NOTES

The authors are, respectively, Counsellor, Intellectual Property Division, WTO Secretariat and Professor, ESSEC (Paris). Professor Jenny is also Vice-Chair, Conseil de la Concurrence, France and has served as Chairman of the WTO Working Group on the Interaction between Trade and Competition Policy since 1997. This chapter draws on material in the various annual reports of the WTO Working Group on the Interaction between Trade and Competition Policy, in Anderson and Holmes (2002), in Anderson and Jenny (2003) and in Jenny (2003). A preliminary version of the first part of the chapter was published in Korea Fair Trade Commission (2002). The views expressed are the personal responsibility of the authors and should not be attributed to the WTO, its Secretariat or any of its members. Helpful discussions with Simon Evenett, Peter Holmes and Adrian Otten are gratefully acknowledged.

1   In August 2004, the General Council of the WTO ruled out the possiblility of negotiations on a multilateral framework on competition policy within the 'single undertaking' of the Doha Development Agenda. The concept of a single undertaking outlined in paragraph 47 of the Doha Ministerial Declaration, recognises that all agreements and instruments contained therein are accepted as elements of a package. Prior to this decision, the European Community had raised the possibility of negotiations that would be conducted outside the single

2. In this chapter, 'competition policy' refers to all measures through which governments seek to promote the efficient and competitive operation of markets. 'Competition law' refers to legislation that prohibits or otherwise deals with specific anticompetitive practices of firms such as cartels, abuses of a dominant position or monopolisation and mergers that create a dominant position or otherwise stifle competition.

3. Notwithstanding the acknowledged importance of these practices, they have not been the main focus of work in the WTO on a possible multilateral framework on competition policy. As discussed below, the focus of that work has been on the development of provisions to deal with cartels, on the promotion of voluntary cooperation and related capacity-building activities, and on 'core principles' (transparency, non-discrimination and procedural fairness) to guide the application of legislation in this area. The reason for the lack of any proposal focused specifically on vertical market restraints relates to the complexity of this area of competition law enforcement and the reluctance of many authorities to reduce the role of prosecutorial discretion and case-by-case analysis in this area. Nonetheless, to the extent that it would play a role in strengthening competition regimes in various respects (including by providing greater political legitimacy and guarantees of independence, transparency and non-discrimination), a multilateral framework could assist in the implementation of this aspect of competition law as well.

4. A related discussion can be found in Working Group on the Interaction between Trade and Competition Policy (2003a) and a useful typology of relevant efficiencies is provided in Kolasky and Dick (2003).

5. This is not to suggest that funding for the competition agency in these countries was necessarily optimal.

6. The draft code was a detailed, ambitious proposal for a binding international agreement on competition law that was put forward by a private group of academics and practitioners.

7. In a statement made prior to the adoption of the declaration, the Chairman of the WTO Ministerial Conference, Mr Youssef Kamal, expressed his understanding that the requirement in paragraph 25 for a decision to be taken, by explicit consensus, on the modalities for negotiations before negotiations on competition policy and other 'Singapore issues' could proceed gave 'each Member the right to take a position on modalities that would prevent negotiations from proceeding after the Fifth Session until that Member was prepared to join in an explicit consensus' (WTO Ministerial Conference, Fourth Session 2001: 2). At the Cancun Ministerial Conference, such a consensus proved elusive.

8. These observations draw on material in Anderson and Jenny (2001), Anderson and Holmes (2002), Anderson and Jenny (2003) and Jenny (2003).

9. The importance of transparency in the formulation of competition policy and its contribution to the evolution of sound enforcement norms in this field is emphasised in the thoughtful analysis in Kovacic (2004), who also stresses the importance of broad scope for experimentation and risk taking in policy formulation in this area.

10. Paragraph 24 of the Doha Ministerial Declaration specified that assistance mandated by the declaration will be provided 'in cooperation with other relevant intergovernmental organisations, including UNCTAD, and through appropriate regional and bilateral channels'.

11. As noted, for some, a further concern was the cost of setting up a national competition agency.

12 Since the Doha Ministerial Conference, the WTO Secretariat has undertaken an extensive program of technical assistance in the area of trade and competition policy (WTO Working Group on the Interaction between Trade and Competition Policy 2003c).
13 As an alternative to development of a multilateral framework on competition policy as foreseen in relevant provisions of the Doha Ministerial Declaration (but rejected by developing countries at Cancun), the European Community raised the possibility of negotiations that would be conducted outside the single undertaking of the Doha Development Agenda and on a plurilateral or 'opt-in/ opt-out' basis (Lamy 2004a and Lamy 2004b).
14 There is no doubt that such concerns were in the minds of the system's founders. Provisions to address 'restrictions imposed by private combines and cartels' were a key element of the US proposal for an International Trade Organisation at the conclusion of World War II. Although this proposal was not, in the end, incorporated into the General Agreement on Tariffs and Trade (GATT) in 1947, its rationale remains instructive: 'when a private agreement divides the markets of the world among the members of a cartel, none of [the goods affected] can move between the zones while the contract is in force. Clearly, if trade is to increase as a result of the lightening of government restrictions, the governments concerned must make sure that it is not restrained by private combinations' (US Department of State 1945: 4; also quoted in Jackson 1969: 522, which provides related context). In a related vein, in 1944 President Franklin Delano Roosevelt had written to Secretary of State Cordell Hull, observing that 'Cartel practices which restrict the free flow of goods in foreign commerce will have to be curbed' (see also Wolff 1994).

REFERENCES

Anderson, Robert D. (2002) 'Intellectual property rights, competition policy and international trade: reflections on the work of the WTO Working Group on the Interaction between Trade and Competition Policy', in Thomas Cottier and Petros Mavroidis (eds) *Intellectual Property: Trade, Competition and Sustainable Development*, Ann Arbor: University of Michigan Press, December.

Anderson, Robert D. and Nancy T. Gallini (1998) *Competition Policy and Intellectual Property Rights in the Knowledge-based Economy*, Calgary: University of Calgary Press for the Industry Canada Research Series.

Anderson, Robert D., Abraham Hollander, Joseph Monteiro and William Stanbury (1998) 'Competition policy and regulatory reform in Canada, 1986–1997', *Review of Industrial Organization* 13(1–2): 177–204.

Anderson, Robert D. and Peter Holmes (2002) 'Competition policy and the future of the multilateral trading system', *Journal of International Economic Law* 5(2): 531–63.

Anderson, Robert D. and Frédéric Jenny (2001) 'Current developments on competition policy in the World Trade Organization', *Antitrust* 16(1): 40–4.

—— (2003) 'The current proposals for WTO negotiations on competition policy: background and overview', paper presented at the Conference on Antitrust Issues in Today's Economy, Conference Board, New York, March.

Birdsall, Nancy and Robert Z. Lawrence (1999) 'Deep integration and trade agreements: good for developing countries?', in Inge Kaul, Isabelle Grunberg and Marc A. Stern (eds) *Global Public Goods: International Cooperation in the 21st Century*, New York: Oxford University Press for the United Nations Development Program.

Blackhurst, Richard (1991) 'Trade policy is competition policy', in *Competition and Economic Development*, Paris: OECD.

Clarke, Julian and Simon J. Evenett (2003) 'A multilateral framework for competition policy?', in State Secretariat of Economic Affairs and Simon Evenett, *The Singapore Issues and the World Trading System: the Road to Cancun and Beyond*, Bern: State Secretariat for Economic Affairs.
Consumer Unity and Trust Society (2003) *Pulling Up Our Socks* (Report based on the 7-Up Project), Jaipur: Consumer Unity and Trust Society, February.
Draft International Antitrust Code (1993) 5 *World Trade Materials*, September, 126–96.
Dutz, Mark A. (2002) 'Competition policy issues in developing and transition markets', presentation at the OECD Global Forum on Competition, Paris, 14–15 February.
Evans, David S. (2002) 'The new trustbusters', *Foreign Affairs* 81(1): 1–19.
Evenett, Simon J., Alexander Lehmann and Benn Steil (eds) (2000) *Antitrust Goes Global: What Future for Transatlantic Co-operation?*, Washington DC: The Brookings Institution.
Evenett, Simon J., Margaret Levenstein and Valerie Suslow (2001) 'International cartel enforcement: lessons from the 1990s', *The World Economy* 24(9): 1221–45.
Frischtak, Claudio C. (1995) *Regulatory Policies and Reform in Industrializing Countries*, Washington DC: The World Bank.
Garcia-Bercero, Ignacio and Stefan Amarasinha (2001) 'Moving the trade and competition debate forward', *Journal of International Economic Law*, 4(3): 481–506.
Gilbert, R. and S. Sunshine (1995) 'Incorporating dynamic efficiency into merger analysis: the use of innovation markets', *Antitrust Law Journal* 63(2): 569–602.
Gilbert, R. and W.K. Tom (2001) 'Is innovation king at the antitrust agencies? The intellectual property guidelines five years later', *Antitrust Law Journal* 69(1): 43–86.
Hoekman, Bernard and Peter Holmes (1999) 'Competition policy, developing countries and the WTO', *The World Economy* 22(6): 875–93.
Hur, J.S. (2002) 'Theories and case study of extraterritorial application of international cartel cases: the international graphite electrodes cartel', mimeo, October.
International Monetary Fund (2002) *World Economic Outlook*, September.
Jackson, John H. (1969) *World Trade and the Law of GATT*, Indianapolis: Bobbs-Merrill.
Jenny, Frédéric (2001) 'Globalization, competition and trade policy: convergence, divergence and cooperation', in Yang-Ching Chao Gee San, Changfa Lo and Jiming Ho (eds) *International and Comparative Competition Law and Policies*, The Hague: Kluwer Law International.
—— (2002) 'International co-operation on competition: myth, reality and perspective', paper presented at the University of Minnesota Law School Conference on Global Antitrust Law and Policy, Minneapolis, 20–21 September.
—— (2003) 'Competition law and policy: global governance issues', *World Competition* 26(4): 609–24, December.
Jordan, W.A. (1972) 'Producer protection, prior market structure and the effects of government regulation', *Journal of Law and Economics* XV(1): 151–76.
Klein, Joel (1996) 'A note of caution with respect to the WTO agenda on competition policy', remarks to the Royal Institute of International Affairs, Chatham House, London, November.
Kolasky, W. and A. Dick (2003) 'The merger guidelines and the integration of efficiencies into antitrust reviews of horizontal mergers', *Antitrust Law Journal* 71(1): 207–51.
Korea Fair Trade Commission (2002) *Seoul Competition Forum 2002*, Seoul: Korea Fair Trade Commission, December.
Kovacic, William E. (2004) 'The modern evolution of U.S. competition policy enforcement norms', *Antitrust Law Journal* 71(2): 377–478.

Krueger, Anne O. (1974) 'The political economy of the rent-seeking society', *American Economic Review* 64(3): 291–303.

—— (1984) 'The problems of trade liberalization', in A.C. Harberger (ed.) *World Economic Growth*, San Francisco: International Centre for Economic Growth.

Lamy, Pascal (Trade Commissioner for the European Communities) (2004a) 'The relaunching of negotiations under the Doha Development Agenda', Strasbourg, 13 January.

—— (2004b) 'Moving the Doha Development Agenda Forward', speech to the European–American Business Council, Washington DC, 26 February.

Levenstein, Margaret and Valerie Suslow (2001) 'Private international cartels and their effect on developing countries', background paper for the World Bank's *World Development Report 2001*, 9 January, available at http://www-unix.oit.umass.edu/~maggiel/WDR2001.pdf.

Marsden, Philip (2003) *A Competition Policy for the WTO*, London: Cameron.

Melamed, Douglas A. (1997) 'International antitrust in an age of international deregulation', remarks to the George Mason Law Review Symposium on Antitrust in the Global Economy, Washington DC, October 10.

Mexico (2002) 'Communication to the Working Group on the Interaction between Trade and Competition Policy: hardcore cartels', WT/WGTCP/W/196, issued 14 August 2002.

Osakwe, Chiedu (2001) 'Poverty reduction and development: the interaction of trade, macroeconomic and regulatory policies', Tenth Joseph Mubiru Memorial Lecture, organised by the Bank of Uganda, 14 December.

Pittman, Russell (2004) 'Abuse-of-dominance provisions of Central and Eastern European competition laws: have fears of over-enforcement been borne out?', Department of Justice (Antitrust Division), Economic Analysis Group, Working Paper 04-1, January.

Posner, Richard (2001) 'Antitrust in the new economy', *Antitrust Law Journal* 68(3): 925–43.

Singh, A. (1999) 'Competition policy, development and developing countries', Working Paper No. 50, Indian Council for Research on International Economic Relations, New Delhi, November.

—— (2002) 'Competition and competition policy in emerging markets: international and development dimensions', Paper No. 18, G-24 Discussion Paper Series, New York: United Nations, September.

Stigler, G.J. (1971) 'The theory of economic regulation', *Bell Journal of Economics and Management Science* 2(1): 3–21, Spring.

Tarullo, Daniel K. (2000) 'Norms and institutions in global competition policy', *American Journal of International Law* 94(3): 478–504, July.

United Nations Conference on Trade and Development (UNCTAD) (1998) *Empirical Evidence of the Benefits from Applying Competition Law and Policy Principles to Economic Development in order to Attain Greater Efficiency in International Trade and Development*, Geneva: UNCTAD, document TD/B/COM.2/EM/10.

US Department of Justice (2000) 'German company pleads guilty to rigging bids on USAID construction contracts in Egypt', press release, 18 August.

US Department of State (1945) 'U.S. proposals for an international trade organization', Publication No. 2411, Washington DC: Department of State.

US Federal Trade Commission (2003) *To Promote Innovation: The Proper Balance of Competition and Patent Law and Policy*, Washington DC: Federal Trade Commission, October.

US International Competition Policy Advisory Committee to the Attorney General and Assistant Attorney General for Antitrust (2000) *Final Report*, Washington DC: Department of Justice, February.

Winters, Alan (2002) 'Doha and world poverty targets', New York: World Bank, mimeo.
Wolff, Alan W. (1994) 'The problems of market access in the global economy: trade and competition policy', Contribution to the OECD Roundtable on Market Access, 30 June.
World Bank (1997) 'Fostering markets: liberalization, regulation and industrial policy', in *World Development Report*, New York: World Bank, chapter 4.
—— (2000) 'Making markets work better for poor people', in *World Development Report*, New York: World Bank, chapter 4.
World Trade Organisation (1997) 'Special study on trade and competition policy', in *Annual Report of the World Trade Organization for 1997*, Geneva: WTO, chapter IV.
WTO Ministerial Conference, Fourth Session (2001) *Summary Record of the Ninth Meeting, Doha*, Geneva: WTO, WT/MIN(01)/SR/9.
WTO Working Group on the Interaction between Trade and Competition Policy (1998) *Report (1998) of the Working Group on the Interaction between Trade and Competition Policy to the General Council*, Geneva: WTO, WT/WGTCP/2.
—— (1999) *Report (1999) of the Working Group on the Interaction between Trade and Competition Policy to the General Council*, Geneva: WTO, WT/WGTCP/3.
—— (2000) *Report (2000) of the Working Group on the Interaction between Trade and Competition Policy to the General Council*, Geneva: WTO, WT/WGTCP/4.
—— (2001) *Report (2001) of the Working Group on the Interaction between Trade and Competition Policy to the General Council*, Geneva: WTO, WT/WGTCP/5.
—— (2002a) *Background Note by the Secretariat on Modalities for Voluntary Cooperation*, Geneva: WTO, WT/WGTCP/W/192.
—— (2002b) *Report (2002) of the Working Group on the Interaction between Trade and Competition Policy to the General Council*, Geneva: WTO, WT/WGTCP/6.
—— (2003a) *Study on Issues Relating to a Possible Multilateral Framework on Competition Policy* (principal author: Simon Evenett), Geneva: WTO, WT/WGTCP/W/228.
—— (2003b) *Report (2003) of the Working Group on the Interaction between Trade and Competition Policy to the General Council*, Geneva: WTO, WT/WGTCP/7.
—— (2003c) *Secretariat Technical Assistance Activities Pursuant to Paragraph 24 of the Doha Ministerial Declaration*, Geneva: WTO, WT/WGTCP/W/230.

5 Competition in electricity markets

Maria Fe Villamejor-Mendoza

INTRODUCTION

In the utilities sector, regulations are used to level the playing field for smaller firms and protect the welfare of consumers. Although there has been a trend away from heavy-handed control of industry and toward minimising regulation to let competition flourish, governments still intervene to protect the welfare of the public. The Philippine electricity industry is an example of where a command-and-control regime has been replaced by a regulatory system that is more facilitative of competition but where the government continues to set rates and prescribe standards of service.

The Philippines has implemented a regulatory pricing system that assures utilities of reasonable returns. The utility gives up its right to charge prices that reflect current supply and demand and thereby loses its ability to acquire scarcity rents or monopoly profits. Instead firms are able to set prices that allow a reasonable return on invested capital after costs are paid. The return should be sufficient to attract capital but not result in windfall gains by being greater than the cost of capital (Hall and Hagler Bailly Services 1999). This pricing structure has been put in place to prevent the abuse of market power, to sanction 'erring' industry players and safeguard the interests of the public.

This chapter chronicles the gradual shift in the Philippines to a regulatory regime designed to introduce competition into the electricity industry. It draws some conclusions from the experience of the Philippines and reflects on the future of regulation and competition in the country.

EARLY REFORMS IN THE ELECTRICITY INDUSTRY

The electricity industry has always been a strategically important sector of the Philippine economy and was largely under state control until the late 1980s. Over the previous eight decades the state had taken an active role in directing and controlling economic activities for development, nationalising industries and intervening on issues of public concern. When the Aquino administration came to power in 1986 sweeping reforms were put in place to make the economy more outward looking and dynamic. Recognising the importance of the private sector as the engine of economic growth, the Aquino government and succeeding administrations introduced a number of policies to open up to the private sector areas that had previously been reserved for the public sector (Table 5.1).

In the late 1980s and early 1990s the Philippines experienced a number of power crises, resulting in sporadic brownouts of up to twenty-four hours. In response the government put in place a number of pro-market policies that lessened the state's control over the electricity sector and encouraged private sector investment to boost the supply of energy.

Ending the monopoly in power generation

Efforts to open the electricity market up to competition began in 1987. Although there were a few private independent power producers (IPPs) in existence, the generation and transmission of electricity was controlled by the National Power Corporation (NPC), a vertically integrated state-owned company (Figure 5.1). The distribution/supply sector was fragmented and inefficient, consisting of seventeen private utilities, 119 rural electric cooperatives, and ten utilities owned by municipal, city and provincial governments (DOE Database 2001).

Figure 5.1 Structure of the electricity industry under initial reforms (1987–2001)

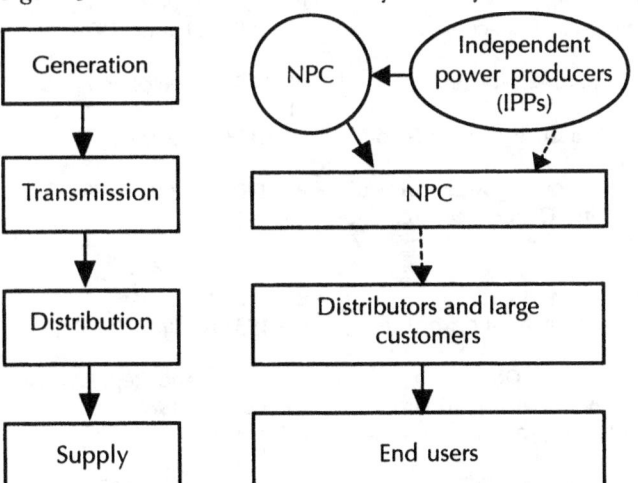

Note: The dotted lines from the IPPs, to the NPC, to distributors represent the initial restriction that IPPs could only indirectly serve distributors through providing power to the NPC. In the late 1990s, the IPPs were allowed to serve distributors directly, provided they paid an access fee for the use of NPC transmission lines. During this period the NPC was still a vertically integrated generation and transmission company under the control of the government.

Table 5.1 Major laws and regulations affecting the electricity industry

Law	Date enacted
The Constitution of the Republic of the Philippines	1935, 1973, 1987
Municipal Franchises Act	Act 667, 6 March 1903
Corporation Law	Act 1459, 1 April 1906
Creation of the Board of Utility Commissioners	Act 2307, 9 December 1913
An Act Creating the Public Service Commission (PSC)	Act 3108, 19 March 1923
Prescribing the Form for Bills for the Granting of Electric Light and Power Franchises	Act 3636, 7 December 1929
Amending the Public Service Act of 1923	Act 3844, 9 November 1931
An Act to Reorganise the PSC, Prescribe its Powers and Duties, Define and Regulate Public Services ... and for Other Purposes	CA 146, 7 November 1936
An Act Creating the National Power Corporation (NPC)	CA 120, 3 November 1936
An Act Amending Section 2 (k) of CA 120	RA 358, 4 June 1949
An Act Revising the Charter of the NPC	RA 6395, 10 September 1971
Establishing Basic Policies for the Electric Power Industry	PD 40, 7 November 1972
An Act Creating the National Electrification Administration (NEA)	PD 269, 6 August 1973
Providing for the Revision of RA 3931, Commonly Known as 'The Pollution Control Law'	PD 984, 18 August 1976
Philippine Environmental Policy	PD 1151, 6 June 1977
Philippine Environment Code	PD 1152, 6 June 1977
Establishing an Environmental Impact Assessment System	PD 1586, 11 June 1978
A Decree Creating the Department of Energy	PD 1206, 6 October 1977
An Act Amending PD 1206	PD 1573, 11 June 1978
An Act Establishing an Oil Industry Commission, and for Other Purposes	RA 6173, 25 April 1977
Granting the Board of Energy the Power to Regulate and Fix the Rates of Pipeline Concessionaires and Amending for that Purpose Section 9 of PD 1206	PD 1700, 10 July 1978
Creating the Energy Regulatory Board	EO 172, 8 May 1987
An Act Providing for the Reorganisation of the Office of Energy Affairs	EO 193, 10 June 1987
Rules of Practice and Procedure Governing Hearings before the Energy Regulatory Board	ERB Rules and Regulations, 15 February 1988
Amending PD 40 and Allowing the Private Sector to Generate Electricity	EO 215, 10 July 1987
The Omnibus Investment Code of 1987	EO 226, 27 July 1987
An Act Authorising the Financing, Construction, Operation and Maintenance of Infrastructure Projects by the Private Sector (The Build-Operate-Transfer Law of 1991)	RA 6957, 1991
An Act Amending Certain Sections of RA 6957	RA 7718, 14 April 1994
An Act Creating the Department of Energy	RA 7638, 19 December 1992

Rules and Regulations Implementing Section 5 (i) of RA 7638	DOE Regulations 1–94
Guidelines and Procedures for the Granting of Financial Benefits under DOE Regulations 1–94	DOE Circular 95–11–009, 1 November 1995
Rules and Regulations Implementing EO 215	DOE Energy Regulations 01–95, 1 February 1995
Providing Additional Guidelines for the Granting of Benefits under DOE Regulations 1–94	DOE Circular 96–08–009, 9 August 1996
Amending Certain Provisions of DOE Energy Regulations 01–95	DOE Circular 97–01–001, 21 January 1997
Rules and Regulations Governing Bulk Power Supply of Industries from the National Power Corporation (NPC)	DOE Regulation 1–97, 5 February 1997
Repealing DOE Regulation 1–97	DOE Circular 98–04–006, 22 April 1998
Further Amending Provisions of ER 1–94	DOE Circular 2000–03–003, 17 March 2000
Act Amending Certain Provisions of RA 7648	RA 7718, 27 April 1994
Anti-Electricity Pilferage Act of 1994	RA 7832, 8 December 1994
Providing for the Segregation and Unbundling of Electric Power Tariff Components of the NPC and Franchised Electric Utilities	EO 473, 17 April 1998
Standard Operating Rules and Regulations Governing the Operation of Electric Power Services	ERB Resolution 95–21,
Open Access Transmission Tariff	ERB Case No. 96–118, 11 June 1997
Existing Pricing Policy for Private Electric Distribution Utility	ERB Pricing Regulation, 6 September 1999
Electric Power Reform Act of 2001	RA 9631, 8 May 2001

The NPC had a monopoly over the transmission network and the construction of generation plants. It sold electricity at rates set by its board, and oversaw all activities and functions related to electricity generation and transmission. The rural electric cooperatives were supervised by the National Electrification Administration (NEA). Policy determination and planning was undertaken by the Department of Energy (DOE). The Public Service Commission, the NEA, local governments and the legislature were all involved in the granting of franchises to utilities. The president made intermittent interventions on critical issues in response to demands from the public.

When Corazon Aquino became president in 1986, the NPC was unable to fulfil the country's demand for power. It was in deep financial trouble and was funding its operations through debt (Viray and Delgado 2002). The NPC's debt was about 75 per cent of the external debt of the Philippines, largely because of its failed investments in infrastructure (Mendoza et al. 2002).

One of the first reforms that occurred in the electricity industry was the abolition of the DOE, seen as a cash cow of the previous Marcos government. Under Executive Order 193, the Office of Energy Affairs (OEA) was created to take over the responsibilities of the DOE.

A number of power crises in the late 1980s resulted in sporadic brownouts, some lasting twenty-four hours. Some of the factors believed to have led to the power crises included delays in constructing base-load power plants, low hydropower generation, failure to raise sufficient capital for new power projects, the breakdown of old plants, delays in project implementation because of environmental and social problems, and the abolition of the DOE (Del Mundo 2002).

The government put in place a number of pro-market policies across the country that opened up state monopolies, including the NPC, to private sector participation. Two laws, Executive Order 215 of 1987 and Republic Act 6957 of 1991 (the Build-Operate-Transfer Law), paved the way for IPPs to build power plants through the build-operate-transfer scheme and its variants (e.g., build-operate-own, rehabilitate-own-lease). Under such schemes private investors construct and operate infrastructure, recoup the investment from users and then transfer the facility to the government.

Executive Order 215 amended the previous law (Presidential Decree 40, issued in 1972) that had given the NPC the monopoly over power generation. It allowed private corporations, cooperatives and similar associations to construct and operate power plants, including cogeneration units, plants intending to sell to the grids, plants intended primarily for the use of the owner but planning to sell excess production to the grids, and plants outside the NPC grids intending to sell directly or indirectly to end users. The aim was 'to promote competition in power generation and increase the responsibility of all utilities to perform their own planning, including the acquisition of an efficient portfolio of generation resources' (section 1, article 1, Executive Order 215). Private participation was lacking and incentive packages had to be offered to lure investment from multinationals, domestic private investors and joint ventures. The NPC's sole responsibility for transmission grids was retained. This meant that the NPC was a monopsony in that it was the sole buyer of generated power and had power over the IPPs because it controlled the grid and did not price transmission openly.

Regulating the industry

Executive Order 215 vested on the NPC and the NEA the authority to formulate rules and regulations to govern private sector involvement in power generation, subject to the approval of the Office of Energy Affairs. Although the NPC's monopoly over power generation was ended, Executive Order 215 did not abandon the command-and-control system of regulation. Although penalties could be imposed on IPPs for not meeting the targets set in their contracts with the government, it became clear later that the incentives offered to private investors far outweighed the sanctions for such breaches of contract.

In 1992 the DOE was re-established under Republic Act 7638. It resumed responsibility for planning and implementing a program for the efficient supply and use of energy. The non-price regulatory jurisdiction, powers and functions held by the Energy Regulatory Board (ERB) were also transferred to the DOE. These include, when necessary, importing, exporting, re-exporting, shipping, transporting, processing, refining marketing, and distribution of energy resources. The Department took over the supervision of the Philippine National Oil Company (PNOC), the NPC and the NEA. The Energy Coordinating Council (ECC) was abolished, and its functions were transferred to the DOE.

In addition the DOE was given the role of implementing the privatisation plan and integrating IPP plants into the national electricity system. Its responsibilities were defined as follows:

1) Develop the Philippine energy program, providing policy direction toward privatising government agencies, deregulating the power and energy industry, and reducing dependency on oil-fired plants.
2) Supervise and control all government energy projects in order to attain the goals of the Act.
3) Regulate private sector energy projects as provided for under existing laws while providing an environment conducive to free and active private sector participation and investment in all energy activities.
4) Devise ways and means of giving direct benefit to local governments and communities, and equitable preferential benefit to the region that hosts the energy resource and/or the generating facility. Ensure that host local governments are not deprived of their energy resources.
5) Encourage private enterprises engaged in energy projects to broaden their ownership and encourage wide public ownership in energy companies.
6) Formulate rules and regulations and exercise other powers as may be necessary to attain the objectives of the Act.

The Energy Regulatory Board, which had been established in 1987, was given regulatory power over the prices set by the NPC and the rural electric cooperatives, meaning that for the first time responsibility for overseeing prices no longer lay with the suppliers of electricity. This was a task some critics believed the ERB did not have the experience or expertise to fulfil (Hall and Hagler Bailly Services 1999).[1] Recall that before 1997, the ERB was focused mainly on oil industry regulation and the NPC was the sole (price) regulator of the electricity sector. The NPC and all franchised utilities with transmission and/or distribution facilities of 69 kilovolts (KV) or above were required to file their interconnection policies and procedures with the ERB for its approval. The ERB was also given responsibility for regulating wheeling tariffs, which are the charges for the use of a distribution system and/or related services.

The Act also set the electricity tariff chargeable by the NPC to not more than 12 per cent by a return-on-rate-base (RORB) methodology, and stated that any increase in power rates had to be approved by the Energy Regulatory Board. In

1993 the increase was not to exceed an average of P0.18 per kilowatt hour (KWH) and households consuming not more than 100 KWH per month were exempt from any increase for five years. Furthermore, the existing subsidy received by households consuming less than 300 KWH per month was to continue. In addition, no rate increase was to be imposed in provinces producing at least 100 megawatts (MW) of geothermal power for one year following the signing of the Act.

Subsequent legislation vested the ERB with additional responsibilities such as the enforcement of the 1994 Anti-Pilferage Act (Republic Act 7832). The law also established a cap on the recoverable rate of system losses by phasing out the component of pilferage losses. System losses refer to the amount of electricity lost in the system through technical problems with power lines, transformers and meters, and non-technical losses from theft, pilferage, illegal connections, and the like. The total system loss is equal to the per kilowatt hour difference between the net energy input and total energy sales (Hagler Bailly Services 2000: 6). The ERB was authorised to determine at the end of the fourth and fifth years after the law was passed whether the caps should be reduced further, taking into consideration the effectiveness of the Act, the viability of private utilities and rural cooperatives, and the interests of consumers. The cap should be no lower than 9 per cent.

On 3 August 1995, the Energy Regulatory Board defined a number of 'Rules and Regulations Governing the Operation of Electric Power Services' (Resolution 95-21) to cover the utilities under its jurisdiction, namely the NPC, private and public utilities, and the rural electric cooperatives. This confirmed the ERB's authority as the industry's quasi-judicial regulator. The resolution required all electric utilities to comply strictly with all the terms and conditions of their certificate of public convenience and necessity (CPCN), franchise rules and regulations, memoranda, orders and circulars, and other regulations issued by the ERB. It required them to operate, maintain and provide safe, reliable, adequate, efficient and continuous services, in accordance with the Philippine Electric Code or, when applicable, the provisions of the US National Electrical Safety Code.

With the deregulation of the oil industry in 1998, the ERB was relieved of its responsibility for oil industry regulation.

INCREASING PRIVATE SECTOR PARTICIPATION

There was a surge of demand for power in the early 1990s as industries were encouraged to increase capacity to propel the nation's development. Although this demand was anticipated, the capacity was insufficient. Interruptions to the electricity supply disrupted the wheels of progress and assumed the magnitude of a public disaster.

In response to the crisis, Republic Act 7648 (the Electricity Power Crisis Act) of 1993 gave emergency powers to then President Fidel Ramos for one year to fast track the implementation of build-operate-and-transfer projects and to negotiate projects to meet peak load requirements. It allowed the president to enter into contracts for the construction, repair, rehabilitation, improvement and maintenance of power plants, projects and facilities.

Republic Act 7648 and Republic Act 7718 (the Expanded Build-Operate-Transfer Law) of 1994 attracted further private participation in power generation. These laws also allowed the self-generation of power by big industries and the direct connection of consumers with power requirements of at least 100 MW to NPC transmission grids. In 2001 privately run power plants accounted for some 61 per cent of the total 12,717 MW capacity, compared with the NPC capacity of 39 per cent (DOE Database 2001). The private sector is now allowed to participate in the design and construction, procurement and project management of power plants. Energy conversion agreements and power purchase agreements facilitate cooperation between the NPC (or other power facilities) and the IPPs.

The IPPs, which are mainly multinational companies or joint ventures between foreign and local firms, have ballooned under the incentives, guarantees and assured profits offered by the national government. The IPPs numbered around thirty as of 2001. In addition to buying electricity from the IPPs, the NPC still generates electricity and sells it at a regulated wholesale price to some 271 major customers directly connected to its transmission lines. These include private utilities and rural cooperatives (126), large industries (ninety-three) and government institutions (fifty-two) (DOE Database 2001).

Before 1994 most multinational IPPs sold power solely to the NPC while the majority of domestic IPPs sold to affiliate distribution utilities (e.g., Meralco, Visayas Electric and Davao Light). For example, First Gas, a Lopez company, produced electricity for Meralco, another Lopez company. After much lobbying, all IPPs were allowed to generate and sell electricity to the NPC and other utilities. However, the private generating capacity that was allowed to the IPPs was restricted to peak-load demand. Thus, the private response was not sufficient (Sicat 2002).

The Build-Operate-Transfer Laws (both the 1991 and 1994 versions) recognised 'the indispensable role of the private sector as the main engine for national growth and development' (section 1, Republic Act 6957). The laws outlined the state's ability 'to provide the most appropriate incentives to mobilise private resources for the purpose of financing the construction, operation and maintenance of infrastructure and development projects normally financed and undertaken by Government. Such incentives, aside from financial incentives as provided for by law, shall include providing a climate of minimum government regulations and procedures and specific government undertakings in support of the private sector' (section 1, Republic Act 6957).

These laws also authorised government agencies to enter into contracts with a prequalified proponent of a private sector infrastructure or development project. Most infrastructure and development projects were opened up to private contractors, allowing the cash-strapped government to reallocate its limited resources to other priorities (Ramos 1997). The laws provided the policy framework and guidelines for contractual arrangements and also authorised the financing, construction, operation and maintenance of private sector projects.

The contractual arrangements or agreements that government-owned or government-controlled corporations, local government units and other government infrastructure agencies may negotiate with the private sector, include any of the below:

1) Build, operate and transfer: the proponent undertakes the construction of infrastructure or a development facility, including the financing, operation and maintenance. The proponent operates the facility over a fixed term and is able to charge users appropriate tolls, fees, rentals and other charges to recoup its investment. The proponent will transfer the facility to a government agency or unit at the end of a fixed term, which shall not exceed fifty years.
2) Build and transfer: the proponent finances and constructs infrastructure or a development facility, and on its completion, turns it over to a government agency or unit. The agency shall reimburse the proponent on an agreed schedule for the total investment expended on the project, plus a reasonable rate of return.
3) Build, own and operate: the proponent finances, constructs, owns, operates and maintains infrastructure or a development facility, and is able to charge users appropriate fees, tolls, rentals and other charges to recoup its investment, operating and maintenance costs plus a reasonable return. Projects need to be recommended by the Investment Coordination Committee of the National Economic and Development Authority and be approved by the president.
4) Build, lease and transfer: a proponent finances and constructs infrastructure or a development facility, and on its completion leases it to a government agency or unit for a fixed period after which ownership is automatically transferred to the government.
5) Build, transfer and operate: the proponent constructs a facility on a turnkey basis, assuming cost overruns, delays and specified performance risks. Once the facility is commissioned satisfactorily, the private entity will operate the facility but the title will be transferred to the government.
6) Contract, add and operate: the proponent adds to an existing infrastructure facility that it is renting from the government. It operates the project over an agreed franchise period.
7) Develop, operate and transfer: favourable conditions external to the infrastructure project that is to be built by the proponent are integrated into an arrangement that gives the proponent the right to develop an adjoining property and thus enjoy some of the benefits the investment creates, such as higher property or rent values.
8) Rehabilitate, operate and transfer: an existing facility is turned over to the private proponent to refurbish, operate and maintain for a franchised period.

When the period expires, the title to the facility is turned over to the government.
9) Rehabilitate, own and operate: an existing facility is turned over to the private proponent to refurbish and operate. No time limit is imposed on ownership: as long as the operator is not in violation of the franchise, the facility can be operated in perpetuity.

Build-operate-and-transfer contractual arrangements included guarantees that in cases of loan default the government or one of its agencies would assume responsibility for repaying the debt incurred by the private operator. Financial incentives were provided and private investors were assured that regulations and procedures would be minimised and that specific government policies would be put in place to support the private sector (Republic Act 6957). The generous guarantees and incentives embodied in the power purchase contracts encouraged a surge of new private power producers.

In a typical contract, the Philippine government shouldered the risk associated with market demand, exchange rate fluctuations, fuel costs, retail tariffs and sovereign risk. In effect, IPPs were riskless investments (Fabella 2002).

An example of an incentive is the controversial 'take or pay' provision, which guaranteed regular payment by the NPC of a fixed fee for a certain capacity regardless of whether the capacity was utilised or dispatched by the project operator. Such a generous incentive may be explained by the recognition that power plants and the fees derived from electricity generation were put up as security in order to obtain finance. The revenues from such projects must be predictable for international financiers to extend loans. Another explanation is that private operators only have a responsibility to make available the capacity they guaranteed in their agreements with the NPC and should not have to bear the risk of the NPC not being able to resell the capacity (DOE Commercial Relations Office, cited in Del Mundo (2002)).

Performance undertakings have also been used to mitigate risk in IPP contracts. The IPPs are assured that if the NPC should fail, the government will meet the NPC's obligations (Viray and Delgado 2002). The rationale for this arrangement is likely to be that at first IPPs were required to sell their capacity exclusively to the NPC.[2] Only the NPC has direct access to consumers and has control over when IPPs are dispatched and how much each facility produces. According to Viray and Delgado (2002), 'it is but fair for NPC to assume the demand or market risk. In addition, these are common arrangements in debt-financed infrastructure projects anywhere in the world.'

Fabella (2002), on the other hand, argues that although increased production from the IPP plants did resolve the power crisis by 1995, the liabilities embodied in these contracts created major problems for the government. The power purchase agreements stipulated that the NPC must continue to pay between 25 and 80 per cent of the agreed rate for power from the IPPs regardless of the level of dispatch (the take-or-pay feature). This stipulation resulted in power costs of up to 25 per cent more than the cost of power generated by the NPC in its own facilities (Tuano 2001; Reside 2001). The appearance of excess power capacity became a fiscal nightmare for the government. The NPC's loss was P5.9 billion in 1999 and P9.9 billion in 2000. When the NPC tried to recoup its losses by raising its tariff, it started a political storm (Fabella 2002).

Nevertheless, the Build-Operate-Transfer Laws generally eliminated the restrictions on the size of generating facilities and allowed self-generation by public utilities. Power consumers with requirements of at least 100 MW were allowed to connect directly to the NPC transmission grid. Thus, a major effect of the laws was to create a strong private sector response, and this led to the quick expansion of power capacity (Sicat 2002).

Between 1996 and 1998 twenty-three new power plants operating in excess of 100 MW came into existence, expanding the total number of IPP power plants to forty-five. These new plants increased capacity by as much as 2,600 MW, thus creating a buffer for industrialisation needs (Table 5.2). The new plants are more efficient, producing electricity at lower cost (Sicat 2002).

When the Asian crisis hit in 1997, the slowdown in the economy dampened the demand for power. Currently there is excess capacity in electricity supply, but this is predicted to service the country's needs only until 2005 (DOE Database 2001).

ONGOING PROBLEMS IN THE PHILIPPINE ELECTRICITY INDUSTRY

The Philippines has one of the highest prices for electricity in Asia, second only to Japan (Table 5.9). The NPC's liabilities represent 25 per cent of the national debt and it continues to be a drain on the nation's finances by providing subsidies of up to P16 billion a year. Over the next ten years the electricity industry needs an annual investment of $1 billion, which the cash-strapped government is unable to provide.

Table 5.2 The number of IPP plants started up between 1986 and 1998

Year and major milestones	Number of plants	Total capacity (MW)
1986 (Aquino Administration, mothballing of the PNPPI nuclear plant)	9	1,988.73
30 June 1992 (start of Ramos Administration)	10	961.95
20 April 1993 (RA 7648, start of one-year effectivity period)	9	896.80
20 April 1994 (end of RA 7648)	14	4,610.25
30 June 1998 (end of Ramos Administration, start of Estrada Administration)	3	766.00
Total	45	9,223.73

Source: DOE (2002).

The high cost of electricity in the country has been blamed on high generation costs, monopoly power at the generating and retail levels, power outages, management inefficiency and the high leverage of power companies, including the NPC (Sicat 2002: 5–9).

High generation costs can be a reflection of the level of technology in power generation, raw material costs or contractual obligations. Many observers, and even the NPC, blame the high cost of contracts signed during the power crisis years for the high generation costs. In recent years the NPC has bought out some of the highest cost contracts and has sought to renegotiate others (Sicat 2002: 6).

Privatising the NPC

In 1994 the Omnibus Power Bill was filed in Congress. It made a number of proposals to address the problems of the Philippine electricity industry, including the restructuring of the industry and the privatisation of the NPC. The much-anticipated legislative fiat came when Republic Act 9136 (the Electric Power Reform Act) was enacted in June 2001 after many years of debate. The restructuring of the Philippine electricity industry is expected to increase efficiency, innovation and consumer choice. A range of mechanisms will be introduced to increase the exposure of the industry to competitive market forces. Such mechanisms include a combination of market actions where competition can be introduced (in generation and supply) and effective regulation in segments that remain natural monopolies (in transmission and distribution) (Abrenica and Ables 2000).

Republic Act 9136 introduces many features from successful international experiences in regulatory and competition policy reform in the power industry. The Act aims to stimulate competition by allowing various mechanisms for the independent production of electricity, to empower users by encouraging greater competition among power suppliers and to set clear regulatory mandates (Sicat 2002: 2).

Figure 5.2 sketches out a picture of the market envisaged by Republic Act 9136.

Republic Act 9136 provides for:

1) the unbundling of electricity into four sectors: generation, supply (which will be competitive and open), transmission and distribution (which are natural monopolies[3] and will be subject to regulation by the Energy Regulatory Commission);
2) the privatisation of the NPC's generation and transmission assets;
3) greater competition in electricity generation and supply;
4) open access in transmission and distribution wires;
5) the unbundling of electricity tariffs to reflect the costs of generating, transmitting, distributing and supplying electricity;
6) the creation of a wholesale electricity spot market;

Figure 5.2 Structure of the electricity industry envisaged in Republic Act 9136

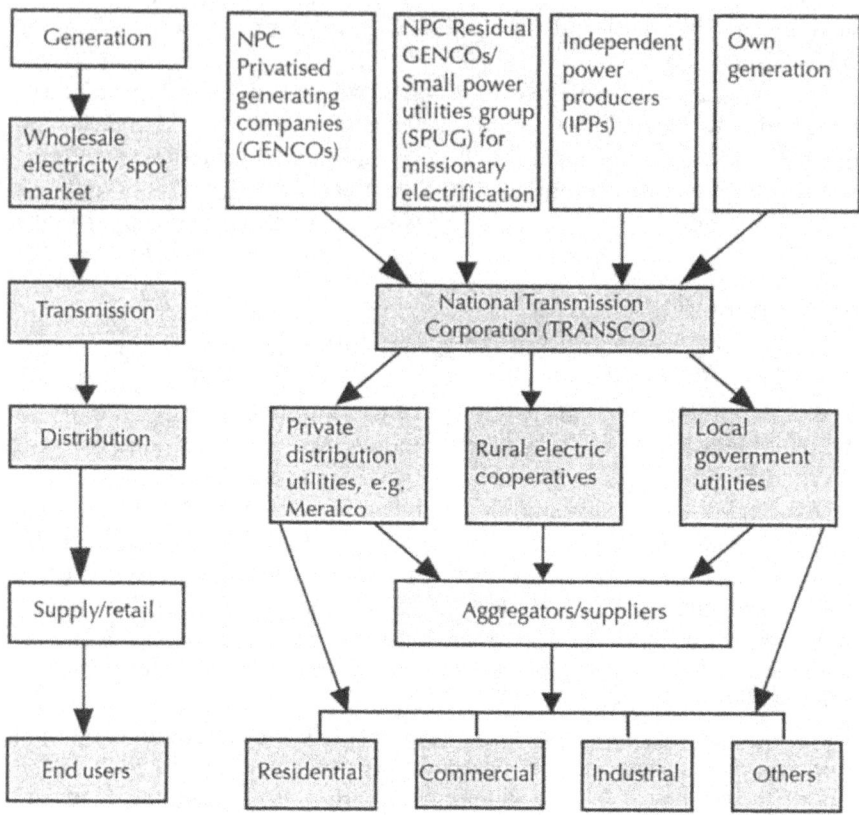

Notes: The ERC regulates the price of transmitting and distributing electricity (transmission charge and distribution wheeling charge); ensures the compliance of the former with performance standards; also ensures the compliance of all generating companies, TRANSCO, distribution utilities and suppliers, with financial capacity, health and safety, and other standards. The DOE regulates the non-pricing activities; supervises the restructuring of the industry; also entrusted to establish and formulate rules on the wholesale spot market. The NEA regulates the franchising of RECs; strengthens the technical capability and financial viability of RECs. The Power Sector Assets and Liabilities Management Corporation (PSALM) manages the privatisation of NPC assets and contracts and the TRANSCO. The Congressional Power Commission oversees the proper implementation of RA 9136.

Source: Adapted from RA9136, DOE Presentation 2001.

7) the promotion of the entry of aggregators and suppliers;
8) the strengthening of the ERB, which will become the Energy Regulatory Commission (ERC);
9) a redefinition of the roles of the DOE, NEA and other government agencies involved in the supervision and administration of the Philippine electricity industry; and
10) a requirement for electricity providers to comply with technical and financial standards for providing a quality service to consumers.

The main aims of the Act are to disengage the state from owning and financing power generation, and to move to greater market determination of outcomes under a fair and transparent (unbundled or segregated) regulatory framework. Electricity generation and supply should be able to be competitive, while transmission and distribution will remain the responsibility of public organisations, subject to the regulation of the strengthened ERC.

The NPC will be privatised, but within the NPC the small power utilities group (SPUG) would be given responsibility for the missionary electrification scheme (the scheme to connect isolated areas to the national grid) and for power generation and power delivery in areas not connected to the transmission system.

The Act prohibits cross-ownership: 'No generation company, distribution utility or stockholder or official thereof shall be allowed to hold ownership in the Transmission Company or its concessionaire and vice versa' (Rule 11, Section 3).[4] It states that 'no company ... can own or control more than 30 per cent of the installed generating capacity of a Grid and/or 25 per cent of the national installed generating capacity' (Rule 11, Section 4). It also prohibits bilateral supply contracts: 'No distribution utility shall be allowed to source from bilateral power supply contracts more than 50 per cent of its total demand from its affiliate engaged in generation' (Rule 11, Section 5).

These rules mean that cross-ownership between generation and distribution is allowed, although transactions between affiliates are limited. Cross-ownership is not allowed in transmission. The ownership and affiliate limitation is intended to inhibit the abuse of market power, discriminatory access, transfer pricing and cross-subsidisation (Fabella 2002).

The unbundling of rates will mean the identification of separate charges for providing services for generation, transmission, distribution or supply to end users. This aims at informing consumers of the true costs of providing each service. Cross-subsidies will be removed within the grid, between grids and between classes of customers. Examples of cross-subsidies include Luzon grid customers subsidising the price of electricity in the Visayan region, industrial users subsidising commercial users, or other users subsidising low-income users. Until cross-subsidies are phased out they should be identified on billing statements. The Act also allows consumers to choose their electricity provider, just like in other utilities such as transportation and telecommunications. Open access provisions allow any qualified person to use the transmission and/or distribution system and associated facilities to sell to consumers. A wholesale electricity spot market is to be developed within one year after Republic Act 9136 is passed, allowing consumers to buy and sell electricity in the spot market for a fee. These changes will make the market more contestable.

The law also provided for the following:

1) The ability in an electricity crisis for Congress to authorise through a joint resolution the establishment of additional generation capacity under whatever terms and conditions it may decide to set. Responsibility for determining an imminent shortage of electricity is vested in the president.
2) Responsibility for reviewing IPP contracts by an interagency committee chaired by the Secretary of the Department of Finance.
3) Renegotiation of power purchase and energy conversion agreements between the NPC and PNOC-Energy Development Corporation.
4) Royalties, returns, rentals and tax rates for indigenous energy resources.
5) Environmental protection.
6) Benefits to host communities.
7) NPC offers of transition supply contracts.
8) Fiscal prudence.
9) Separation of benefits from the privatisation of the NPC and the unbundling of the industry into generation, transmission, distribution and supply.
10) Education and protection of end users.
11) Fines and penalties for non-compliance with financial and technical standards.

Although Republic Act 9136 is considered a milestone in electricity sector reform, a number of issues remain, especially in relation to the debts of the NPC.

The Act created a new government agency, the Power Sector Assets and Liabilities Management Corporation (PSALM), to formulate and implement a program for the sale and privatisation of NPC assets and IPP contracts, and for the liquidation of NPC debts and stranded contract costs.

PSALM will take over the stranded debts and stranded contract costs of the utilities (the NPC, eligible private utilities and the rural cooperatives) and take ownership of all NPC generation assets, IPP contracts, real estate and other disposable assets. Any liabilities that have not been met by the proceeds from the sale of NPC assets will be assumed by the national government. Stranded debts refer to any unpaid obligations of the NPC. Stranded contract costs refer to the excess of electricity costs under eligible contracts over the market price of the contracted energy output. The law allowed private utilities to recover stranded contract costs resulting from the restructuring of the industry during the first year of open access. Approval is subject to the review and approval of the ERB.

The calculation of stranded debts and contract costs of the NPC will form part of a universal charge to be determined, fixed and approved by the ERC within one year from the passing of the Act. It will be imposed on all electricity users for the following purposes:

1) payment for stranded debts in excess of the amount assumed by the government (P200 billion) and for the stranded contract costs of private utilities;
2) missionary electrification;
3) the equalisation of taxes and royalties applied to indigenous or renewable sources of energy vis-à-vis imported energy fuels;
4) an environmental charge equivalent to one-fourth of one centavo per kilowatt-hour; and
5) a charge to account for all forms of cross-subsidies for a period not exceeding three years.

When a government asset is privatised the state usually assumes any liabilities to make the asset more attractive to prospective buyers. This increases the government's debts, eroding any profits that might be gained from the sale. The Freedom from Debt Coalition (FDC), a militant non-government organisation in the country, and others who opposed the bill estimate that privatisation of the NPC will fetch between US$4.5 billion and US$5.2 billion, against the government's target of US$14.7 billion. This will leave a US$9.5 billion (P352 billion) shortfall. Previous DOE Secretary Jose Camacho said the government had committed to absorb up to P200 billion of stranded costs,[5] reducing the total to P152 billion, which is still a substantial sum (Doronila 2001).

The Act mandates a rate reduction of thirty centavos per kilowatt hour (P0.30/ KWH) for all residential end users. The reduction will appear as a separate item on consumers' bills. It also provides for a lifeline rate for marginalised consumers. The rate will be set by the ERC and will be exempted from the cross-subsidy phase-out under the Act for a period of ten years, unless extended by law. Each utility is to file a petition with the ERC recommending the level of consumption that should qualify for the lifeline rate.

Inefficiencies in energy distribution

Since 1999 the country has been experiencing an oversupply of power. In 2002 DOE Secretary Vince Perez estimated excess capacity to be around 11 per cent, or 1,235 MW. Of the total dependable capacity of 11,191 MW, slightly more than half comes from hydro (23 per cent) and geothermal (30 per cent) sources (as cited in Viray and Delgado 2002). The reserve margin, or the capacity required to provide a secure supply of power, is between 22 per cent and 30 per cent, or at least 2,462 MW. The demand for electricity, however, has decreased (Viray and Delgado 2002).

Table 5.3 describes the country's energy generation mix from 1990, projected to 2004. It shows the increasing reliance on imported energy, for example oil and coal, and a decreasing reliance on indigenous resources, particularly water and geothermal energy. This implies a possible overuse of indigenous resources,

Table 5.3 The national energy generation mix, 1990–2004 (per cent)

Fuel Type	1990	1995	2000	2004
A. Imported	50	46	58	54
Oil	47	38	47	45
Coal	3	8	11	9
B. Indigenous	50	54	42	46
Hydro	24	18	4	4
Geothermal	22	25	7	7
Coal	4	11	3	3
New & Renewable	–	–	28	32

Sources: For entries in 1990 and 1995, '1991 power development program, NPC', as cited in *Ibon* (1992): 15(7), 15 April; for 2000 and 2004 entries, 'The medium-term Philippine development plan, 1999–2004', National Economic Development Authority.

inefficiency in their operations, the aging of NPC power plants (which generate indigenous resources), or a combination of the above and other factors. In 1992 most NPC plants were already over ten years old, suggesting capacity and productivity have been low in electricity generation

The under-utilisation of power generating capacity by industrial and commercial users resulted in an increase in the cost of electricity to all consumers because of the take-or-pay provisions in the IPP contracts. Part of the fixed liabilities owed by the NPC and private utilities to the IPPs, these payments are reflected in electricity bills through the purchased power adjustment or PPA, which averages more than 60 per cent of the total bill (DOE Electricity Price Watch, July 2002). The take-or-pay provision has been onerous on the government and consumers.

To address this problem a review was held of the thirty-five IPP contracts negotiated in the 1990s. Of these, nineteen were found to be financially and legally valid. Sixteen were identified as having legal and financial issues that needed appropriate study, renegotiation or possible legal action (DOE Electricity Price Watch, July 2002). Of the latter group, five contracts were found to be defective and prejudicial to the government and the public. These were the Binga Hydroelectric Plant, the Cavite EPZA Diesel Plant, the Sual Coal-fired Thermal Plant, the Casecnan Multipurpose Project and the San Roque Multipurpose Project (*Philippine Daily Inquirer*, 6 July 2002).

The NPC's high-voltage transmission systems require enormous rehabilitation and upgrading to ensure sustainable quality, reliability and security of power supply (DOE 2000). The NPC is still the sole transmitter of bulk electricity to distributors and large industrial customers through the Luzon, Visayas and Mindanao grids. It is also responsible for constructing the grid that will connect the main islands of the country.

Table 5.4 The age of NPC plants, 1992

Age in years	Hydro	Geothermal	Coal	Oil
< 5	0	0	0	4
5–10	6	5	2	4
10–15	7	4	1	9
15–20	0	0	0	1
>20	8	0	0	2

Source: 'Philippine power system development map, NPC', as cited in *Ibon* (1992): 15(7), 15 April.

In 1998 the Luzon-Visayas grid was unified through a cable linking Leyte (in the Visayas) to the Luzon mainland. A national transmission grid will be created when the Mindanao island grid is connected to the Visayas grid between Leyte and Surigao (in Mindanao) in 2004. Owing to its geography and isolation, the Philippines has no means of importing power from elsewhere, unlike countries that share a common land boundary or short waterway distance (Sicat 2002: 5).

The distribution of electricity at a usable voltage to consumers is largely a private sector enterprise, but with government participation through the rural electric cooperatives that it organises and funds. Distribution is undertaken by seventeen private utilities, 119 rural electric cooperatives and ten utilities owned or operated by municipal, city or provincial governments.

Private utilities sell electricity to some 4.5 million residential, commercial and industrial customers nationwide. The rural electric cooperatives, meanwhile, provide approximately 4.7 million interconnections in Luzon, Visayas and Mindanao (DOE Database 2001). Table 5.5 shows that the private utilities served around 90 per cent of the total customer base in 2000 (by number not power requirements). The Lopez-owned Manila Electric Company (Meralco) was by far the largest private utility in the distribution sector, serving 79.5 per cent of the country's total customer base, followed by the Visayas Electric Company (VECO) at 5.1 per cent and Davao Light at 4.2 per cent.

Meralco distributes 59 per cent of the total electricity requirements of the Philippines across a 9,328 square kilometre franchise area that covers only 23 per cent of the population. It buys 80 per cent of all NPC and IPP-generated power, which it sells to its 3.6 million customers.[6] It holds the exclusive franchise to distribute, supply and market electricity through its own wires to its franchise area. VECO is the second largest distributor but accounts for only 2.5 per cent of total electricity sales.[7] The Alcantaras are the major stockholders of VECO while the Aboitizes control Davao Light.

Meralco is believed to have undue market power because it owns and controls both generation and distribution facilities. Among the generation facilities it

Table 5.5 Market share of private utilities, by number of customers, 2000–03

Private utilities	Number of customers	Per cent share of total
Luzon		
Angeles Electric Corp.	66,096	1.45
Bauan Electric Light System	–	–
Cabanatuan Electric Corp.	41,144	0.90
Dagupan Electric Corp.	63,781	1.40
Ibaan Electrical & Engineering Corp.	4,800	0.11
La Union Electric Co.	25,427	0.56
Manaoag Utility Inc.	–	–
Manila Electric Co.	3,623,798	79.54
Mansons Corp.	11,704	0.26
Pud-Olongapo	–	–
San Fernando Electric Light & Power	44,460	0.98
Tarlac Enterprises, Inc.	43,488	0.95
Subtotal	3,924,698	86.14
Visayas		
Mactan Electric Co.	–	–
Panay Electric Co.	48,454	1.06
PPUD-Bohol	16,210	0.36
Visayas Electric Co.	234,273	5.14
Subtotal	298,937	6.56
Mindanao		
Cagayan Electric Power & Light Co.	78,298	1.72
Cotabato Light & Power	23,383	0.51
Davao Light & Power	192,357	4.22
Iligan Electric Light & Power Co.	38,341	0.84
Subtotal	332,379	7.29
Total	4,556,014	100.00

Note: The number of customers includes residential, commercial and industrial customers, as well as government authorities.
Source: ERB (2001a).

controls are First Private Power, Panay Power, First Gas, FGP Corporation, Duracom, and Bauang Private Power. These facilities have a combined installed capacity of 3,800 MW (DOE Database 2001).

Cross-ownership in generation and distribution gives companies undue information advantages and opens up opportunities for discriminatory self-dealing, cross-subsidisation and cost shifting. The likelihood of the abuse of interlocking holdings relates to the possibility of funnelling profits from retail distribution to power generation. This poses a challenge to regulation and competition in the electricity industry, as monopoly power could be gained in power generation.

Table 5.6 Average systems loss of electric cooperatives, 1997–2000 (per cent)

Grid	Average loss
Luzon	18.9
Visayas	13.2
Mindanao	15.9
Philippines	16.9

Source: ERB (2001b).

In addition to opening the sector to competition and private sector participation, the government has moved to address such issues as unbundling and open access in preparation for the restructuring of the electricity industry and the privatisation of the NPC, which would require the separation of the corporation's generation and transmission functions. Executive Order 473, passed on 17 April 1998, ordered the ERB to formulate and adopt guidelines to identify unbundled tariffs and the different services provided by the NPC and all franchised utilities, and also the corresponding tariffs charged to customers. Unbundled tariffs include, but are not limited to: generation charges; transmission, sub-transmission and distribution charges; ancillary service charges; and service costs for the supply of electricity.

In a policy statement in 1999, the ERB reiterated its support for the RORB pricing system it adopted to regulate the electric utilities (ERB 1999). The statement presented the rationale for the regime and the legal bases for its use.[8] It stated that the RORB system provided a 'just and reasonable' basis for setting rates that allow for operating costs and a reasonable rate of return. The return must be high enough for the utility to maintain its credit rating and attract whatever capital may be required for maintenance, expansion and technological innovation. The return must also be comparable to that earned by other businesses that face similar risk.

The distribution system is highly fragmented with limited economies of scale. System losses and inefficiencies are prevalent. The allowable system loss chargeable against revenues is 14 per cent but the average system loss of a rural electric cooperative over the four-year period between 1997 and 2000 was 17 per cent. Rural electric cooperatives in Luzon registered the highest loss at 19 per cent, followed by Mindanao rural electric cooperatives at 16 per cent. For a private utility (Cagayan Electric Power and Light), the average loss over the same period was 6.9 per cent.

Although system losses have fallen – in 1997 Luzon rural electric cooperatives made an average 21 per cent loss and Mansons Corporation cooperatives made an average 35 per cent loss – there is a great deal of room for improvement. There are no sanctions imposed against utilities with high systems losses, nor

Table 5.7 Average systems loss of private utilities, 1997–2000 (per cent)

Private utility	Average loss
Luzon	
Angeles Electric Corp.	8.5
Bauan Electric Light System	30.2
Cabanatuan Electric Corp.	14.1
Dagupan Electric Corp.	11.5
Ibaan Electrical and Engineering Corp.	25.3
La Union Electric Co.	21.9
Manaoag Utility Inc.	22.9
Manila Electric Co.	11.4
Mansons Corp.	30.9
Pud-Olongapo	32.6
San Fernando Electric Light and Power	8.8
Tarlac Enterprises, Inc.	13.2
Visayas	
Mactan Electric Co.	12.6
Panay Electric Co.	11.3
PPUD-Bohol	18.0
Visayas Electric Co.	12.6
Mindanao	
Cagayan Electric Power and Light Co.	6.9
Cotabato Light and Power	10.4
Davao Light and Power	9.1
Iligan Electric Light and Power Co.	11.8

Source: ERB (2001b).

do utilities have any incentive to improve efficiency while they can recover 14 per cent of their systems losses.

In comparison with other Asian countries, the Philippine electricity industry registered the worst transmission and distribution (T&D losses) at 19 per cent in 1994. Singapore has the most efficient system, with T&D losses of only 3.4 per cent, followed by South Korea (5.3 per cent), Malaysia (8.9 per cent) and Thailand (9.7 per cent). Indonesia's losses stood at 12.5 per cent (Table 5.8).

CONCLUSION

Efforts to open the Philippine electricity industry only began in 1987 and it has been a difficult road to create a competitive energy sector after eight decades of active state involvement in electricity generation, transmission, distribution and supply. It would be naive to expect competition to flourish instantly.

The industry has had a dismal financial performance and contributes a substantial share of the national debt. The demand for electricity has grown

Table 5.8 Comparison of transmission and distribution losses in selected Asian countries, 1994

Country	Gross generation	T&D losses	Per cent losses
Singapore	20,234	686	3.4
South Korea	164,993	8,678	5.3
Japan	727,102	3,456	6.0
Malaysia	39,975	3,550	8.9
Thailand	71,177	6,867	9.7
Indonesia	61,370	7,650	12.5
Philippines	24,507	4,657	19.0

Source: 'Electric Power in Asia and the Pacific, 1993 and 1994', Economic and Social Commission for Asia and the Pacific, as cited in 'The medium-term Philippine development plan, 1999–2004', National Economic Development Authority, pp. 5–10.

Table 5.9 Average rates of Asian utilities, 1997 (peso per KWH)

Country	Residential	Commercial	Industrial	Overall
Japan	7.18	5.05	5.05	5.64
Singapore	3.55	3.09	2.71	3.01
Malaysia	2.34	3.78	2.86	3.12
Thailand	1.69	–	1.24	1.65
Indonesia	1.69	2.80	1.67	1.65
Philippines (Meralco)	3.46	3.48	3.18	3.36
Philippines (NPC)			1.70	1.72
Luzon	–	–	1.94	1.77
Visayas	–	–	2.07	1.94
Mindanao	–	–	1.41	1.31
Taiwan	2.94	3.63	1.87	2.00
South Korea	3.90	3.92	2.11	2.74

Source: DOE Database (2001), cited in 'The Medium-Term Philippine Development Plan, 1999–2004', National Economic Development Authority, pp. 5–8.

rapidly, and is projected to grow further, but the rapid expansion of the sector will require huge capital investment.

The Electric Power Reform Act of 2001 put in place reforms to restructure the industry and privatise the NPC. The Act will create a wholesale electricity spot market, segregate components of the industry and allow the unbundling of tariffs. However, these reforms raise policy issues and legal challenges. For example, is it morally right for the Filipino people or the government to pay the stranded costs of power generation by the NPC and the rural electric cooperatives? Will the prices of electricity remain exorbitantly high under the new universal charge to be imposed on electricity users?

The reforms of the Philippine electricity sector have not removed the NPC's monopoly over transmission nor Meralco's domination of the distribution sector. These monopoly positions may only be solved by such action as divestment or contracting out. The issue of cross-ownership in generation and distribution also continues to be a problem. There is the potential for affiliate private power producers and utilities like Meralco to use this market power to their advantage by channelling profits from one sector to another.

Moreover, the designation of power generation and power supply as businesses that can be opened to competition poses questions as to how these markets will promote competition. Public utilities have responsibilities to provide efficient and affordable services as widely as possible. When utilities are no longer considered public services, meaning common carriers performing recognised public functions for public service, how will such responsibilities be assured?

Nevertheless, these reforms are moving the industry in the right direction in that they will minimise inefficiencies and losses as competition is gradually introduced. They also accentuate the ability of the Energy Regulatory Commission to penalise abuses of market power while also promoting competition, encouraging market development and ensuring customer choice in the power industry.

NOTES

1. Under Executive Order 172, the ERB's regulatory and legal powers over the energy sector only included oversight of the petroleum industry, and the shipping and transportation of petroleum products and coal, but not utilities involved in generation and distribution.
2. This was true for most of the early build-operate-transfer programs, but the requirement was relaxed a little in later years, allowing IPPs to sell to distributors and other utilities.
3. Natural monopolies usually exist in capital-intensive industries where there are large economies of scale, fluctuating demand, an inability to store the good, a specificity to a set location, a public need and direct interaction with consumers (Berg and Tschirhart 1999).
4. Many believe this to be a diluted version of the original 1994 provision and an accommodation to the powerful distribution sector.
5. Section 32 of Republic Act 9136 states that 'the national government shall directly assume a portion of the financial obligations of NPC in an amount not to exceed P200 billion'.
6. See <www.npc.gov.ph/npcstrat.htm>; 'Asian utilities', Deutsche Bank, November 1999.
7. See 'Asian utilities', Deutsche Bank, November 1999; DOE (2000); Villasenor. (2000).

8 See, e.g., Meralco vs. Public Service Commission, 18 SCRA 651; and Republic of the Philippines vs. Medina, 41 SCRA 643.

REFERENCES

Abrenica, Ma Joy and Adelardo C. Ables (2000) 'Competition policy in the power sector', Philippine Institute for Development Studies, mimeo.
Berg, Sanford and E. Tschirhart (1999) 'Developments in best practice regulation: process vs. performance', paper prepared for the Australian Competition and Consumer Commission conference on Incentive Regulation and Overseas Development, 18–19 November, Sydney, Australia.
Del Mundo, Rowaldo R. (2002) (Understanding IPPs and PPA', technical briefing paper on the power industry for the House of Representatives' Committee on Energy, 3 June.
Department of Energy (DOE) (2000) Presentation to the Senate on privatising the Philippine electricity industry, 20 August.
DOE Database (2001) 'Philippine electricity players, performance and other statistics', Manila: Department of Energy.
DOE (2002) 'Report on the Philippine Power Emergency Act', Manila: Department of Energy.
Doronila, Amando (2001) 'Macapagal faces severe test in power reform bill', *Philippine Daily Inquirer*, 28 May, A1, A6.
Energy Regulatory Board (ERB) (1999) 'Existing pricing policy for private electric distribution utilities', 6 September, Manila: Energy Regulatory Board.
— (2001a) 'Philippine electricity industry players and their market shares', Manila: Energy Regulatory Board.
— (2001b) Statistics on the Philippine electricity industry, Manila: Energy Regulatory Board.
Fabella, Raul (2002) 'The regulatory environment of the energy sector in the Philippines', paper presented at the 2002 annual conference of the Centre for Regulation and Competition, Manchester, UK, 2–4 September, accessed at <www.idpm.man.ac.uk/crc/>.
Hagler Bailly Services (2000) 'Utility technical performance standards and allowable levels of energy loss', paper presented at a workshop on Developing Performance Standards for the Philippine Power Sector, DOE Conference Room, Manila, May.
Hall, George and Hagler Bailly Services (1999) 'An assessment of the Philippine regulatory scheme', interim report submitted to the Asian Development Bank, October.
Mendoza, Maria Fe V., Juvy Gervacio, Rene Lopos and Clarissa Isa (2002) 'Public enterprise reform and privatization in the Philippines', paper presented at a seminar on Public Enterprise Reform and Privatization in the Philippines: An Assessment of Experience and Proposals for a New Policy Agenda, Centre for Policy and Executive Development, University of the Philippines, and AusAID, Manila.
Ramos, Fidel V. (1997) 'Liberalization and privatization of utilities and services', policy statement to the Philippine Congress, June.
Reside, Renato Jr. (2001) 'The future of the Philippine power sector: reason to be cautious (lessons from California and the United Kingdom)', in Dante Canlas and Yasuhiro Nimura (eds) *Socio-Economic Reform Program in the Philippines – Impacts and New Directions*, Tokyo: Institute of Developing Economies, Japan External Trade Organisation.

Sicat, Gerardo P. (2002) 'Electricity reform in the Philippines and the prospects for competition', remarks to the Twenty-Eighth Pacific Trade and Development Conference on Competition Policy in the New Millennium, September.

Tuano, Philip Arnold (2001) 'Privatization of a state enterprise: the NAPOCOR case', in *Economic Reforms and Governance in the Philippines – Eight Case Studies*, Quezon City: Ateneo School of Government and Ateneo Center for Social Policy and Public Affairs.

Villasenor, Yolanda (2000) 'Asian utilities', report to the Department of Energy.

Viray, Francisco L. and Guido Alfredo A. Delgado (2002) 'All things being equal, we still would have forged IPP contracts', *Philippine Daily Inquirer*, 10 September, B4.

6 Telecommunications

Christopher Findlay, Roy Chun Lee, Alexandra Sidorenko and Mari Pangestu[1]

INTRODUCTION

This chapter examines a number of issues in the application of policy affecting competition in the telecommunications sector. This sector is quite highly regulated because of the risk of market failure associated with the ownership and operation of essential infrastructure by incumbent operators. Some of the questions addressed here are: What are the trends in policy across APEC economies? What are the emerging issues and problems especially with respect to competition policy? How do economies in the region deal with these issues? What are the most effective measures used?

These questions are examined by reviewing policy in a number of economies around the Asia Pacific region. All policy that affects competition is considered, not just the actions related to institutions set up for the purpose of regulating the competitive process. Trade policy also affects the process of competition. One of the themes of the chapter is that international commitments made through trade policymaking institutions, in this case in GATS negotiations, can help the design of policy affecting competition.

This chapter provides information on policy in terms of commitments made under the General Agreement on Trade in Services (GATS), and on their implementation, for a sample of fifteen economies in the Asia Pacific region: Australia, Canada, China, Hong Kong, Indonesia, Japan, Korea, Malaysia, New Zealand, the Philippines, Singapore, Taiwan, Thailand, the United States and Vietnam. Actual policy is compared with the GATS commitments of economies in the sample and the chapter comments on the degree to which policy has been implemented. The policy environment in those economies is set against the performance of their telecommunications sector. The chapter comments on the impact of technological change on competition and highlights the challenges for competition, especially the terms of access to essential infrastructure. It concludes with a discussion of the contribution of international cooperation to telecommunications sector policy.

OVERVIEW OF POLICY

A summary of policy on telecommunications in the sample is provided in Annex 6.1, with information given on local services, long distance domestic services, international long distance and the mobile segments of all these markets. Within each market, three dimensions of policy are examined: (1) GATS commitments, (2) statements of policy, and (3) the actual situation. GATS commitments are those made during the GATS negotiations and the accession negotiations. Statements of policy are those available up to 2002.

There are various combinations of these dimensions of policy. For example, actual policy could be more liberal than commitments made in the GATS, but the current situation may lag behind the ambitions laid out in policy documents. On the other hand, all these options could be more closely aligned.

Fink et al. (2001) performed a similar comparison using information from 1999. They compared policy that had been announced with the GATS commitments of each economy, although they did not draw a distinction with the actual situation.[2] The conclusions of Fink et al. are combined with observations from the sample in this chapter to identify the key factors that shape competitive processes in these markets, including privatisation, barriers to entry (to both local and foreign firms), the role of regulators and rules on anticompetitive behaviour.

Sequencing of competition and privatisation

In relation to policy relevant to fixed line sectors, there is a diversity of approaches. Some countries have allowed new firms to enter in competition with a government-owned carrier. In other countries, privatisation has preceded the introduction of competition. In other cases, the changes have been simultaneous.

There is now a consensus, however, that privatisation, including through the provision of market access to foreign providers, should not precede the introduction of competition. When privatisation occurs without competition in domestic markets, the effect is to hand rents to private investors, who then become a new source of resistance to further reform.

Sequencing of market opening

Countries also differ in terms of which market was first opened to entry by domestic and foreign suppliers. Some moved first on local lines, others on long distance services and others on international services. For instance, Thailand opened up local services in the Bangkok metropolitan area to several private operators through the form of build-operate-transfer (BOT) contracts with the state-owned monopoly, but decided to keep both long distance and international services under state control until 2006. Indonesia issued an extra local service licence in August 2002, while domestic long distance and international services are scheduled to be opened sometime in 2003. On the other hand, Korea has so far maintained a duopoly for local services, but has opened up its long distance and international markets over the past four years. Another approach adopted by some countries in the region, such as Singapore and Taiwan, has been to allow integrated carriers to provide a bundle of local, long distance and international services.

The mobile segment of these markets has always been the first to be opened to competition, sometimes years ahead of other services. In the sample, where there are restrictions on the number of licences for fixed line services, there are either more licences or no restrictions applying in the mobile sector. Hong Kong, Indonesia, Korea, the Philippines, Malaysia, Singapore, Taiwan, Thailand and Vietnam all followed this pattern. In China two more new entrants are due to enter what has been a duopoly mobile market.

Fink et al. (2001) found that policy for the mobile sector is usually more flexible than that for the fixed line sector but noted that several barriers such as handset taxes and interconnection pricing remain.

Restrictions on further entry

While competition is evident in many markets, entry is not necessarily unrestricted. There may be a number of licences on issue but no new licences available. For instance, it is expected that neither Korea nor Taiwan will issue new licences for network-based services in the foreseeable future. Alternatively, the market might be segmented and separate licences offered for each segment. This is what has occurred in China. Indonesia has segmented its mobile markets based on both geographic and technical criteria. Other forms of segmentation include Thailand's BOT concessions for local networks mainly in the Bangkok metropolitan area and Vietnam's for allowing foreign operators to deploy and manage local networks in designated areas through business cooperation contracts.

Rules on foreign participation

Fink et al. noted that many economies placed more restrictions on foreign participation than on domestic operators, through limits on foreign equity. In the sample of fifteen economies, these limits are also common, but as Fink et al. also noted, limits are generally easing. In the sample, Hong Kong is perhaps the most liberalised market with no limits on foreign ownership from 2003. A second group of countries – Australia, Japan, New Zealand and Singapore – post no restrictions on foreign equity except for incumbents that had previously been publicly owned.

GATS and actual policy

Fink et al. find that some countries did bind themselves to their actual policy at the conclusion of the GATS negotiations on basic telecommunications. Examples of those economies, which are also in the sample, are Hong Kong and Malaysia. Other countries bound themselves at less than the actual policy, and Fink et al. refer to Indonesia as an example. Economies that made substantial policy change as part of the negotiations were Japan (which removed limits on foreign equity except for NTT and KDD), Singapore (which brought forward its commitment to introduce competition) and Korea (which raised foreign equity limits and accelerated its liberalisation timetable).

The most significant examples of advancements in actual policy relative to GATS commitments can be seen in China and Indonesia. The former has raised restrictions on foreign investment for basic telecommunications services to 49 per cent from 2002, five years earlier than its accession timetable. In draft legislation Indonesia also promised to review market entry constraints from 2003 instead of 2011 as in its GATS commitment.

Of the sample countries, Hong Kong has also further liberalised its policy beyond its GATS commitments. Malaysia's and Taiwan's limits on foreign ownership are more relaxed than their GATS commitments. Singapore currently has no limits on foreign ownership, but its GATS commitments are more restricted.

Overall, there are a number of examples of significant changes in policy that are well in advance of GATS commitments.

Policy and actual practice

A high level of consistency between policy and actual practice is commonly observed, but in some cases there is still a lag between the two. One obvious example is the case of Singapore, where the government announced there would be full competition in the telecommunications sector from April 2000 with no restrictions on the number of operators for all services. To date only one extra local service licence has been granted, creating a duopoly market structure with the incumbent Singtel. In comparison, Hong Kong, with a similar geography and policy context, has six local service carriers.

Adoption of the Reference Paper

As a result of the GATS negotiations, economies made commitments to a number of principles of regulation applying to basic telecommunications. These principles were described in the Reference Paper on Telecommunications Services (24 April 1996). The Reference Paper refers to the prevention of anticompetitive practices in telecommunications, the rights to set universal service obligations, the presence of a regulator 'separate from, and not accountable to, any supplier of basic telecommunications services', and the allocation of 'scarce resources' (e.g., spectrum) in ways that are 'objective, timely, transparent, and non-discriminatory', as well as the public availability of information.[3]

There is one remaining principle that Fink et al. (2001) refer to as 'perhaps the most important'. This is the requirement that interconnection should be provided by a major supplier on non-discriminatory terms, at rates and of a quality no less favourable than that provided for its own like services, in a timely fashion, and at additional points on the network (subject to charges that reflect the cost of doing so).

In the sample reported in this chapter, the following countries have adopted the Reference Paper: Australia, China, Indonesia, Japan, Korea, Malaysia (partial),

New Zealand, the Philippines (partial), Taiwan and Thailand (partial). Hong Kong has 'additional commitments on regulatory principles'.

In all economies in the sample, the regulator is independent of the operators. However, if a more demanding test of independence is applied – namely, that the regulators are appointed to positions independent of other government agencies, such as ministries responsible for telecommunications policy – then China has no separate regulator, nor does Indonesia, Japan, Korea, New Zealand, Taiwan or Thailand.

The regulator's powers also vary. In some cases, its powers are extensive, but in others, for example Korea, Singapore and Taiwan, it can only arbitrate on interconnection rates fixed by the dominant operator.

This review of the information available suggests that there is a significant variation between economies in policy affecting competition in telecommunications markets. But evidently there has also been substantial change in policy over time, including change well beyond international commitments on market access and national treatment. How can the significance of variations in policy between economies and the extent of change in actual policy in recent years be assessed and compared? Can variations in policy be linked to differences in the performance of telecommunications sectors?

COMPARING TELECOMMUNICATIONS POLICIES

In order to compare policies affecting fixed and mobile telecommunications in selected APEC economies, and to examine changes over time, a set of indexes is constructed to measure impediments to trade and investment in telecommunications. This methodology follows that developed by Warren (2000a, 2000b), who constructed indexes based not only on GATS commitments but also on actual policies. The source of the original data was the International Telecommunications Union's report on telecommunications reform (ITU 2002). The above policy data on the fifteen countries in the sample is used to update the calculation of the indices to the current year. Index values can then be compared across countries and over time.

Policy measures included in the calculation of indexes have been split into five components, according to their primary impact. The indexes measure impediments to cross-border trade in telecommunications, impediments to market access through establishment (foreign direct investment) and ongoing operations, and limitations to national treatment.

The components of the policy index are defined as follows:

i. MA/Trade

This index captures policies discriminating against both domestic and foreign entrants to the telecommunications market seeking to supply cross-border services. It is based on the actual policies toward domestic and international leased lines/networks, third-party resale, and connections of leased lines/networks to the public switched telephone network (PSTN). When one of these options is allowed, a score of 1 is awarded. This leads to an index value ranging from 0 and 6, which is then rescaled to the percentage out of the maximum of 6 in the calculation of the average policy index.

ii. MA/Invest (fixed)

This index captures policies discriminating against all entrants (both domestic and foreign) seeking to supply fixed network services through investment. It is calculated as a weighted average of three components – the number of firms providing fixed telephony (a score capped at a maximum of 3), taken with a weight of 3; the degree of competition in the local, long distance, international, data and leased line services (with 0 standing for monopoly and 1 for full competition), taken with a weight of 2; and the percentage of the incumbent privatised, taken with a weight of 1.

iii. MA/Invest (mobile)

This index captures policies discriminating against all entrants (both domestic and foreign) seeking to supply cellular mobile network services through investment. It is calculated as a weighted average of three components – the number of firms providing mobile services (capped at a maximum of 3), taken with a weight of 3; the degree of competition in analogue and digital mobile phone services (with 0 standing for monopoly and 1 for full competition), taken with a weight of 2; and the percentage of the incumbent privatised, taken with a weight of 1.

iv. NT/Trade

This index captures discrimination against cross-border suppliers of telecommunications services. Its value equals 1 if the callback services are allowed.

v. NT/Invest

This index measures discrimination against foreign providers seeking access to domestic fixed or mobile markets through investment. The index value equals the percentage of foreign ownership allowed in competitive carriers. It follows from the construction of the indexes that the higher the value of each of the components (i)–(v), the less restrictive (more liberal) are the policies.

An aggregate policy index can be formed in many different ways. One is by taking a simple average of the five components. An alternative approach is to combine the components (i)–(v) by choosing the weights endogenously, to maximise the correlation between the individual components and their weighted averages (Sidorenko 2001). This chapter uses the simple average of the sub-indexes (i)–(v) to build an average telecommunications policy index for 2002, although it also refers to results based on the use of a weighted average. Index values of the component and the simple average are presented in Table 6.1.[4]

All of the APEC economies liberalised their fixed and mobile telecommunications markets to various degrees between 1998 and 2002 (see the last pair of columns in Table 6.1). Comparisons of the liberalisation scores in 1998

Table 6.1 Individual components of the policy index, 1998–2002

	MA/Trade		MA/Inv(f)		MA/Inv(m)		NT/Trade		NT/Invest		Policy (ave.)	
	1998	2002	1998	2002	1998	2002	1998	2002	1998	2002	1998	2002
Australia	6	6	0.90	0.90	0.90	0.90	1.00	1.00	1.00	1.00	0.96	0.96
Canada	3	6	0.97	1.00	0.83	1.00	0.00	1.00	0.49	0.49	0.56	0.90
China	0	2	0.30	0.50	0.67	0.67	0.00	0.00	0.00	0.49	0.19	0.40
Hong Kong	3	6	0.47	1.00	1.00	1.00	1.00	1.00	1.00	1.00	0.79	1.00
Indonesia	0	2	0.57	0.57	0.71	0.75	0.00	0.00	0.35	0.35	0.33	0.40
Japan	6	6	0.89	0.91	0.89	0.91	1.00	1.00	1.00	1.00	0.96	0.96
South Korea	0	6	0.55	0.70	0.71	1.00	0.00	0.00	0.33	0.49	0.32	0.64
Malaysia	0	2	0.89	0.89	0.89	0.89	0.00	0.00	0.30	0.49	0.42	0.52
New Zealand	6	6	1.00	1.00	0.83	1.00	1.00	1.00	1.00	1.00	0.97	1.00
Philippines	2	6	1.00	1.00	1.00	1.00	0.00	0.00	0.40	0.40	0.55	0.68
Singapore	2	6	0.26	0.64	0.70	0.84	1.00	1.00	0.49	1.00	0.56	0.90
Thailand	0	2	0.20	0.50	0.67	0.80	0.00	0.00	0.20	0.20	0.21	0.37
United States	6	6	1.00	1.00	1.00	1.00	1.00	1.00	1.00	1.00	1.00	1.00
Vietnam	2	2	0.27	0.70	0.83	0.50	0.00	0.00	0.00	0.00	0.29	0.31

and 2002 for the set of economies and the change in the measured index that occurred over this period are presented in Figures 6.1–6.3. Economies in the sample differ in terms of the achieved degree of liberalisation of the fixed and mobile telecommunications markets, and the pace of the reform toward liberalisation. In 2002 five economies (the United States, New Zealand, Hong Kong, Japan and Australia) had achieved at least 95 per cent liberalisation in their telecommunications sectors (Figure 6.1). China and Korea made the largest improvements in the degree of openness and competitiveness of their telecommunications sectors. Their index values more than doubled, with China starting from a particularly low point in terms of market liberalisation. Figure 6.2 compares the absolute increases in the policy scores for the set of countries from 1998 to 2002, and also expresses them as percentages of the average score in 1998.

The pace of policy reform is necessarily slower at the higher levels of liberalisation. The state of liberalisation and its dynamics can be examined by plotting the degree of liberalisation, as measured by the aggregate policy index, against the percentage increase in the index over 1998–2002 (Figure 6.3). As mentioned above, a group of five countries have already achieved almost full liberalisation, with Hong Kong standing out in terms of the magnitude of the reform effort since 1998. Canada and Singapore also achieved a high degree of liberalisation and an above-average rate of policy reform over 1998–2002, with the policy index in both countries standing at 0.9 and showing a 60 per cent

118 *Christopher Findlay et al.*

Figure 6.1 Index values in selected economies, 1998 and 2002 (ranked by 2002 scores)

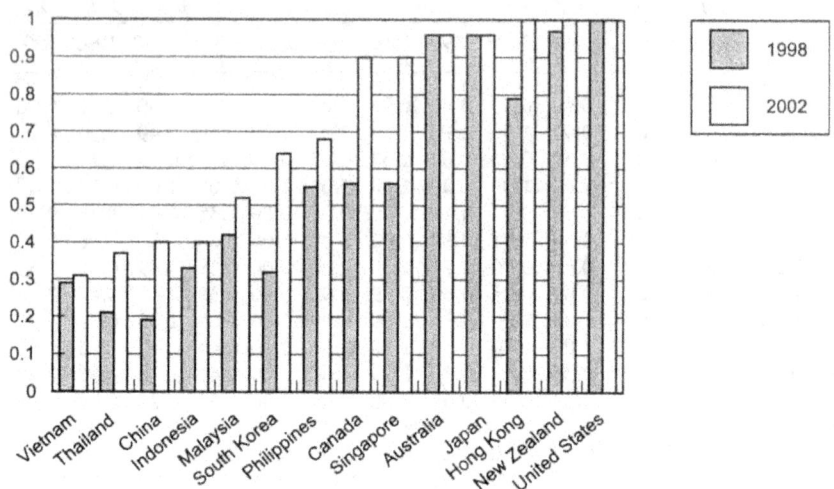

Note: Higher index values represent fewer impediments.

Figure 6.2 Policy changes in selected economies in absolute and percentage terms

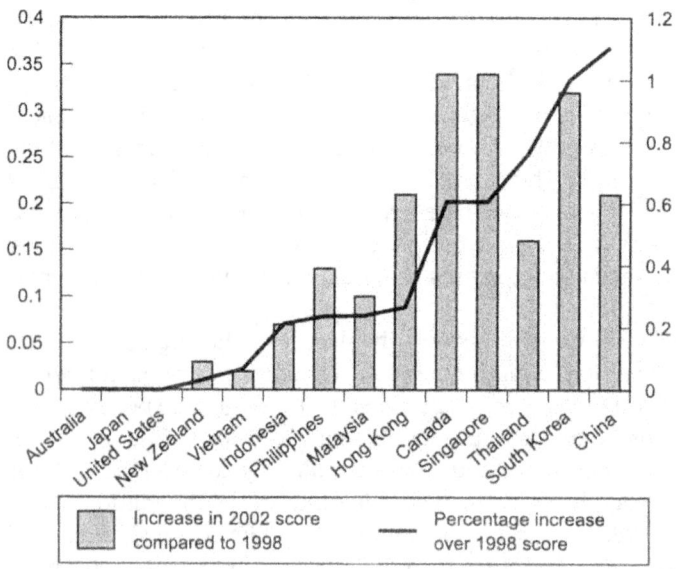

Figure 6.3 The state of telecommunications policy liberalisation and the rate of liberalisation over 1998–2002

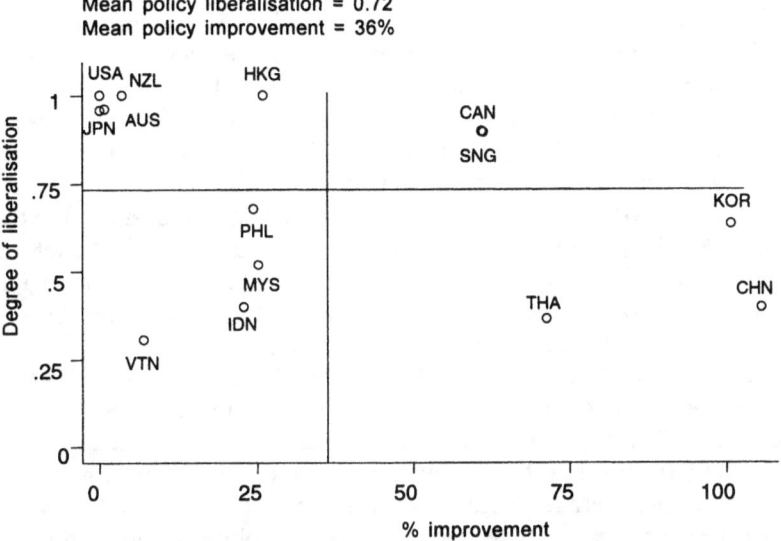

Note: The two lines intersect at the sample mean of the level of policy liberalisation and the sample mean of the degree of policy improvement; for instance, the countries in the top left of the quadrant have higher than average scores for policy liberalisation but have not improved policy by as much as those in the top right quadrant.

improvement since 1998. Thailand and China have been liberalising rapidly, yet the overall level of liberalisation is still below the mean level of 0.72 for the sample. Reform undertaken in Korea since 1998 has been impressive, with the overall score for policy improvement having doubled over this time, but the degree of liberalisation is still below the average. The degree of policy liberalisation in the Philippine telecommunications sector is approaching the average from below, at a modest pace. Vietnam, Indonesia and Malaysia are moving more slowly and have achieved a relatively low degree of liberalisation.

In general the assessment based on the change in index values supports the evidence discussed earlier of significant changes in policy affecting competition in this sector, but with a wide range of outcomes in the sample. The impact of these changes can be assessed by linking them to their expected effects on the price of telecommunications services.

IMPACT OF POLICY ON PERFORMANCE

The above comparison of the telecommunications sectors in the sample countries shows that there have been changes in the aggregate indicator of policies in markets for fixed and mobile services. A more disaggregated examination of these policies and their impacts on market outcomes can be made by looking at the extent of telecommunications penetration in each economy.

Warren (2000b) completed a regression analysis of penetration rates in a sample of 136 countries, measured as the number of fixed telephone lines and the number of mobile subscribers per 100 inhabitants in 1998. The estimated equations included variables such as GDP per capita (up to the cubic term), population density (including a quadratic variable), the quality of fixed lines measured as the percentage of mainlines attached to a digital switch, and one of the policy indexes defined above, as well as the aggregate index. It could be expected that a policy regime associated with more impediments (and therefore lower index scores) will lead to markets where the use of competitive strategies is less evident and where the rate of penetration is lower, allowing for the influence of the other determinants of that indicator.

Table 6.2 reproduces Table 6.5 in Warren (2000b). Model 1 includes the policy index MA/Trade, Model 2 has MA/Invest (fixed), Model 3 has NT/Trade and Model 4 has NT/Invest. Model 5a is based on the weighted index approach of Sidorenko (2001), and performs marginally better than Model 5, which is based on the simple average of the policy indexes (i)–(v) presented above.

A similar regression analysis was performed on mobile penetration rates (Warren's Model 6 is not reported here). The set of explanatory variables contained GDP per capita (up to the quadratic term) and population density.

As expected, all the regression models apart from Model 3 (callback services) and Model 1 (MA/Trade) establish a strong and positive relationship between the policy index and the penetration rate, controlling for incomes, population density and the quality of lines.

After the structural form of the regression model was estimated, the coefficients were used to predict the effect of a move to full liberalisation. A prediction was obtained by setting a corresponding policy index equal to 1. The predicted market outcome (penetration rate) was then compared to the actual outcome, with the difference expressed as a percentage of actual output and attributed to the policy restrictions. This percentage output loss was further translated into a tariff equivalent of the policy measure, under the assumption of a constant own-price elasticity of demand equal to 1.2.

Notwithstanding the shortcoming of the assumption that no structural change in the relationship between policy and performance has occurred since 1998, the new policy index was applied to MA/Invest (fixed) to estimate the loss of output due to this policy measure and its tariff equivalent, all things being equal. The results are listed in the 2002 column of Table 6.3.[5] The estimates of the price impact of the 1998 policy measures are shown in the adjacent column. The 'additional liberalisation' column shows whether a reduction in the price impact or the quantity impact has been achieved from a liberalisation of market access policies in fixed telecommunications over 1998–2002. Changes in policy are associated with significant downward shifts in the price of fixed line services

Table 6.2 Regression analysis of the influence of policy on penetration rates

Variable	Model 1	Model 2	Model 3	Model 4	Model 5	Model 5a
MA/Trade	-0.9253					
St. error	(2.2795)					
MA/Inv(f)		5.4122#				
St. error		(2.7933)				
NT/Trade			-0.0085			
St. error			(1.9369)			
NT/Invest				4.1678**		
St. error				(1.4109)		
Policy ave.					6.6254*	
St. error					(2.9696)	
Weighted ave.						7.0493*
St. error						(3.0985)
Y	0.0045**	0.0046**	0.0045**	0.0044**	0.0045**	0.0045**
St. error	(0.0005)	(0.0004)	(0.0004)	(0.0004)	(0.0004)	(0.0004)
Y^2	-1.280E-07**	-1.410E-07**	-1.320E-07**	-1.300E-07**	-1.420E-07**	-1.430E-07**
St. error	(3.280E-08)	(3.110E-08)	(3.140E-08)	(3.010E-08)	(3.090E-08)	(3.090E-08)
Y^3	1.430E-12*	1.710E-12**	1.500E-12**	1.460E-12**	1.700E-12**	1.720E-12**
St. error	(5.940E-13)	(5.690E-13)	(5.700E-13)	(5.480E-13)	(5.630E-13)	(5.640E-13)
HD	0.0290*	0.0299*	0.0302*	0.0337**	0.0328**	0.0327**
St. error	(0.0126)	(0.0121)	(0.0123)	(0.0119)	(0.0121)	(0.0121)
HD^2	-1.680E-05*	-1.640E-05*	-1.720E-05*	-1.930E-05**	-1.840E-05*	-1.830E-05*
St. error	(7.530E-06)	(7.350E-06)	(7.450E-06)	(7.240E-06)	(7.320E-06)	(7.310E-06)
Qual	-0.1297**	-0.1324**	-0.1304**	-0.1195**	-0.1252**	-0.1255**
St. error	(0.0236)	(0.0232)	(0.0236)	(0.0231)	(0.0232)	(0.0232)
Constant	10.4448**	8.6315**	10.1610**	7.7537**	7.6724**	7.4796**
St. error	(2.0728)	(2.0791)	(1.9570)	(2.0561)	(2.2156)	(2.2469)
Adjusted R^2	0.8926	0.8956	0.8925	0.8995	0.8966	0.8967

Notes: Standard errors in brackets; # significant at the 90 per cent level; * significant at the 95 per cent level; ** significant at the 99 per cent level
Sources: Warren (2000b) and Sidorenko (2001).

in China and Thailand (located in the bottom right quadrant in Figure 6.3). On the other hand, policy in this sector in Indonesia continues to generate a large impact on prices, equivalent to a 48 per cent tariff. Many economies have lessened their discrimination against foreign suppliers of fixed and mobile telecommunications services, and these measures are captured in the NT/Invest index. A number of economies made significant changes to their policy settings, resulting in a significant reduction in prices, especially in China and the Philippines (see Table 6.4).[6]

The effect on prices of mobile services from shifts in market access policy was significant in Thailand, Indonesia and Korea, while policy in China did not shift over this period (Table 6.5).

Table 6.3 Price and quantity impacts from market access policy in fixed telecommunications, index = MA/invest (fixed)

	Quantity impact (per cent)		Tariff equivalent (per cent)		Additional liberalisation?
	2002	1998	2002	1998	
Australia	1.15	1.15	0.96	0.96	
Canada	0.00	0.32	0.00	0.27	✓
China	112.46	286.16	93.71	238.47	✓
Hong Kong	0.00	5.53	0.00	4.61	✓
Indonesia	57.91	57.91	48.26	48.26	
Japan	0.79	0.96	0.66	0.80	✓
South Korea	4.08	6.25	3.40	5.21	✓
Malaysia	3.14	3.14	2.61	2.61	
New Zealand	0.00	0.00	0.00	0.00	
Philippines	0.00	0.00	0.00	0.00	
Singapore	2.92	6.19	2.43	5.16	✓
Thailand	24.53	46.02	20.44	38.35	✓
United States	0.00	0.00	0.00	0.00	

Overall, policy changes over the period 1998 to 2002 have had significant effects on the size of price distortions in telecommunications markets. Even outside the formal negotiating processes of the GATS, the rate of policy change in the sample countries has been impressive, and not just in the mobile sector, although the openness of the mobile sector may have driven policy changes affecting fixed line services. Despite these developments, price distortions remain high in a number of economies, according to this analysis.

FACTORS AFFECTING PERFORMANCE

The above discussion of the state of telecommunications sectors in the sample countries has offered one way of demonstrating a link between policy characteristics and performance in markets for telecommunications services. There are a number of issues in the application of this assessment. These include the stability of the statistical relationships and the manner in which the aggregate indices of the policy environment are formed, as noted above.

Another issue is that the policy regime was characterised in terms of structural variables, which were linked to market performance through the estimated statistical relationship. A particular structure could in principle be associated with different market outcomes depending on the behaviour of the market participants. Even in a highly concentrated market, highly vigorous competition

Telecommunications 123

Table 6.4 Price and quantity impacts from national treatment policy, index = NT/invest

	Quantity impact (per cent)		Tariff equivalent (per cent)		Additional liberalisation?
	2002	1998	2002	1998	
Australia	0.00	0.00	0.00	0.00	
Canada	4.48	4.48	3.73	3.73	
China	96.90	2,755.20	80.75	2,296.00	✓
Hong Kong	0.00	0.00	0.00	0.00	
Indonesia	95.32	98.27	79.43	81.89	✓
Japan	0.00	0.00	0.00	0.00	
South Korea	3.88	7.46	3.23	6.22	✓
Malaysia	12.50	18.86	10.41	15.72	✓
New Zealand	0.00	0.00	0.00	0.00	
Philippines	21.89	50.76	18.24	42.30	✓
Singapore	0.62	3.24	0.52	2.70	✓
Thailand	26.29	35.93	21.91	29.94	✓
United States	0.00	0.00	0.00	0.00	

Table 6.5 Price and quantity impacts from market access policy in mobile telecommunications, index = MA/invest (mobile)

	Quantity impact (per cent)		Tariff equivalent (per cent)		Additional liberalisation?
	2002	1998	2002	1998	
Australia	1.73	1.73	1.45	1.45	
Canada	0.00	2.77	0.00	2.31	✓
China	151.51	151.51	126.26	126.26	
Hong Kong	0.00	0.00	0.00	0.00	
Indonesia	60.66	77.93	50.55	64.94	✓
Japan	1.08	1.32	0.90	1.10	✓
South Korea	0.00	8.39	0.00	7.00	✓
Malaysia	6.14	6.14	5.12	5.12	
New Zealand	0.00	3.15	0.00	2.63	✓
Philippines	0.00	0.00	0.00	0.00	
Singapore	1.54	2.93	1.28	2.44	✓
Thailand	19.74	37.36	16.45	31.13	✓
United States	0.00	0.00	0.00	0.00	

might be observed. A market in which there was only one operator, but in which the operator felt constrained by the threat of entry, could show performance levels close to those expected under competition. In other words, important behavioural variables may have been omitted from the estimated relationships. Their impact is more likely to be revealed in detailed case studies of the experiences of particular economies than in cross-section analysis.

There are a number of other factors that affect performance and that are highly relevant to the design and implementation of policy in this sector. These factors include the impact of new technology, the design of regulatory arrangements and the effect of community service policies.

Impact of new technology

A key feature of telecommunications markets and one of the most important parameters that regulators must monitor is the impact of technology. Technological change affects the views of policymakers designing regulatory systems, and the extent to which market power might be sustainable. The differences in access to technologies in various markets, although not independent of the policy environment, also complicate the identification of a relationship between policy and competition or performance.

An example of the impact of new technology is in China's markets where fixed line operators have come under new competitive pressures from closely substitutable services (Pangestu and Mrongowius 2002).

A step on the way to convergence of different types of telecommunications services is the evolution of the voice over internet protocol (VOIP). The possibility of long distance rates that are 70 per cent lower than those charged by the fixed line provider (China Telecom) has led to intense competition for the provision of this service in China.

Knowing that it would be difficult to control such developments, China's regulatory body legalised VOIP. Incumbents have seen their revenues drop by US$130 million owing to the increase in VOIP usage. Thus far the substantial price differential has more than compensated for the lower quality of VOIP. Mobile operators are also now providing internet access, allowing subscribers to use VOIP services through their mobiles as well. In terms of expansion facility, IP networks can be built and deployed more rapidly than PSTN or local area networks (LAN).

As a result, the telecommunications regulator was forced to allow the incumbents to provide these services as well. Five of the seven telecommunications carriers in China are now licensed to provide VOIP services. Foreign network providers and local paging companies have been forming alliances to obtain a share of the market (Pangestu and Mrongowius 2002).

Apart from competition from within the telecommunications sector, the impact of new technologies can also be observed in the form of joint provision from other sectors. For example, with upgraded hybrid fibre-coaxial (HFC) networks and the digitalisation of information, cable television (CATV) operators are now capable of delivering both telephony and broadband internet services. With a higher than average CATV density in some of the sample countries, cross-sector competition will become a major regulatory issue in the near future.

Cross-sector convergence highlights the inconsistency of regulatory policy, which has often resulted from the common practice of dividing telecommunications and broadcasting into two distinct jurisdictions to be governed by two separate regulators. Policy inconsistency can create regulatory barriers that restrain competition and market development instead of enhancing it. Nevertheless, an increasing number of countries in the sample, notably Australia, Canada, Hong Kong, Malaysia and Singapore, have started to establish unified frameworks and cross-sector regulators to tackle this development, while draft legislation to create a new cross-sector regulator is under consideration in Taiwan.

Administrative practice

Another reason for the lack of a unique relationship between the structures observed in a market and its performance, as assumed in the regression analysis, is the choice of regulatory systems.

The significance of this problem is illustrated by reference to the experience of Singapore. Impediments to international business in services in Singapore, particularly in telecommunications, were revealed in interviews with business people conducted as part of the evaluation of the costs and benefits of a free trade agreement between Australia and Singapore (Access Economics 2001). The concerns of potential entrants interviewed in Australia included the lack of a fully independent and enforceable competition policy, and the lack of transparency in interconnection prices. While the work by the Info-Communications Development Authority in Singapore to improve the competition environment was also noted in the report by Access Economics, there are clearly concerns, at least among potential entrants, about the design of competition policy.

The best regulation is designed to minimise administrative costs and errors that may arise in the attempts to resolve market failures. More extensive regulation incurs higher administrative costs. It also runs the risk of inducing a higher level of 'gaming' by entrants to seek protection against the competitive strategies of the incumbents.

There are two types of errors to be considered (Warren and Findlay 2000). One is that of incorrectly condemning competitive behaviour as anticompetitive (a regulatory failure, or a type 1 error). The other is the error of exonerating anticompetitive behaviour (a market failure or a type 2 error). There is a trade-off between these two types of errors. A more extensive regulatory regime that provides the regulator with a higher degree of discretion can reduce the risk of type 2 errors but at the same time may increase the risk of type 1 errors. A more extensive regime also adds to administrative costs and may induce a higher level of gaming by potential entrants.

The choice of regime therefore depends on the assessment of the two types of errors and the costs associated with them. When designing interconnection policy, for example, the regulatory failure of condemning a reasonable proposal for an access regime and driving down the access price, while promoting the position of the entrant, can have significant effects on the incentives for further investment in the network.

On the other hand, a lighter degree of regulatory intervention (or a circumstance in which the capacity to operate such a complex regime does not exist) may fail to identify an anticompetitive practice, for example an interconnection designed deliberately to discourage entry. The cost of this market failure is that associated with the incumbent's use and abuse of its market power in this and other markets.

Rapid technological change facilitates the entry of new suppliers and reduces the cost of type 2 errors. In that case, the choice of regulatory regime might be biased toward a lighter hand (or the concern about the lack of regulatory capacity to deal with these issues might be ameliorated).

Recent work by the Productivity Commission on the Australian regulatory regime has stressed the value of a lighter hand. This position arose from the commission's concerns that 'risky greenfields investments will be particularly vulnerable to regulatory risk' (Banks 2002: 14). The commission has paid particular attention to other options for reform, including 'access holidays' (a temporary waiver from access obligations for certain greenfield infrastructure projects).

Service quality

In the regression analysis, the assessment of performance in telecommunications was based on average levels of service across the whole economy. There will, however, be significant variations in service levels around these average values. The degree of dispersion may be related to the extent of competition in each market and to the degree that companies are induced to supply universal services to remote and rural areas. There is some evidence that greater competition will actually increase access to networks (Petrazzini 1996: 37). Competition through new technology such as mobile services can add to teledensity. But the extent of coverage will also depend on the application of policy. The Reference Paper states that:

> Any Member has the right to define the kind of universal service obligation it wishes to maintain. Such obligations will not be regarded as anticompetitive per se, provided they are administered in a transparent, nondiscriminatory and competitively neutral manner and are not more burdensome than necessary for the kind of universal service defined by the Member.[7]

The Reference Paper provides general principles, but these can be implemented in a variety of ways.

Pangestu and Mrongowius (2002) review a number of models for meeting community service obligations. China's current penetration rate of fixed lines is 20 per cent of the population while the mobile penetration rate is 10 per cent. Penetration rates in rural areas might be as low as 6 per cent. Despite the reference to meeting service obligations, the two market leaders in China appear to have been given no explicit mandate on universal service. There has been some discussion of establishing a fund for extending services to areas with poor access but no details have been finalised and the focus so far has been on introducing competition.

Pangestu and Mrongowius review the experience of Chile, where subsidies from a public fund were allocated through competitive bidding to provide public telephones in rural areas. They also discuss other models such as the imposition of mandatory service obligations on all operators including new entrants (funded by cross-subsidies between consumer groups), charges paid by telecommunications operators to cover the access deficits of incumbents, and universality funds. They stress their preference for the last of these models but make the following recommendations for its application:

- The target should be specified clearly.
- Financing should be transparent, be it from direct government funding, contributions from operators or proceeds from privatisation.
- The administration and disbursement of the funds must be done by a body that is independent from the operators. It should also be market neutral in not favouring the incumbent over new entrants, and be subject to competitive bidding.
- Subsidies should only cover the uneconomic portion of the cost of providing the services, and the operators, be they private or government, should finance the rest of the cost from their revenues.
- The scheme could: (1) be combined with roll-out requirements for new and foreign entrants to provide services to isolated areas before they compete in larger and more developed areas; and (2) incorporate a strategy that allows operators to tailor their services and technical choices to meet the needs of rural areas.
- Services should be charged according to costs and not a geographical average since lower-cost services could be offered as alternatives to the standard service to meet the needs of rural populations.
- Options can be differentiated by service quality and price, and customers can decide which option is the most suitable. Rural areas could be offered higher quality services through low upfront charges, low fixed recurrent charges and the ability to make small, frequent payments.

CONCLUSION

This chapter has reviewed the recent changes in telecommunications policy in the region, the impact on market performance, and some of the complications in the relationship between policy and performance. Is it possible to achieve better performance in telecommunications markets through international cooperation on the design of policy or the conditions of entry and of regulatory principles that affect the choices of competitive strategies?

Markets open to entry by both domestic and foreign suppliers are more competitive and are expected to deliver better performance. This relationship is evident in the empirical work reported earlier in this chapter. As Fink et al. (2001) explain in more detail, the GATS provides a forum in which to undertake market access negotiations based on reciprocity, and in that context they observe that the gap between actual and bound policy provides scope for improving commitments without significant changes in national policy. That gap has widened even further since their study, as this chapter has shown.

Fink et al. also comment that using the GATS can lend credibility to current policy. They note that 'in principle a clear GATS commitment not to restrict entry could add significantly to the contestability of markets'. They argue that the credibility of current commitments can be increased by 'purging' the schedules of language such as 'licences may be granted' and of references to approval to enter being contingent on ill-defined criteria.

Fink et al. commend the scope to develop procompetitive regulation in the GATS through the adoption of the Reference Paper which has, in many cases, stimulated domestic regulatory reform. The paper's principles cover all the anticompetitive issues likely to arise in this sector.

This chapter has commented on the flexibility available to implement the principles of the Reference Paper, the judgement open to regulators, and the trade-off between the two types of regulatory errors. Fink et al. cite examples where signatories have not guaranteed to provide interconnection at cost-based prices or where those who have apparently adopted the Reference Paper have not committed to explain why a licence might not be issued. Their concern is that in these cases the multilateral approach has created an 'illusion of reform'. Moving closer to a common practice on the application of regulatory principles is another contribution of international cooperation.

Structures in some markets will be the result of competition policy choices made in others. This issue provides another area for discussion, at least among regulators.

For example, a competition authority may permit two service providers to merge without a substantial reduction in competition in a market in its jurisdiction. But in a smaller foreign market, the consequence could be a reduction in the number of suppliers. The smaller market might re-examine its entry policy, but because of its size, and despite its GATS commitments, further credible entry (at least under the existing technology) may be unlikely. Depending on the behaviour of the incumbents, prices may rise. There are a number of steps and qualifications in the sequence leading to this conclusion, but it does illustrate the possibility that the extent of market power of incumbents in one market need not be independent of policy choices applying to other markets. A forum for discussing these linkages would be valuable.

In such circumstances, Fink et al. (2001) argue for: (1) an end to the exemption from national competitive laws of collusive agreements that affect only foreign markets; and (2) the right for foreign consumers to take action in the courts of countries whose companies abuse their market power overseas. These procedures could also be added to the GATS provisions.

Finally, there is scope for international cooperation in the sharing of experience in the design and operation of the institutions of competition policy, especially as they apply to the telecommunications sector. Examples of items to put on this agenda include the prospects for further technological change and its impact on competition, the choice of institutional design to deal with the dilemma of the trade-offs between the two types of errors in regulatory policy, and the adoption of innovative policies to fulfil community service obligations.

NOTES

1   The contribution of Findlay and Sidorenko to this chapter was supported in part by a grant from the Australian Research Council.
2   The sample used by Fink et al. (2001) had a greater focus on developing economies and included more South Asian economies: their list included Bangladesh, Cambodia, China, Hong Kong, India, Indonesia, Japan, Korea, Malaysia, Nepal, Pakistan, the Philippines, Singapore, Sri Lanka, Thailand, Taiwan and Vietnam.
3   Available at < http://www.wto.org/english/tratop_e/serv_e/telecom_e/tel23_e.htm>, accessed 12 November 2003.
4   Taiwan was not included in the original study, so it is not possible to make meaningful comparisons of the liberalisation processes in this economy over 1998–2002.
5   All other explanatory variables were held constant at their 1998 levels.
6   The price impact refers to the prices for fixed lines.
7   The use of profits earned in one market to subsidise sales in another in order to drive out competitors (cross-subsidisation) is considered by the Reference Paper as an anticompetitive practice that should be prevented.

REFERENCES

Access Economics (2001) 'The costs and benefits of a free trade agreement with Singapore', paper prepared for the Department of Foreign Affairs and Trade, Canberra, September.

Banks, Gary (2002) 'Regulating Australia's infrastructure: looking forward', paper presented to the Australian Financial Review and AusCID National Infrastructure Summit, Melbourne, August.

Fink, Carsten, Aaditya Mattoo and Randeep Rathindran (2001) 'Liberalizing basic telecommunications: the Asian experience', paper prepared for the conference on Trade, Investment and Competition Policies in the Global Economy: the

Case of the International Telecommunications Regime, Hamburg, Germany, January.
International Telecommunications Union (ITU) (2002) 'Competition policy in telecommunications', background paper, Geneva: ITU.
Pangestu, Mari and Debbie Mrongowius (2002) 'Telecommunications services in China: facing the challenges of WTO accession', May, World Bank Group, mimeo.
Petrazzini, Ben A. (1996) 'Competition in telecoms – implications for universal service and employment', Public Policy for the Private Sector Note No. 96, World Bank Group, available at <http://rru.worldbank.org/viewpoint/HTMLNotes/96/96ptrazzini.pdf>.
Sidorenko, A. (2001) 'Construction of the optimal weighted policy index', Australia Pacific School of Economics and Management, the Australian National University, mimeo.
Warren, T. (2000a) 'The identification of impediments to trade and investment in telecommunications services', in C. Findlay and T. Warren (eds) *Impediments to Trade in Services*, London: Routledge.
Warren, T. (2000b) 'The impact on output of impediments to trade and investment in telecommunications services', in C. Findlay and T. Warren (eds) *Impediments to Trade in Services*, London: Routledge.
Warren, T. and C. Findlay (2000) 'Sins of commission and omission: measuring regulatory impediments to trade in services', in Productivity Commission and the Australian National University, *Achieving Better Regulation of Services, Conference Proceedings,* Canberra: Ausinfo.

ANNEX 6.1: POLICY INFORMATION BY ECONOMY

Australia

A. Background:

GATS commitments
No limitations to services except: Foreign equity limited to 35% of the sale of one-third of the government's equity in Telstra on 1 May 1997, which is about 11.7% of the total equity; A limit of 5% of one-third of the government's equity (about 1.7% of total equity) would be available for individual or associated groups of foreign investors; Limitations on the share of equity that any individual foreign shareholder can hold of Optus may apply. Adoption of Reference Paper.
Regulatory status
Separate regulators established: Access and interconnection regulation – Australian Competition and Consumer Commission; Industry standard, spectrum management – Australian Communications Authority. Incumbent not privatised (Telstra minority privatised: 49%).

B. Local services (including leased lines):

Actual policy on market entry and foreign equity
Competition. No limitations on number of carrier licences. No limitations on foreign equity except for Telstra and Optus.
Actual market status
Competition.

C. Long distance services: same as local services.

D. International services: same as local services (resale and callback permitted).

E. Mobile services:

Actual policy on market entry and foreign equity
Competition. No limitations on foreign equity except for Vodafone.
Actual market status
Competition.

Canada

A. Background:

GATS commitments
No limitations on services except: Foreign investment in facilities-based telecommunications service suppliers permitted up to a cumulative total of 46.7% of voting shares, based on 20% direct investment and 33% indirect investment.
Regulatory status
Separate regulator established (Canadian Radio-Television Telecommunications Commission). Incumbent privatised.

B. Local services (including leased lines):

Actual policy on market entry and foreign equity

Competition except:
    A common carrier* must comply with the following:
        Not less than 80% of the board of directors must be Canadians;
        Canadians should own, directly or indirectly, in the aggregate and otherwise than by way of security only, not less than 80% of the corporation's voting shares issued and outstanding.

Actual market status
Competition.

*A common carrier is a company that owns or operates a transmission facility for its own use or for another company's use to provide telecommunications services to the public for compensation

C. Long distance services: same as local services.

D. International services: same as local services (resale and callback permitted).

E. Mobile services: same as local services.

China

A. Background:

Accession commitments
6-year phasing-in of competition for local, long distance and international services: Within 3 years after WTO accession: foreign service suppliers permitted to establish joint ventures in and between Shanghai, Guangzhou and Beijing with less than 25% equity holding; no quantitative restrictions; Within 5 years after accession: 14 more cities opened to foreign service suppliers with investment ceiling at 35%; Within 6 years after accession: no geographic restrictions and foreign investment ceiling at 49%. 5-year phasing-in of competition for mobile services: On accession: foreign service suppliers permitted to establish joint ventures in and between Shanghai, Guangzhou and Beijing with less than 25% equity holding; no quantitative restrictions. Within 1 year after accession: 14 more cities opened to foreign service suppliers with investment ceiling at 35%. Within 3 years after accession: Foreign investment shall be no more than 49%; Within 5 years after accession: no geographic restrictions. Adoption of Reference Paper.
Regulatory status
No separate regulator. Incumbent not privatised (China Telkom and China Netcom). Drafting of Telecom Act underway.

B. Local services (including leased lines):

Actual policy on market entry and foreign equity
Duopoly with partial (regional) competition. The unbundling of China Telkom in May 2002 into China Netcom (northern China) and China Telkom (southern China) with two regional minor competitors. Cross-border competition between China Netcom and China Telkom permitted. Foreign equity participation raised to 49% through joint ventures. Leased lines: competition.

134 *Christopher Findlay et al.*

Actual market status
Duopoly with partial (regional) competition.
Two dominant carriers: China Telkom and China Netcom (62.1% and 36.8% respectively as of June 2002).
Two minor regional competitors: China Unicom and China Railcom (1.1% each as of June 2002).

C. Long distance services: same as local services.

D. International services: same as local services (resale and callback not permitted).

E. Mobile services:

Actual policy on market entry and foreign equity
Duopoly.
Issuing of new licences to China Telkom and China Netcom envisaged.
Foreign equity participation raised to 49% through joint ventures from 2002.
Actual market status
Duopoly (China Mobile and China Unicom).

Hong Kong

A. Background:

GATS commitments
Competition.
Four licences for local fixed network services issued in 1995. New licences will not be considered before June 1998.
Additional commitments on regulatory principles.
Regulatory status
Separate regulator established.
Incumbent privatised.

B. Local services (including leased lines):

Actual policy on market entry and foreign equity
Competition (10 licences).
No restrictions on number of licences and foreign equity after 01/01/2003.
Actual market status
Competition.

C. Long distance services: not relevant.

D. International services: competition (resale and callback permitted).

E. Mobile services: competition.

Indonesia

A. Background:

GATS commitments

Local services: monopoly arrangement before 2011.
   Local services provided exclusively by Telkom and 5 regional joint-operation schemes;
   Foreign equity participation limited to 35% for all services;
   Foreign management and technical experts (natural persons) for a joint venture limited to 20 persons for all services;
   The period of exclusivity for local services expires in 2011. Review of new entry on expiry.
Long distance services: monopoly arrangement before 2006.
International services: duopoly arrangements before 2005.
Mobile services: competition. Legal form of foreign participation required: joint ventures only.
Adoption of Reference Paper.

Regulatory status
No separate regulator. Incumbent not privatised (PT Telkom, minority privatised: 24%).

B. Local services (including leased lines):

Actual policy on market entry and foreign equity
Monopoly – transition to competition. New legislation proposed 2003 as the date of expiry for exclusivity arrangements. Review of new entrants on expiry. Foreign equity participation limited to 35% through joint ventures. Leased lines: partial competition.
Actual market status
Wire lines, fixed: monopoly (Telkom, including 5 private consortia). Wireless fixed, local: duopoly (Indosat and Satelindo). Leased lines: partial competition.

C. Long distance services:

Actual policy on market entry and foreign equity
Monopoly (transition to competition). New legislation proposed 2004 as date of expiry for exclusivity arrangements. Review of new entrants on expiry. Foreign equity participation limited to 35% through joint ventures.
Actual market status
Monopoly (Telkom).

D. International services:

Actual policy on market entry and foreign equity
Duopoly (transition to competition). New legislation proposed 2003 as the date of expiry for exclusivity. Foreign equity participation limited to 35% through joint ventures. Resale and callback not permitted.
Actual market status
Duopoly (Indosat and Satelindo).*

*Joint venture between Telkom, Bimagraha Telekomindo and Deutsche Telkom's affiliate, DeTeAsia Holding GMBH.

E. Mobile services:

Actual policy on market entry and foreign equity
Competition, global system for mobile telecommunications (GSM). No plan for new entry. Regional monopoly or duopoly for specific systems. Foreign equity participation limited to 35% through joint ventures only.
Actual market status
Nordic Mobile Telephones (NMT) 450: regional monopoly (Mobisel*) (analogue mobile systems utilising the 450 MHz frequency band to differentiate from the NMT 900 system using the 900 MHZ). Advanced mobile phone system (AMPS): regional monopoly (Komselindo*, Metrosel* and Telesera). Nationwide GSM: competition (Satelindo*, Excelcomindo and Telkomsel**).

*Affiliated with Telkom
** Telkom major shareholder

Japan

A. Background:

GATS commitments
Competition except: 　Foreign capital (direct and/or indirect) in Nippon Telegraph and Telephone (NTT) and Kokusai Denshin Denwa (KDD) must be less than one-fifth; 　Board members and auditors in NTT and KDD are required to have Japanese nationality. Adoption of Reference Paper.
Actual regulatory status
No separate regulator. Incumbent privatised (NTT, majority privatised: 54.1%).

B. Local services (including leased lines):

Actual policy on market entry and foreign equity
Competition. No restrictions on number of licences. No restrictions on foreign equity except for NTT and KDD.
Actual market status
Competition.

C. Long distance services: same as local services.

D International services: same as local services (resale and callback permitted).

E. Mobile services: same as local services.

Korea

A. Background:

GATS commitments
Competition except: 　Aggregate foreign investment cannot exceed 49%; 　The largest shareholder of Korea Telecom (KT) must be Korean government or Korean individual; 　The aggregate foreign shareholding in KT must be no more than 33%. Adoption of Reference Paper.

138 *Christopher Findlay et al.*

Actual regulatory status
No separate regulator. Incumbent privatised.

B. Local services (including leased lines):

Actual policy on market entry and foreign equity
Duopoly. Aggregate foreign investment cannot exceed 49%. The largest shareholder of KT must be Korean government or Korean individual. The aggregate foreign shareholding in KT must be no more than 33%.
Actual market status
Duopoly (Korea Telecom, Hanaro Telecom). Leased lines: competition.

C. Long distance services: competition (with foreign equity limitations the same as local limitations).

D. International services: competition (resale permitted, callback not permitted).

E. Mobile services: competition (with foreign equity limitations the same as local limitations).

Malaysia

A. Background:

GATS commitments

Competition except:
   Only through acquisition of shares of existing licensed public telecommunications operators;
   Foreign shareholding of up to 30% in these service providers allowed.
Partial adoption of Reference Paper.

Actual regulatory status
Separate regulator established. Incumbent not privatised (Telecom Malaysia, minority privatised: 36%).

B. Local services (including leased lines):

Actual policy on market entry and foreign equity
Competition. 61% of foreign equity allowed in basic telecommunications carriers for 5 years, after which equity reverts to 49%.

Actual market status
Competition.

C. Long distance services: same as local services.

D. International services: same as local services (resale and callback not permitted).

E. Mobile services: same as local services.

New Zealand

A. Background:

GATS commitments
Competition except: The Articles of Association of the Telecom Corporation of New Zealand Ltd limit the shareholding by any single overseas entity to 49.9%. At least half the board of directors must be New Zealand citizens. Adoption of Reference Paper.
Actual regulatory status
No separate regulator. Incumbent privatised.

B. Local services (including leased lines): competition.

C. Long distance services: same as local services.

D. International services: same as local services (resale and callback permitted).

E. Mobile services: same as local services.

Philippines

A. Background:

GATS commitments

Competition except:
Entry subject to the following requirements and conditions:
  Franchise from Congress of the Philippines;
  Certificate of public convenience and necessity (CPCN) from regulator.

Foreign equity permitted up to 40%. Partial adoption of Reference Paper.
Actual regulatory status
Separate regulator established. Incumbent privatised, Philippine Long Distance Telephone Company (PLDT).

B. Local services (including leased lines):

Actual policy on market entry and foreign equity
Competition except: Total foreign equity limited to 40%; The participation of foreign investors in the governing body of any public utility enterprise shall be limited to their proportionate share in its capital; All executive and managing officers of such corporations or associations must be Philippine citizens.
Actual market status
Competition.

C. Long distance services: same as local services.

D. International services: same as local services (resale permitted, callback not permitted).

E. Mobile services: same as local services.

Singapore

A. Background:

GATS commitments
Phasing in of competition: Up to two additional operators will be licensed in 1998 to provide these services from 1 April 2000, thereafter additional licences will be granted; A cumulative total of 73.99% foreign shareholding, based on 49% direct investment and 24.99% indirect investment, in these operators allowed.
Actual regulatory status
Separate regulator established. Incumbent not privatised (Singtel, minority privatised: 22%).

B. Local services (including leased lines):

Actual policy on market entry and foreign equity
Competition: No restrictions on number of carriers; No restrictions on foreign equity except for Singtel (max. 40%).
Actual market status
Duopoly (Singtel and Starhub).

C. Long distance services: not relevant.

D. International services: same as local services (resale and callback permitted).

E. Mobile services: competition.

Taiwan

A. Background:

Accession commitments
Competition except: A service supplier shall be a limited company incorporated in Taiwan; Foreign direct investment in a service supplier cannot exceed 20%; Aggregate of direct and indirect foreign investment in a service supplier permitted to 60%, except for Chunghwa Telecom, which cannot exceed 20%; The chairman and a majority of the board of directors shall be Taiwan nationals. Adoption of Reference Paper.
Actual regulatory status
No separate regulator (separate regulator planned). Incumbent not privatised (Chung Hwa Telecom, minority privatised: 33%).

B. Local services (including leased lines):

Actual policy on market entry and foreign equity
Competition (4 licences). Consultation paper on full competition (unlimited number of licences) of local services (including integrated fixed line service) released on August 2002. 49% of direct and 60% indirect foreign direct investment permitted except for Chunghwa Telecom.
Actual market status
Competition.

142   *Christopher Findlay et al.*

C. Long distance services: same as local services.

D. International services: same as local services (resale permitted, callback not permitted).

E. Mobile services: same as local services.

Thailand

A. Background:

GATS commitments
Exclusivity arrangements before 2006:   Foreign equity participation not exceeding 20% of registered capital and the number of foreign shareholders not exceeding 20% of total shareholders;   Introduce market access elements from 2006, when all necessary Communications Acts come into force.   Partial adoption of Reference Paper.
Actual regulatory status
No separate regulator (separate regulator planned).   Incumbents not privatised, Telephone Organisation of Thailand (TOT) and Communications Authority Thailand (CAT), state owned. TOT and CAT are separate and independent public-owned enterprises: TOT is charged with providing fixed line local and domestic long distance services, while CAT is assigned with the provision of international services.

B. Local services (including leased lines):

Actual policy on market entry and foreign equity
Duopoly.   Foreign equity participation cannot exceed 20% for all services.   Partial competition for leased lines.
Actual market status
Duopoly (TOT and CAT).

C. Long distance services: monopoly (TOT).

D. International services: monopoly (resale and callback not permitted).

E. Mobile services: competition.

United States

A. Background:

GATS commitments

Competition except:
   Direct foreign investment may not be granted to or held by:
     A foreign government or the representative thereof;
     a non-US citizen or the representative of any non-US citizen;
     any corporation not organised under the laws of the United States;
     or any US corporation of which more than 20% of the capital stock
     is owned or voted by a foreign government or its representative,
     non-US citizens or their representatives or a corporation not organised
     under the laws of the United States.
Adoption of Reference Paper.

Actual regulatory status
Separate regulator established. Incumbent privatised.

B. Local services (including leased lines):

Actual policy on market entry and foreign equity

Competition.
No restrictions on foreign investment except:
   Direct foreign investment on common carrier radio licences limited to
   20% except on waiver from the Federation Communications
   Commission (FCC);
   Must satisfy FCC's 'public interest' test criteria.
Competition for leased lines.

Actual market status
Competition.

C. Long distance services: same as local services.

D. International services: same as local services (resale and callback permitted).

E. Mobile services: same as local services.

Vietnam

A. Background:

GATS commitments
Not relevant (non-WTO member).
Actual regulatory status
No separate regulator. Incumbent, Vietnam Post and Telecommunication (VNPT), state owned.

B. Local services (including leased lines):

Actual policy on market entry and foreign equity
Competition. Leased lines: partial competition. Foreign investment through only business cooperation contract (BCC) with local operators for fixed network deployment, operation and maintenance.
Actual market status
Competition.

C. Long distance services: same as local services.

D. International services: same as local services.

E. Mobile services: duopoly.

7 The airline industry

Ralph Huenemann and Anming Zhang

INTRODUCTION

This chapter defines competition policy in the broadest sense as encompassing any government policy, undertaken by individual states or jointly, that may protect or enhance consumer interests. In the context of the airline industry, competition policy could include traditional antitrust measures such as prohibitions on price collusion, but could also include, for example, policies implemented to reduce congestion or monopolisation of slots at key airports, or policies designed to assure that all airlines receive equal treatment on computer reservation systems (CRSs). As these examples are meant to suggest, competition policy has some rather unusual aspects where the airline industry is concerned.

Ever since the Chicago Convention was negotiated in 1944, virtually all commercial aspects of international air transportation have been governed by bilateral air services agreements (ASAs). The US delegation at Chicago pressed for a liberal multilateral agreement, in the contemporaneous spirit of Bretton Woods and the proposed International Trade Organisation, but failed to persuade many other representatives, who opposed such an arrangement for military and commercial reasons, especially a fear of being unable to compete with American carriers (Kaduck and Hooper 2002: 31–2; Yergin et al. 2000: 38–41).

ASAs are based on the principle of reciprocity within a single industry – that is, an 'equal and fair exchange' of air transport rights between countries with, possibly, different market size, geographical characteristics and economic interests, and with airlines of different strength. Some ASAs go so far as to pool revenues between carriers. Thus, ASAs quite consciously reject the logic of comparative advantage as the basis for trade in airline services. In one sense, this bilateral system was an interesting solution to a competition issue, because countries feared unilateral application of monopoly power by a trading partner. However, it introduced another set of competition problems by constraining entry, especially to routes between countries (see, e.g., Warren and Findlay 1998).

In discussing the exchange of rights for air services between nations, a vocabulary has emerged that is referred to as the nine freedoms of the air.[1] It is important to note, however, that although the jargon refers to 'freedoms' and 'rights', these are not in any sense entitlements. An airline enjoys these rights only if they have been specifically negotiated by the relevant national governments, and even then only if the airline has been included in the list of designated carriers in the ASA.

The first two freedoms (to transit air space and to stop for refuelling or repairs) are considered 'transit' rights by contrast to the remaining freedoms, which are characterised as 'traffic' rights. The third freedom refers to the right of an airline to carry traffic from the home country to the foreign country, while the fourth freedom refers to the right to carry traffic on the return trip. The fifth freedom is the right to carry traffic between a first foreign country and a second, as an extension of flights that start out as third and fourth freedom rights. Fifth freedom rights are often called 'beyond rights', although these terms are not synonyms. For example, on a Vancouver–Hong Kong–Bangkok flight by a Canadian carrier, the aircraft may be permitted to pick up additional passengers/cargo in Hong Kong, or may only be permitted to continue onward with passengers who boarded in Vancouver. Either way, it is a beyond right, but strictly speaking only the former is a fifth freedom right. Beyond rights of any sort, but the more generous fifth freedom rights in particular, are often highly contentious. The less controversial sixth freedom is a combination of the third and fourth (a bridging flight, with the home country as the midpoint). The seventh freedom (often referred to as the 'change of gauge' right, because it permits an airline to use a smaller aircraft on the final leg of a fifth freedom flight) is the right to pick up traffic in one foreign country and carry it to another foreign country, using an aircraft stationed abroad. Finally, the eighth and ninth freedoms, the right to provide air services between points within a single foreign country (cabotage), either as a continuation of a flight from the home country or with a separate aircraft, have traditionally been almost non-existent, although they are beginning to emerge within such agreements as the single aviation market between Australia and New Zealand established in 1996 and the integrated air market for the European Union established in 1997 (Findlay and Kissling 1997: 189; Oum and Yu 2000: 139). It is noteworthy that Donald Carty, the CEO of American Airlines, has recently suggested that Canada and the United States should negotiate reciprocal cabotage rights and thereby 'treat aviation like any other industry, free from nationalistic constraints' (*Globe and Mail*, 9 July 2002, B2).

Following the precedent of the first US–UK bilateral agreement (Bermuda I) in 1946, ASAs generally specify services (passenger, cargo) and routes to be operated between the two countries, and stipulate fare-setting mechanisms. They usually specify the airlines with the rights to fly on each route and determine the capacity that can be provided by each of those designated airlines. At British insistence, the US–UK agreement was renegotiated in 1977 (Bermuda II), with significantly more restrictive terms (Oum and Yu 2000: 134). However, more recent renegotiations of ASAs, beginning with the US–Netherlands agreement of 1992, have definitely moved in the direction of greater liberalisation and therefore are referred to generically as 'open skies' agreements, although it is important to note that this is a misleading label, since these agreements generally exclude third-country airlines, prohibit cabotage, and so on, and thus still fall well short of establishing completely free trade in airline services. Despite these limitations, however, the open skies agreements have certainly increased competition on many international routes, to the clear benefit of consumers.

The liberalising tendencies exhibited by open skies agreements internationally followed upon – and were undoubtedly encouraged by – the substantial domestic liberalisation (deregulation and privatisation) of airlines in many countries, beginning with the United States in 1978. In a rare episode of deliberate bureaucratic self-effacement, the economist Alfred Kahn used his position as head of the US Civil Aeronautics Board (CAB) to lay the groundwork for passage of the Airline Deregulation Act, which gave US airlines unprecedented latitude to choose routes, set fares, pursue mergers, and so on. The Act even provided for the demise of the CAB itself (Yergin et al. 2000: 42–5). There were no doubt many reasons why the United States took the lead in domestic airline deregulation, but one important factor was surely the absence of a government-owned airline in the United States. As the experience of other countries amply demonstrates, government ownership of the dominant airline creates a major impediment to deregulation, which is why deregulation and privatisation have usually been implemented in tandem in other countries that have followed the US precedent.

Despite the substantial liberalisation of domestic and international air services that occurred in the 1980s and 1990s, the Uruguay Round of the General Agreement on Tariffs and Trade (GATT) succeeded in applying multilateral trade disciplines to only three relatively minor aspects of the air transport sector, in the form of a separate 'Annex on Air Transport Services' under the General Agreement on Trade in Services (GATS).[2] The three aspects were aircraft repair and maintenance, selling and marketing of air transport services, and CRS services. However, the annex specifically excluded measures affecting traffic rights and services directly related to the exercise of traffic rights.[3] Although the GATS rules provide that the annex will be reviewed at least every five years, the first review in 2000 did not accomplish much. Ironically, a major barrier to change was the position of the US government. By contrast to the American support for a multilateral agreement at Chicago in 1944, the American delegation to the World Trade Organisation (WTO) in 2001 strongly opposed bringing air transport services into the GATS, arguing that bilateral open skies ASAs are a more effective tool for liberalising the sector than the multilateral GATS negotiations could be (WTO 2001).

THE KEY CHARACTERISTICS OF THE AIRLINE INDUSTRY[4]

The economic realities of airlines are shaped by complex spatial and technological considerations. Spatially, airlines face the paradox that each city pair is, to a substantial degree, a separate product,[5] yet these city pairs are embedded in extensive networks that span the globe. A customer who wants to travel (or send cargo) between A and B on a given day generally has no use for flights going from A to C, never mind flights from C to D. However, the same traveller may wish to go from A to C on another day, and may be influenced by brand loyalty, especially if that loyalty is reinforced by membership in a frequent flyer program. This means that competition between carriers, whether in pricing or in other service characteristics like frequency and convenience of departures, has both route-specific and network-wide aspects.

At the same time, the cost side of the industry (especially the efficient utilisation of aircraft and flight crews) is also shaped by both route-specific and network-wide considerations. For example, on some routes there may not be enough traffic to keep an aircraft busy, so the passenger who wants to go from A to B may be served at lower cost if the same aircraft is used on other routes when it is not shuttling between A and B. At the same time, however, larger aircraft have lower costs per seat kilometre and greater range, while smaller aircraft will have fewer empty seats (a higher load factor) for a given level of traffic, which means that an aircraft that minimises costs on one route may or may not suit the other route. Yet the substantial economies in maintenance and training that arise from operating a uniform fleet may also mean that the 'intelligent misuse' of aircraft (using the 'wrong' aircraft on a certain route) is the rational way to minimise costs (King and Burrows 2002: 10).

Further significant complications arise because cargo shipments have a very different pattern from passenger movements. Most passengers prefer daytime flights, but freight shipments are often sent at night by preference. Passenger traffic is largely bi-directional, because most travellers return to their point of origin, whereas freight is heavily uni-directional – much more cargo flies from Asia to North America than the other direction, for example. Even within Asia, the air freight flows are unbalanced, as can be seen in Table 7.1. The pattern for freight is so different from that of passengers that some of the world's largest airlines (such as UPS and FedEx) are pure freight operations. However, because modern jets have significant excess cargo capacity in their holds, beyond the space needed for luggage and supplies, many passenger airlines also earn substantial revenues from freight shipments, and must manage aircraft movements accordingly. This is particularly true in Asia. For example, Cathay Pacific earns nearly 30 per cent of its revenues from cargo shipments (*Asian Wall Street Journal*, 17–23 June 2002, 17).

It is clear that even the short-run problem of allocating an airline's existing fleet across its network is a major management challenge, which is compounded by the variability of peak/off-peak traffic flows (which vary by time zones and by culture) and by the uncertainties caused by bad weather, mechanical problems, airport congestion, no-show passengers, and so on. Long-term planning for fleet expansion or renewal is further complicated by technological uncertainty (when will the super-jumbo Airbus A380 become available; will Boeing ever build the Sonic Cruiser?) and by the fact that the income elasticity of demand

Table 7.1 Projected airfreight shipments in Asia Pacific, 2000 (tons)

	South Asia	Southeast Asia	Northeast Asia
Imports from South Asia	37,700	62,500	47,000
Exports to South Asia	37,700	80,500	55,500
Imports from SE Asia	80,500	570,500	666,000
Exports to SE Asia	62,500	570,500	1,001,800
Imports from NE Asia	55,500	1,001,800	2,019,700
Exports to NE Asia	47,000	666,000	2,019,700

Source: International Air Transport Association 1995 Airfreight Forecast (adapted from The Logistics Institute – Asia Pacific, 'Air Cargo White Paper', September 2000).

for air transport is significantly greater than one, which means that the airline industry is particularly vulnerable to the fluctuations of the business cycle (Tretheway and Oum 1992: 14–15). The airline industry is, under the best of circumstances, an industry with good years and lean. These difficulties were exacerbated for many Asian airlines by the financial crisis of 1997 and then of course for airlines around the world by the trauma of September 11, 2001.

Where airlines are concerned, the simple textbook concept of economies of scale is not particularly useful, since an airline can grow bigger either by adding cities to its network or by carrying heavier traffic on an existing network, and the cost consequences of these two types of expansion are very different.[6] There are very significant cost advantages to increased traffic density on a given route, but there do not seem to be any significant economies of network scale once medium network size is attained (Caves et al. 1984; Tretheway and Oum 1992: 1–10). As suggested earlier, however, the situation on the demand side is quite different, since there are significant marketing advantages to a large network, due to increased customer convenience, brand loyalty, and so on.

Traditionally (that is, prior to deregulation), airline networks tended to display an undifferentiated pattern that is usually labelled a linear network, although direct might be a better term. That is, there were non-stop flights from most points on the network to most other points. On low-density pairs, flights were infrequent and there was little competition between carriers, both because regulators restricted entry and because it was uneconomical to divide the passenger load between two half-empty aircraft (which creates substantial first mover advantages, as a business school professor would say, or reduces contestability, as an economist would say). Just in case the obvious barriers to entry did not serve to discourage new entrants, predatory pricing was a possible second line of defence against newcomers, although it was little needed in the cosy world prior to deregulation. Recently, predatory behaviour has become a more salient issue. For example, the US Department of Transportation has sponsored a study of predatory pricing (Oster and Strong 2001); the Australian Competition and Consumer Commission (ACCC) has brought court action against Qantas for adding extra capacity on the Brisbane–Adelaide route in an attempt to force Virgin Blue to withdraw as a competitor; and Japan's Fair Trade Commission has warned the major Japanese airlines against predatory pricing aimed at newcomers Skymark and Air Do.[7]

Following deregulation, and reinforced by the development of larger aircraft, which are cost-effective only on higher-density routes, the old linear networks tended to evolve into 'hub-and-spoke' networks. In a hub-and-spoke configuration, one aircraft brings passengers from a smaller city to a larger central hub, where they are transferred to other aircraft to complete their journeys. By eliminating some direct routes, this pattern permits airlines to capture economies of density on the remaining routes. Many passengers who previously travelled direct now travel on a more circuitous route, and generally have to change planes, so the new pattern provides clearly inferior service in some respects, but the increased density on remaining routes also permits more flights per day, which is a definite improvement in service. Whether, on balance, hub-and-spoke is better or worse for consumers depends on individual needs and the specifics of network geography.[8]

Another strong trend that emerged with deregulation in the United States and elsewhere was the disappearance of weaker airlines through bankruptcies or mergers, but at the same time the birth of upstart competitors. Well-established brands like PanAm and Western disappeared, while new brands like Virgin, Dragonair, EVA Air and Asiana emerged. As already mentioned, there are beginning to be a few regional exceptions to the traditional prohibition on cabotage. Also, a few instances are emerging of local airlines that are owned by foreign interests, such as Deutsche BA, which is incorporated and operates in Germany, but is owned by British interests. However, despite these precedents, it is still largely true that national rules against foreign ownership or operation effectively prevent transnational mergers of airlines. Yet the advantages of larger networks are just as compelling internationally as they are domestically. Competitive pressures have therefore pushed the airlines into various forms of quasi-merger, referred to generically as alliances. The specific mechanisms of alliance can include interlining (whereby a single ticket can be used for connections on to partner airlines), code sharing (a more integrated form of interlining, in which partner airlines use each other's identity codes on their own flights), and the coordination of frequent flyer reward programs. It should be noted that these mechanisms of alliance can only be implemented if they receive approval from domestic authorities, which does not always happen. It should also be noted that although alliances generate marketing advantages and perhaps cost advantages for the airlines, these benefits may or may not be passed along to customers.

In addition to the economic characteristics just described, there are also a number of important political issues that affect the airline industry. In the postwar years, as many former colonies achieved independence, the establishment of a national airline (a 'flag carrier') became an important symbol of sovereignty. Issues of security have also been important. At first, the security concerns were primarily about overflights, which could be used for spying. Later, as it became apparent that intelligence-gathering flights use specialised aircraft and will take place even without permission, commercial overflights became less sensitive politically – so much so that in recent years even Russia and China have granted substantial first freedom rights to foreign airlines. Since the terrorist attacks of September 11, 2001, security issues of a different sort have become important. In addition to issues of national pride and national security, there is also the classic protectionist issue of jobs. It is worth noting, however, that it has long been common practice for airlines, even national flag carriers, to hire foreign pilots, while many other airline jobs, whether for flight crews or on the ground, would go primarily to local people in any event, as a matter of the airlines' own interest in cost minimisation, even if ownership were foreign. Thus, the protection of jobs in itself should not be an insuperable political obstacle to cabotage or foreign ownership, although it must be noted that the airline unions in a number of countries are vociferous in their opposition, out of fear that foreign airlines may be non-union.

COMPETITION POLICY AND CONSUMERS

In classical economic theory, monopolies and oligopolies are seen to have two different sorts of failings – inefficiency and inequity. The inefficiency arises because simple profit maximisation equates marginal cost to marginal revenue, not to price, so some customers who could be served at marginal cost go unsatisfied (there is a deadweight efficiency loss). But airlines, with their sophisticated yield-management systems (which offer highly diverse fares by selling cheaper tickets to passengers who can book in advance or meet other restrictions), are to a considerable extent engaging in marginal cost pricing. So the little triangle of deadweight loss is arguably not a major policy concern in this industry.

Inequity (excess profit) is another matter. The marginal traveller may be paying marginal cost, but the intra-marginal traveller is still a potential source of rents, at least in good years of the business cycle and in the absence of pesky newcomers. A study by the US Department of Transport, which compared route pairings of equal distance and passenger volume, found the following average one-way fares in late 1997:

Atlanta–Greensboro	US$224
Atlanta–Mobile	US$110
Chicago–Cincinnati	US$259
Chicago–Louisville	US$72

Denver–Des Moines	US$255
Denver–Kansas City	US$104
Detroit–Philadelphia	US$226
Detroit–St Louis	US$81

In each of these city pairs, the first route was served only by major carriers, while the second route was also served by one of the low-cost newcomers like Southwest or Vanguard. As the study concluded, 'the number of competitors in a market is far less important than the type of competitors in a market' (US Department of Transport 1999: 3).[9] Five years later, the low-cost carriers continue to put heavy pricing pressure on the majors. For example, Northwest's round-trip fare for Detroit–LaGuardia was US$318 until Spirit Airlines announced a US$154 fare, which Northwest has been forced to match (*New York Times*, 18 August 2002).

Of course, beginning with the Asian financial crisis and the recent US recession, and strongly reinforced by the impact of September 11, many airlines now face a situation in which, in the near term, excess profitability is hardly the issue (although calcified rents from earlier periods of prosperity are undoubtedly part of the current problem). Major airlines such as Swiss Air, Sabena, Ansett and US Airways, and even the giant United Airlines, have all gone into bankruptcy, as have newcomers Canada 3000, Air Do and Vanguard.[10] These events have made headlines around the world. But other significant developments are less well known. The following thumbnail sketch outlines some recent developments in the APEC region.

AIRLINE DEVELOPMENTS IN SELECTED APEC ECONOMIES[11]

Australia and New Zealand[12]

Airline deregulation came to New Zealand in 1983, when government fare setting and regulatory barriers to entry were abolished. In 1989 Air New Zealand was privatised, with the government retaining only a single 'Kiwi share' that was not meant to constrain commercial operations. Foreign ownership in Air New Zealand was limited to 35 per cent, but full foreign ownership of other airlines was permitted. Deregulation came to Australia in 1990, and Qantas was privatised a few years later (25 per cent to British Airways, and the remainder widely held). The other major Australian carrier, Ansett, had always been private, and since 1979 had been owned 50 per cent by TNT (an Australian logistics firm) and 50 per cent by Rupert Murdoch's News Corporation (US).

The foreign ownership pattern has evolved in complex ways. In 1996 Air New Zealand bought TNT's 50 per cent of Ansett. In 1999 Singapore International Airlines (SIA) tried to buy Murdoch's 50 per cent of Ansett, but Air New Zealand exercised a right of first refusal on the Murdoch shares and thus ended up with 100 per cent of Ansett. SIA responded the next year by buying 24.9 per cent of Air New Zealand, an indirect way of getting a piece of Ansett. This proved to be an extremely unwise purchase. Heavy losses by Air New Zealand, due to its ownership of Ansett and exacerbated by September 11, forced the New Zealand government to recapitalise Air New Zealand, effectively renationalising it (and drastically diluting SIA's share). Ansett itself grounded its aircraft in September 2001, made a few sputtering efforts to restart its business, but finally ceased all operations in March 2002. Thus, SIA spent a great deal of money to acquire a negligible share of Air New Zealand, which in turn owned a defunct Ansett. British-owned Virgin Blue moved quickly to capture some of Ansett's previous market share, but needed capital to finance an expanded fleet for this purpose, so Virgin's Richard Branson sold a 50 per cent interest to the Australian logistics firm Patrick Corporation. Meanwhile, SIA acquired 49 per cent of Virgin Atlantic (Branson's full-service European airline) in 1999, and recent rumours say that SIA is trying to buy 25 per cent of Virgin Blue as well. Qantas has proposed an alliance with Air New Zealand, but its bid for 22 per cent of the airline was rejected by the ACCC. And further rumours suggest that Dragon Air, which is based in Hong Kong but whose largest shareholder is in Beijing, may be bidding for Ansett's operating certificate. All in all, it seems fair to conclude that the jockeying for ownership and control of antipodean airlines has not yet stabilised.

On the policy front, Australia and New Zealand signed their Single Aviation Market Agreement in 1996. As mentioned earlier, this very liberal agreement permits the airlines of each country full cabotage rights in the other country. In 2001 New Zealand joined with four other APEC countries to sign a plurilateral open skies agreement, but Australia – although a participant in the negotiations – chose not to sign, on the grounds that the agreement was not liberal enough. More is said about this agreement and its implications further below.

China

Following deregulation in the 1980s, China developed a highly fragmented domestic airline industry, with more than two dozen carriers, some with only two or three planes. At present, at Beijing's insistence, the industry is being restructured to create three large airline consortia (consolidating the ten carriers under central government control), each of which will have assets of about US$6 billion and fleets of more than 100 aircraft (*China Daily*, 23–29 July 2002, 8; *Far Eastern Economic Review*, 17 January 2002, 32–6). The three anchoring carriers are Air China, China Eastern and China Southern; the three consortia will account for about 80 per cent of flights inside China. Outside the consortia, highly successful upstart Hainan Airlines, whose largest shareholder is George Soros and which emulates such low-cost carriers as Southwest and Ryanair, will almost certainly survive and prosper (with assets of about US$2.4 billion and 68 planes, and growing rapidly, Hainan may even catch up to the Big Three in size).

What will this consolidation mean for consumers? Certainly the three large consortia should be able to achieve major cost reductions through fleet rationalisation, shared maintenance facilities, and so on. One outside estimate puts these potential savings at US$440 million a year (*South China Morning Post*, 2 May 2002). Whether these savings will be passed along to consumers depends very much on the competition policies enforced by the government. At present, air tickets in China often sell at deep discounts to their officially regulated prices, as the small airlines engage in cut-throat competition to fill seats. After the smaller airlines are absorbed into the three big consortia, and the tiny airlines probably wither away, these price wars may well disappear. That is certainly the hope of the central authorities, who are feeling subsidy fatigue. Somewhat paradoxically, the end of the price wars may create an environment in which the regulatory authorities are willing to permit the majors to engage in more flexible pricing practices (yield management), and thus may actually move the market closer to an efficient outcome (reduced costs, coupled with marginal cost pricing). But whether this will actually be the outcome will depend on the evolving patterns of competition and on the enforcement decisions of regulators.[13]

Internationally, China's airline policies are becoming more liberal, in line with its broader trade expansion goals and its accession to the WTO. Here are two examples. First, a new ASA was signed between Beijing and Hong Kong in 2000, allowing carriers to increase their capacity by a combined 60 per cent and partly remedying the capacity imbalance between Dragonair and mainland carriers. In late 2002 Cathay Pacific applied for operating rights to Beijing, Shanghai and Xiamen. How quickly and generously Hong Kong and Beijing respond to this request will be an important indicator of Beijing's degree of commitment to liberalisation. Second, in 1999 China and the United States implemented an expanded ASA, which included a fourth carrier from each side and an increase in weekly services from twenty-seven to fifty-four (US Department of Transportation News Release 52-99, 9 April 1999). Because some important US carriers (Delta and American) are not included in the designated four, expanded code-sharing arrangements (Delta with China Southern and American with China Eastern) are an important additional mechanism of liberalisation.

Consistent with its increasingly liberal bilateral policy, China has recently made important concessions allowing foreign companies to take larger equity stakes in domestic airlines. Since the summer of 2002, foreign investors have been allowed to take stakes of up to 49 per cent (so long as no single investor holds more than 25 per cent), compared with the maximum 35 per cent allowed under earlier regulations. China Southern, the country's largest carrier, is already 35 per cent held by foreign investors, while China Eastern is about 33 per cent foreign owned. China Eastern has indicated that it will apply to increase its foreign participation. The company has good working relationships with Air France and American Airlines and may introduce them as strategic shareholders.

Hong Kong

In the airline industry, as in much else, Hong Kong as a Special Administrative Region of China functions in an environment of considerable ambiguity. Governments everywhere struggle to find a balance between their own producers (airlines and airports) and consumers (passengers and shippers). The Hong Kong government has the additional complexity of having to decide how to respond to Beijing's interests as well. For purposes of designation in ASAs, Cathay Pacific functions nominally as Hong Kong's flag carrier, although this identification has always been weak, both because the Hong Kong authorities have traditionally espoused liberal free market ideals and because Cathay Pacific was never owned by the Hong Kong government. In October 2002, after protracted and highly contentious negotiations, a new bilateral open skies pact with the United States was finalised. Cathay Pacific was granted its long-sought alliance with American Airlines, which will give Cathay access to many more US cities, although only on a code-share basis. In return, US carriers will be permitted many more fifth freedom flights, both passenger but especially freight, to other Asian destinations through Hong Kong, thus expanding Chek Lap Kok's role as a regional hub (*South China Morning Post*, 19 October 2002). In reaching this agreement, the negotiators apparently chose to disregard the objections that had been lodged by United Airlines and by major Dragonair shareholders China National Aviation Corporation and Citic Pacific (*South China Morning Post*, 29 May 2002 and 15 June 2002).

Japan[14]

Airline liberalisation has come slowly and reluctantly to Japan, but it has come. Japan Air Lines (JAL) was privatised in 1987, but for many years thereafter there was still little competition between the three majors – JAL, All Nippon Airways (ANA) and Japan Air System (JAS). Fares were set by the regulators and were identical for all carriers. Discount fares were highly regulated and ungenerous in their terms, compared with fares in North America and Europe. Low-cost carriers, such as Skymark and Air Do, have appeared only recently. However, the new Civil Aeronautics Law, passed in 1999, substantially liberalised the operating licensing system, fare approval system and other regulatory provisions. Following September 11, in the face of heavy losses, JAL sought permission to merge with JAS. At first, the Fair Trade Commission refused permission, fearing the anticompetitive consequences, but permission was finally granted after JAL and JAS agreed to give up nine of their landing slots at Haneda and promised to reduce their fares by 10 per cent across the board (*Agence France Presse*, 10 May 2002).

In the international sphere, liberalisation has also advanced slowly. The Memorandum of Understanding signed on 14 March 1998 with the US government was the outcome of long negotiations. Owing to strong resistance from the Japanese government, the MOU was not the liberal agreement that the United States had sought. Japan has long argued that there exists an inequality of rights and interests in the Japan–US bilateral agreement, and that this inequality has hampered fair competition in air transport markets between the two countries. The latest MOU equalises the number of 'full rights' carriers between the two countries, but leaves deeper conflicts unresolved.

Malaysia

Writing in 1996, John Bowen and Thomas Leinbach posed the question 'is privatisation always the best option for improving the performance of state-owned carriers?' (Bowen and Leinbach 1996). In discussing this question, they cited the positive effects that privatisation had seemingly brought to Malaysia Airlines (MAS). The privatisation of MAS had begun in 1985, and was completed in 1994 with the sale of the government's remaining 32 per cent to a well-connected Malay entrepreneur, Datuk Tajudin Ramli. However, the ink was barely dry on the Bowen–Leinbach essay when MAS's success collapsed with the 1997 currency crisis, and the airline has suffered massive losses for the last five years. In December 2000, when the government bought back Tajudin's shares of MAS, it created a major political crisis by paying him 8 ringgit a share, which was nearly three times the price on the KL Stock Exchange (*Far Eastern Economic Review*, 14 February 2002, 44–45, and 27 June 2002, 40–44). Through this and other purchases, the government now effectively controls 83 per cent of the airline's shares. Most recently, MAS has announced that it will try to escape its problems through some elaborate financial re-engineering. The aeroplanes and other tangible assets are being sold to, and leased back from, a newly created government company, thus creating a 'virtual' airline. As Dr Mahathir himself has pointed out, this arrangement means that 'MAS will be like a hotel operator ... which runs and manages the hotel but does not own the building' (*Business Times* [Malaysia], 30 January 2002). In addition, MAS is being relieved of its previous obligation to cover the heavy losses on domestic routes, where government regulators have deliberately set fares low to encourage tourism and regional development, and it has been shedding many of its prestigious but costly long-haul international routes and reconfiguring itself as a regional carrier. Whether MAS will emerge from these reforms (which could be described as Chapter 11 with Malaysian characteristics) as a viable airline will depend very much on the terms of the leaseback arrangements, which are confidential (and controlled by government), and on the profitability of flying regional routes, which are governed by ASAs (also controlled by government).

Philippines

After World War II, Philippine Airlines (PAL) emerged as the only significant airline in the country, a monopoly position that was formally legitimated when a 'one airline' policy was promulgated in 1973. The underlying rationale for this policy was that PAL was required to serve many unprofitable local ('missionary') routes, so was permitted to recover its losses by charging high fares on the main routes, domestic and international. However, this policy was diluted in 1976, when the government agreed to give foreign carriers somewhat greater access to the international routes. The negative impact on PAL's profitability was significant, and in 1977 the government nationalised the airline. Some minor steps toward liberalisation were taken in 1988, when the government sold off some of its shares in PAL and diluted the 'one airline' policy somewhat, but major change came only in 1992, when majority control of PAL was auctioned off to private interests.[15] Deregulation of the industry followed in 1995, with the promulgation of Executive Order 219. In the following months, five new airlines began operations, and by 1999 PAL's domestic market share had fallen to 49 per cent. Two of the newcomers, Cebu Pacific and Air Philippines, had captured 24 per cent and 22 per cent market shares, respectively, although another newcomer, Grand Airways, had already gone out of business (Austria 2000: 16–18).

Recently, the government has been under increasing pressure to further liberalise the rules governing the industry. Foreign pressure is coming from two different directions. A bilateral open skies agreement was negotiated with the United States a few years ago, but the Philippines side has argued for, and received, substantial delays in implementation, because of the 1997 currency crisis and subsequent difficulties (cash flow problems and a pilots' strike grounded PAL for a time in 1998). However, the American goal is undoubtedly still to achieve full implementation – and sooner rather than later. The other source of external pressure comes from discussions of a possible regional open skies agreement within ASEAN, which will be discussed below. Domestically, the liberalisation agenda has been supported vocally by the 'Freedom to Fly' coalition (aligned with the tourism industry) but is opposed by the equally vocal 'Save Our Skies' coalition (aligned with the airlines).

In the face of these conflicting pressures, President Macapagal-Arroyo announced in May that she had asked the Finance Secretary to study the possibility of renationalising PAL. In explaining her thinking, President Macapagal-Arroyo focused on the needs of the tourism industry, and cited Malaysia and Thailand as countries where money-losing national airlines are used as loss leaders to attract tourists. The reaction to this trial balloon was immediate and vociferous. The critics pointed out that such a policy would violate the President's commitment to a free market economy where 'the excellent survive and the inefficient, the protected, and the mediocre fall by the wayside', that it would require subsidies to PAL that the government simply could not afford, and that the real impediment to increased tourism was fear of terrorism, not the price of air tickets (*Business World* [Philippines], 4 June 2002, quoted from OneSource Information Services, June 2002).

It is likely that the proposal to renationalise PAL will be quietly shelved after it has been 'studied'. However, the deeper issues (what version of open skies, how quickly, and with whom?) remain unresolved.

South Korea

Korean Air (KAL) took over the state-run Korean National Airlines in 1969, and was the only national flag carrier until 1988, when Asiana Airlines entered the industry. The increased capacity and competition following Asiana's entry, together with the country's rapid economic growth, resulted in a large increase in air traffic volume. Ten new domestic routes were introduced between 1988 and 1993, as compared to only two routes between 1980 and 1987. On the international routes, the market share of Korean carriers was 48 per cent in 1990 when KAL was a monopoly, but it rose to 67 per cent in 1998 with the duopoly (Park 2000). One consequence of the entry was that it became more difficult to allocate air traffic rights, as the Korean government had to negotiate on behalf of the two airlines. Often it had to get permission for double tracking[16] from other countries. During this period, the government has attempted to award the traffic rights in a balanced pattern (broadly 60:40) so that both carriers could grow in international markets. But the government's tolerance for comfortable duopoly market sharing has its limits, and in 2001 the Fair Trade Commission imposed substantial fines on KAL and Asiana for colluding on domestic airfares (*Air Transport World*, July 2001, 10).

Major recent developments include the liberalisation of airfare setting for the domestic routes in August 1999, and the signing of an open skies agreement with the United States a year earlier. The agreement provides Korean and US carriers with unlimited service rights on any city pair between the two countries, unlimited fifth freedom rights, as well as the right to determine flight frequency and fares on those routes. In addition, unlimited seventh freedom rights were granted to the US carriers. The fifth and seventh freedoms are particularly important for developing the new Incheon International Airport, opened in 2001, as a major regional hub airport. Incheon's ambitions as a regional hub are strengthened by KAL's success in the cargo realm (second only to Lufthansa in freight carried), by capacity constraints at Narita and cost constraints at Kansai, and by KAL's participation in the SkyTeam Alliance (with Delta, Air France, and others).

Taiwan

The airline industry in Taiwan has a number of parallels to airlines elsewhere, including the emergence of EVA Airlines as a successful challenger to traditional flag carrier China Airlines, but for purposes of this chapter only a single issue is raised: the likelihood that direct flights between Taiwan and the mainland will be permitted, possibly as early as 2003. Such a development would have important implications for other airlines in the region, most obviously for Cathay Pacific. Because of the heavy flow of indirect travel between Taiwan and the mainland, the Taipei–Hong Kong route is one of the most lucrative in the world – this despite the number of airlines serving the route (at least seven) and despite significant competition from other routes (especially through Macao, but also from connections through the Philippines, Vietnam, etc.). Recently, Cathay Pacific agreed to share the Taipei route with Dragonair, presumably to strengthen its own bargaining position in requesting permission to initiate flights to mainland cities.

AIRLINES IN THE WTO DOHA ROUND

Although there have been concerted efforts, and considerable progress, in liberalising air services trade over the last decade, these have largely occurred outside the GATT/WTO negotiations. The Uruguay Round succeeded only in applying multilateral trade concepts to three secondary areas of air transport. So far, efforts to bring traffic rights under the multilateral purview of the GATS have failed. Given the characteristics of the airline industry and the history of bilateral ASAs in international aviation, the direct application of GATS concepts to air services is difficult for two reasons, hinging on the most favoured nation (MFN) and national treatment principles. Application of the national treatment principle to air services would require that foreign airlines be treated the same as comparable domestic airlines. Applying this principle to non-traffic rights is relatively straightforward, as illustrated by the coverage of three ancillary services in the GATS Annex on Air Transport Services. If the principle is applied to traffic rights, however, national treatment becomes much more problematic.

Specifically, there exist large asymmetries in domestic regulatory policy for the airline industry. While the United States, Canada, the European Union and Australia/New Zealand have deregulated their internal air markets (e.g., free domestic entry, free price setting), regulation is the norm for most other countries. The national treatment principle would effectively increase market access for airlines from nations with closed domestic markets without expanding access for airlines whose domestic markets have already been deregulated. In particular, national treatment would be sufficient to assure foreign airlines access to the deregulated US, Canadian, EU and Australia/New Zealand internal markets. However, it would not necessarily help the carriers of these markets to obtain access in foreign markets where, for instance, regulatory limits on entry apply to both domestic and foreign carriers. So long as some nations still practise restrictive domestic regulatory policies, therefore, the national treatment principle does not help resolve the problem of equal access to all markets.

Another key GATT principle is the MFN clause, meaning that a concession that one country yields to another country extends automatically to all other WTO members. On balance, it is not clear that liberalisation would be facilitated by the application of unconditional MFN to traffic rights. In particular, MFN may permit 'free riding' by countries that are unwilling to open their own markets. As a result, more liberal nations would probably be unable to agree among themselves on air transport reforms so long as unconditional MFN is in place. It appears that even the most liberal nations find it necessary to discriminate in granting traffic rights in order to offset severe restraints experienced by their own airlines in foreign markets (Kasper and Hindley 1999). Given the difficulties that arise for air transport from unconditional MFN, a key question is whether conditional MFN could be developed for application specifically to air transport. Conditional MFN may be described as opening only to other countries that have taken similar measures. Conditional MFN was introduced into the WTO for the first time with the Agreement on Government Procurement (GPA), to which only some member governments are parties, and which is therefore characterised as plurilateral rather than multilateral. So the precedent does exist. But it is an uncomfortable one in the WTO context, where unconditional MFN is the long-established principle. And the precedent of the GPA is a frail foundation for air transport reform in particular, since many governments, including those that are parties to the GPA, require their employees to travel on national carriers when flying, even on foreign trips.

Despite these potential drawbacks with the multilateral mechanism, the approach offers some obvious advantages for the air cargo sector. If the sector were under the GATS umbrella, then several issues of key importance to the cargo carriers could be addressed relatively easily. For example, customs clearance procedures for transshipments can be dealt with under the WTO trade facilitation program, while restrictions on intermodal and airport handling rights fall under the market access program. Since substantial multilateral liberalisation of passenger traffic rights is not likely to occur in the near future, the current debate among specialists in the field centres on: (1) whether air cargo rights should be negotiated separately from passenger issues, and (2) whether such negotiations should be undertaken in the global Doha framework or through more fragmented regional initiatives.

EMERGING REGIONAL DEVELOPMENTS

US bilateral open skies initiatives

Since the early 1990s, the United States has been promoting bilateral open skies agreements with individual nations in preference to a multilateral approach. The first open skies deal was signed in September 1992 between the United States and the Netherlands – an agreement nurtured by the strong mutual interests of KLM and Northwest. The United States negotiated an open skies agreement with Canada in 1995. By the end of 1996, the United States had successfully signed such deals with ten European countries. Reaching agreement with the United Kingdom has been more difficult, and these negotiations continue.

In January 1997 Singapore became the first Asian country to sign an open skies agreement with the United States. Recent bilateral agreements between the United States and some Asia Pacific economies – Taiwan, the Philippines, Brunei and Singapore – have included seventh freedom traffic rights on cargo (the hubbing or change of gauge rights in a foreign territory), although limits were imposed on the fifth freedom rights for passenger travel. These provisions have enabled Federal Express and UPS to set up mini-hubs in Asia.

An important explanation for the differing viewpoints of the United States and many Asian countries is their fundamental dissimilarity of geography, which shapes airline network operations. The US carriers enjoy the economies of density that arise from an extensive hinterland network that is entirely domestic (open to them but closed to their foreign competitors). The formation of an integrated air market within the European Union is creating analogous advantages for European carriers. Asia, however, has a more fragmented political geography. Many Asian carriers do not enjoy the advantages of an extensive domestic network. Singapore Airlines and Cathay Pacific are extreme examples of a more general problem.

If enough Asian countries grant fifth or seventh freedoms to the United States, then US carriers may be able to serve intra-Asia spokes more freely than the home carriers on those spokes, particularly if the two countries concerned have restrictive bilateral agreements between themselves. The United States' enthusiasm for bilateral open skies is sometimes characterised as a strategy of 'surround and conquer' (Button 1997). Bilateral open skies agreements can also create a dynamic effect, since countries that do not enter such agreements with the United States risk a diversion of traffic to routes that are more competitive (Findlay 2002). At recent count, the United States has fifty-six bilateral open skies agreements worldwide. These agreements generally provide each party with 'beyond rights', but they do not cover domestic routes. As of May 2000 ICAO reported twenty-six similar types of agreements not involving the United States.

The plurilateral or club approach

Although the plurilateral (conditional MFN) approach is an uncomfortable fit in the WTO, it can certainly be pursued outside the WTO. This approach, which is often referred to as the bloc or club approach, is the mechanism that led to liberalisation within NAFTA and within the European Union.[17]

The European Union was active in deregulating its internal market through a sequence of three packages for liberalisation, in 1988, 1990 and 1993. In 1997 the European Union created a single aviation market similar to the US domestic market. Any EU-registered carrier has the right to operate flights between or within any of the fifteen EU member countries, as well as in Norway and Iceland. National ownership rules have been replaced by EU ownership criteria. Airlines have been given freedom to set fares, with safeguards against predatory pricing through the EU competition rules. So far, these changes do not apply to extra-EU agreements, and joining the European Union is not easy. So this is not an 'open club' as the literature understands that term (Elek et al. 1999).

Another example of the club approach is the Multilateral Agreement on the Liberalisation of International Air Transportation, signed at its inception in 2001 by the United States, Singapore, New Zealand, Chile and Brunei Darussalam, and joined later by Peru. Since all of these countries are member economies of APEC, it has sometimes been referred to as an APEC agreement, although it is not really that. It did not arise through APEC negotiating mechanisms, it encompasses only six of APEC's twenty-one member economies, and it does not provide MFN treatment for the other fifteen. As already mentioned, Australia stayed out because the agreement did not go far enough, while Japan stayed out because it went too far. The agreement could more accurately be described as a US plurilateral open skies agreement. Its provisions are much less liberal than the EU club. In particular, the eighth and ninth freedoms (cabotage rights) remain off limits. However, the agreement does represent progress toward liberalisation in certain limited dimensions. For example, for cargo traffic it is not required that flights pass through the home country. Thus, it is now possible for Singapore Airlines to operate cargo services direct between the United States and New Zealand. Also, the agreement's rules on designation permit participation by airlines provided they are effectively controlled by, and have a principal place of business in, a party to the agreement. That is, the usual requirement of 'substantial ownership' found in bilateral ASAs has been softened a bit. Despite these small steps toward liberalisation, however, the overall impact of the agreement on actual airline operations will probably be quite limited, and – as Findlay (2002) notes – 'other economies are not rushing to join'. Like the EU single aviation market, the US plurilateral agreement is not a particularly open club and hence does not provide a promising foundation for further liberalisation of the air transport sector.

An open skies bloc for Northeast Asia?

There has recently been increased interest in economic cooperation among the Northeast Asian countries. In November 1999 China, Japan and South Korea held a tripartite summit on the sidelines of the formal ASEAN summit in Manila and agreed to conduct joint research to seek ways of institutionalising economic cooperation among the three countries. In particular, the three countries will commission their research institutes to identify ten areas, including commerce, shipping, fisheries and customs, as the target sectors for cooperation.

Air transport is not explicitly identified as a target sector for cooperation, but it will be interesting to see whether an open skies bloc among China, South Korea and Japan can be formed. There is certainly an economic and trade basis for liberalising air transport in Northeast Asia. China, South Korea and Japan all have enjoyed rapid economic growth for two to three decades, and – as shown in Table 7.2 – trade among the three countries has grown rapidly in recent years. China is now the second largest exporter to Japan (after the US). Since China–Korea trade and Korea–Japan trade have also been rising, the share of intraregional trade among the three countries increased from 12.4 per cent in 1990 to 18.7 per cent in 1997 (Lee 1999). Such extensive trade and economic linkages would be further enhanced if a liberalised and integrated airline market existed among the three countries.

However, there are many obstacles that must still be overcome. First, the three countries differ in their economic systems, as well as in their level of development. Second, major Chinese airlines are state-owned firms. Until these airlines are privatised, both central and local governments are likely to have too large a stake in their success to allow for regional liberalisation of air services. Third, the airline industries in all three countries have been tightly regulated for a long time, and their international aviation policies have traditionally been restrictive.

Table 7.2 China's trade with Japan and South Korea (US$ billion)

	Total trade with		Exports to		Imports from	
	Japan	Korea	Japan	Korea	Japan	Korea
1991	20.3	5.3	10.3	3.9	10.0	1.4
1992	25.4	5.1	11.7	2.4	13.7	2.6
1993	39.0	8.2	15.8	2.9	23.3	5.4
1994	47.9	11.7	21.6	4.4	26.3	7.3
1995	57.5	17.0	28.5	6.7	29.0	10.3
1996	60.1	20.0	30.9	7.5	29.2	12.5
1997	60.8	24.0	31.8	9.1	29.0	14.9
1998	57.9	21.3	29.7	6.3	28.2	15.0
1999	66.2	25.0	32.4	7.8	33.8	17.2
2000	83.2	34.5	41.7	11.3	41.5	23.2
2001	87.8	35.9	45.0	12.5	42.8	23.4

Source: *China's Customs Statistics*, various issues.

ASEAN

Many ASEAN countries are still cautious about exposing their domestic carriers to competition from foreign airlines. This contradicts visions of making the primary domestic airport a regional hub and promoting tourism – ambitions shared by Singapore, Malaysia, and Thailand, among others. The ASEAN nations have established a framework for negotiations in trade in services known as the ASEAN Framework Agreement on Services (AFAS).[18] So far, the negotiations under AFAS have been focused on seven 'priority sectors', including air transport. A review of the outcome of these negotiations shows that few additional commitments have been made at the regional level, which reflects the members' unwillingness to open up their aviation industry even among neighbours (Nikomborirak 1999). Consequently, the idea of establishing a regional open skies policy within ASEAN, as proposed by Singapore, will require more work and evaluation before it has any chance of being endorsed (Findlay and Nikomborirak 2002).[19]

APEC

The first APEC Transportation Ministers' Meeting in 1995 focused heavily on air transport issues and created an expert Air Services Group under APEC's Transportation Working Group (TPT-WG) to explore options for liberalising the sector. After consultations with member economies, the Air Services Group tabled a report in early 1998 entitled 'Comprehensive Report on the Options'.[20] The eight options were prioritised as follows:

High:
- Doing Business Matters
- Air Freight
- Multiple Airline Designation
- Airlines' Cooperative Arrangements

Medium:
- Air Carrier Ownership and Control
- Tariffs (Fares)
- Charter Services
- Market Access

This report was endorsed by the TPT-WG later in 1998, and in 1999 in Auckland the APEC Leaders declared that '[w]e support implementation of the eight steps for more competitive air services, and the identification of further steps to liberalise air services in accordance with the Bogor goals'. The Air Services Group surveys member economies annually to measure progress toward implementation of the eight options. The survey results do suggest some movement, albeit gradual, toward liberalisation. However, the report from the third Transportation Ministers' Meeting in Lima in 2002 and the TPT-WG's own statement of current priorities both focus almost entirely (and understandably) on air safety and counterterrorism. But the TPT-WG and the Air Services Group continue to work on other issues, and to discuss these priorities with non-APEC governments at such forums as the ICAO World Wide Conference, held in March 2003.

CONCLUSION

Rarely is a given city pair served by more than two or three carriers – routes like Taipei–Hong Kong, with seven carriers, are quite unusual. Hence competition policy in air transport will always confront oligopoly behaviour. The temptation and the ability to collude will remain strong. And, even though the new low-cost carriers are rewriting the rules, they have not yet made their presence felt on international routes. State ownership is another factor that hampers liberalisation under the current bilateral system. The overall trend has been toward privatisation, but this has been partially reversed by recent difficulties (Air New Zealand, MAS, etc.).

With the exception of special situations like the EU and the Australia/New Zealand single aviation markets, eighth and ninth freedoms (cabotage) are unlikely to be granted to foreign carriers by most countries in the foreseeable future. In addition, majority ownership by foreign interests is still resisted by most countries. The continuing resistance to cabotage and foreign ownership means that alliances will remain important. The implications for consumer welfare are ambiguous, and regulators will have difficulty deciding which alliances to sanction.

Efforts to liberalise air services trade have largely occurred outside the WTO. For passenger traffic, prospects for significant multilateral liberalisation through the GATS are not promising, although prospects for cargo are somewhat better. Although bilateral open skies agreements represent genuine progress toward liberalisation, they fall well short of free trade in services. Open clubs are difficult to achieve through plurilateral open skies agreements, so these agreements promise only small benefits while they remain relatively closed.

As for progress in Asia Pacific forums, the difficulties of many ASEAN airlines following the financial crisis of 1997 and exacerbated by September 11 make ASEAN-based regional liberalisation difficult to achieve. Within the wider APEC group, attitudes toward air transport liberalisation are widely divergent, as evidenced by the number of member economies that have chosen not to join the US plurilateral.

For the foreseeable future, air transport liberalisation globally will proceed by small increments.

NOTES

1. The first five freedoms are specified in the Chicago documents (the Chicago Convention itself and the complementary International Air Services Transit Agreement), while the others have been articulated subsequently. Aviation issues of international interest are discussed under the aegis of the International Civil Aviation Organization (ICAO), an inter-governmental agency that was also a product of the Chicago negotiations. Another important organisation, the International Air Transport Association (IATA), whose members are airlines not governments, dates from 1919.
2. A fourth aspect, namely, ground-handling services, was considered until late in the Uruguay Round, but eventually discarded.
3. Traffic rights were defined in the widest sense to include routes, capacity, pricing and the criteria for the designation of airlines. Specifically, paragraph 6(d) of the annex states: 'traffic rights mean the right for scheduled and non-scheduled services to operate and/or carry passengers, cargo and mail for remuneration or hire from, to, within, or over the territory of a member, including points to be served, routes to be operated, types of traffic to be carried, capacity to be provided, tariffs to be charged and their conditions, and criteria for designation of airlines, including such criteria as number, ownership and control'.
4. The literature on the economics of the airlines industry is an extensive one. A good introduction to many of the basic issues can be found in Tretheway and Oum (1992). Other useful sources include Caves et al. (1984); Morrison and Winston (1986); Gillen et al. (1988); Butler and Huston (1989); Baumol and Lee (1991); Hanlon (1996); Oster and Strong (2001); and Clougherty (2002).
5. Even separate airports within a given city are, for many travellers, imperfect substitutes. Gatwick is not Heathrow, Narita is not Haneda and Pudong is not Hongqiao.

6   Because each city pair is, to a significant degree, a separate product, adding cities to the network should probably be labelled a change of scope rather than a change of scale.
7   Despite the Fair Trade Commission's intervention, Air Do went into bankruptcy in June 2002.
8   See, e.g., Brueckner and Spiller (1991); Oum et al. (1995); Hendricks et al. (1995, 1999); Zhang (1996); Berechman et al. (1998); and Barla and Constantatos (2000) for discussions of the economics of hub-and-spoke networks. Southwest, a very profitable regional carrier in the United States, deliberately retains a linear network, thus sacrificing the potential economies of density created by hub-and-spoke networks, but attracts passengers with the convenience of direct flights. Southwest achieves economies of fleet utilisation in other ways: a fleet of uniform smaller aircraft (all 737s) with crowded seating patterns, and aggressive discount fares. Because their flights do not need to wait at hubs for connections, and because no meals are served (which eliminates catering time), Southwest's turnaround times are superior to those that a hub-and-spoke airline can achieve. But it remains to be seen whether an airline like Southwest can compete for long-haul business – this is now being tested, because Southwest has recently opened its first coast-to-coast routes.
9   A recent study by Morrison (2001) showed that the presence of Southwest Airlines has had a significant impact on fares and social welfare. The estimated savings – due to actual, adjacent and potential competition from Southwest – were US$12.9 billion in 1998. These savings amounted to 20 per cent of the US airline industry's 1998 domestic scheduled passenger revenue and slightly more than one-half of the fare reductions attributed to airline deregulation.
10 Many commentators have noted that Chapter 11 in reality is not exactly bankruptcy. As the iconoclastic Donald Carty has noted, barriers to exit in the airline industry may be greater than barriers to entry (quoted in the *Economist*, 29 June 2002, 60).
11 These summaries are drawn from diverse sources in the financial media, only some of which will be specifically cited.
12 Readers interested in a detailed account of the evolution of events in Australia and New Zealand are referred to King and Burrows (2002); Forsyth (2002); and Findlay and Kissling (1997).
13 Although our perspective focuses on benefits to consumers, we note that tax-subsidised price wars between state-owned airlines are an ambiguous blessing, since consumers are also taxpayers.
14 Excellent background discussions on the situation in Japan can be found in Yamauchi and Ito (1996); Yamauchi (2000); and Oum and Yu (2000).
15 In the opinion of Bowen and Leinbach, this was not a 'quality privatisation', since there were few ready buyers (Bowen and Leinbach 1996: 87). The government was able to find a buyer only by agreeing to absorb all of PAL's accumulated debts.
16 See, for example, the op-ed piece 'To take a stand' in *Business World* (Philippines), 4 June 2002.
17 In return for access for its two carriers, the Korean government engaging in bilateral negotiations has had to open Korean airports to two carriers from the other country. This has been problematic when the other country has more than two airlines vying for participation in the agreement.
18 See Kim (2001) for a discussion of other cases of subregional multilateral air transport cooperation.
19 The basis for negotiation is based on commitments members made in the GATS. That is, each member is to offer additional commitments to liberalise

relevant service markets beyond what has already been committed in the GATS, known as 'GATS plus' offers. At the same time, members also submitted specific requests for other members to liberalise. For example, Singapore submitted a request for Thailand to abolish regulations that require transmission of data through public networks only (Findlay and Nikomborirak 2002).
20 The APEC documents referred to can be found on the APEC website (www.apecsec.org.sg) and the TPT-WG's own website (www.iot.gov.tw/apec_tptwg/).

REFERENCES

Austria, Myrna S. (2000) 'The state of competition and market structure of the Philippine air transport industry', Manila: Philippine Institute of Development Studies, mimeo.
Barla, Philippe and Christos Constantatos (2000) 'Airline network structure under demand uncertainty', *Transportation Research Part E* 36: 173–80.
Baumol, William and Kyu Sik Lee (1991) 'Contestable markets, trade and development', *The World Bank Research Observer* 6(1), New York: World Bank.
Berechman, Joseph, S. Plodder and Oz Shy (1998) 'Network structure and entry in the deregulated airline industry', *Keio Economic Studies* 35: 71–82.
Bowen, John T., Jr. and Thomas R. Leinbach (1996) 'Development and liberalization: the airline industry in ASEAN', in Gary Clyde Hufbauer and Christopher Findlay (eds) *Flying High: Liberalizing Civil Aviation in the Asia Pacific*, Washington DC: Institute for International Economics.
Brueckner, Jan K. and Pablo T. Spiller (1991) 'Competition and mergers in airline networks', *International Journal of Industrial Organization* 9: 323–42.
Butler, R.V. and J.H. Huston (1989) 'How contestable are airline markets?', *Atlantic Economic Journal* 17: 27–35.
Button, Kenneth (1997) 'Developments in the European Union: lessons for the Pacific Asia region', in Christopher Findlay, Chia Lin Sien and Karmjit Singh (eds) *Asia Pacific Air Transport: Challenges and Policy Reforms*, Singapore: Institute of Southeast Asian Studies.
Caves, D.W., L.R. Christensen and M.W. Tretheway (1984) 'Economics of density versus economics of scale: why trunk and local service airline costs differ', *Rand Journal of Economics* 15(Winter): 471–89.
Clougherty, Joseph A. (2002) 'US domestic airline mergers: the neglected international determinants', *International Journal of Industrial Organization* 20: 557–76.
Elek, A., ?. Hooper, C. Findlay and T. Warren (1999)
Findlay, Christopher (2002) 'Plurilateral agreements on trade in air transport services: the US model', discussion paper, Asia Pacific School of Economics and Management, Australian National University, August.
Findlay, Christopher and Christopher Kissling (1997) 'Flying towards a single aviation market across the Tasman', in Christopher Findlay, Chia Lin Sien and Karmjit Singh (eds) *Asia Pacific Air Transport: Challenges and Policy Reforms*, Singapore: Institute of Southeast Asian Studies.
Findlay, Christopher and D. Nikomborirak (2002) 'Liberalization of air transport services', in W. Martin and M. Pangestu (eds) *Options for Global Trade Reform: A View from the Asia Pacific*, Cambridge: Cambridge University Press.
Forsyth, Peter (2002) 'Low cost carriers in Australia: experiences and impacts', paper presented to the Air Transport Research Society, Seattle, July.
Gillen, D.W., T.H. Oum and M.W. Tretheway (1988) 'Entry barriers and anti-competitive behaviour in a deregulated airline market: the case of Canada', *International Journal of Transport Economics* XV(1): 29–41.

Hanlon, Pat (1996) *Global Airlines: Competition in a Transnational Industry*, Oxford: Butterworth-Heinemann.

Hendricks, Ken, Michele Piccione and Guofu Tan (1995) 'The economics of hubs: the case of monopoly', *Review of Economic Studies* 62: 83–99.

Hendricks, Ken, Michele Piccione and Guofu Tan (1999) 'Equilibria in networks', *Econometrica* 67: 1407–34.

Kaduck, Raymon and Paul Hooper (2002) 'Airline domestic ownership requirements: the cases of Canada and Australia', in *Transportation Visioning – 2002 and Beyond*, proceedings of the Thirty-Seventh Annual Conference, Canadian Transportation Research Forum, Saskatoon, Canada: University of Saskatchewan Printing Services.

Kasper, Daniel M. and Brian Hindley (1999) 'Liberalization in the transport sector: will GATS fly?', paper delivered at the Services 2000: New Directions in Services Trade Liberalization Conference, Washington DC, 2 June.

Kim, K.S. (2001) 'A study on the air transport cooperation in Northeast Asia between China, Japan and Korea', paper presented at the Sixth Air Transport Research Group (ATRG) Conference, JeJu Island, South Korea, July.

King, John M.C. and Geoffrey H. Burrows (2002) 'Antipodean agony: the unnecessary end of a 65-year-old Ansett', paper presented to the Air Transport Research Society, Seattle, July.

Lee, C.-J. (1999) 'A new approach towards enhanced Asian economic cooperation', in *Proceedings of the Conference on 'The Road to Greater Northeast Asian Economic Cooperation in the 21st Century'*, Seoul: Korea Institute for International Economic Policy, 159–76.

Morrison, Steven A. (2001) 'Actual, adjacent and potential competition: estimating the full effect of Southwest Airlines', *Journal of Transport Economics and Policy* 35: 239–56.

Morrison, Steven A. and Cliff Winston (1986) *The Economic Effects of Airline Deregulation*, Washington DC: Brookings Institution.

Nikomborirak, D. (1999) 'A survey of the ASEAN airline industry: what lies ahead after the crisis', Research Paper, Bangkok: Thailand Development Research Institute Research Paper.

Oster, Clinton V., Jr. and John S. Strong (2001) 'Predatory practices in the U.S. airline industry', http://ostpxweb.dot.gov/aviation/domestic-competition/predpractices.pdf.

Oum, Tae Hoon and Chunyan Yu (2000) *Shaping Air Transport in Asia Pacific*, Aldershot: Ashgate.

Oum, Tae Hoon, Anming Zhang and Yimin Zhang (1995) 'Airline network rivalry', *Canadian Journal of Economics* 28: 836–57.

Park, Yonghwa (2000) 'Reducing legal and institutional barriers to liberalize the air transportation market: Korea's perspective', paper presented at the EWC/KOTI Conference on Northeast Asia Transportation, Hawaii, August.

Tretheway, Michael W. and Tae H. Oum (1992) *Airline Economics: Foundations for Strategy and Policy*, Vancouver: Centre for Transportation Studies, University of British Columbia.

US Department of Transport (1999) 'Competition in the U.S. domestic airline industry: the need for a policy to prevent unfair practices', http://ostpxweb.dot.gov/aviation/domav/comp_rev.pdf.

Warren, Tony and Christopher Findlay (1998) 'Competition policy and international trade in air transport and telecommunications services', *The World Economy* 21: 445–56.

World Trade Organisation (WTO) (2001) 'Communication from the United States: review of the GATS Annex on Air Transport Services', S/C/W/198, Geneva: WTO.

Yamauchi, Hirotaka (2000) 'Air transport policy in Japan: policy change and market competition', paper presented at the EWC/KOTI Conference on Northeast Asia Transportation, Hawaii, August.

Yamauchi, Hirotaka and Takatoshi Ito (1996) 'Air transport policy in Japan', in Gary Clyde Hufbauer and Christopher Findlay (eds) *Flying High: Liberalizing Civil Aviation in the Asia Pacific*, Washington DC: Institute for International Economics.

Yergin, Daniel, Richard H.K. Vietor and Peter C. Evans (2000) 'Fettered flight: globalization and the airline industry', Cambridge, Mass: Cambridge Energy Research Associates.

Zhang, Anming (1996) 'An analysis of fortress hubs', *Journal of Transport Economics and Policy* 30: 293–308.

8 The shipping industry

Deunden Nikomborirak

INTRODUCTION

Despite the fact that Indonesia and the Philippines are island-states and that the Southeast Asian region contributes approximately 15 per cent of world container traffic (Containerisation International 1998), Singapore is the only country in the Association of Southeast Asian Nations to operate a shipping liner on an international scale.

Regional trade is highly dependent on foreign shipping operators. In Thailand, for example, 94 per cent of goods trade, or over 130 million tons, went by sea in 2000. Only 10.4 per cent of shipments were transported by Thai ships (Thai Farmers Research Centre 2001). The heavy reliance on foreign shipping liners leaves ASEAN countries vulnerable to the collusive practices of major foreign liners operating beyond the control of domestic legal jurisdictions. Sudden price hikes and arbitrary charges are the most common examples of the abuse of the superior bargaining power of large shipping companies operating in legal cartels called liner conferences. Major industrialised countries such as the United States, Japan and the European Union have countenanced liner conferences by providing antitrust exemptions for the industry at a cost to shippers worldwide.

Many empirical studies have shown that shipping cartels increase freight rates. Fink et al. (2001) illustrate that private anticompetitive practices are more responsible for high freight rates than are government restrictions. High transport costs have a marked impact on the competitiveness of developing countries. The World Trade Organisation estimated that transport costs made up 8.3 per cent of the value of goods transported by developing countries in 1997 (WTO 1998: 3).[1]

These practices have been denounced by shippers worldwide, as well as by international organisations such as the World Bank, the United Nations Conference on Trade and Development (UNCTAD) and the Organisation for Economic Cooperation and Development (OECD). Despite the clear impact that liner conferences have on transport costs, and therefore trade, past negotiations over maritime services in the General Agreement on Trade in Services (GATS) have concentrated narrowly on 'free trade' (market access) rather than 'fair trade'.

In recognition of this problem, regional governments have attempted to develop national shipping companies or attract foreign vessels to register domestically. These efforts have been mostly in vain. This chapter assesses the various options the governments and shippers could take to counter the formidable market power of liner conferences. It considers the possibility of cooperation between governments and private associations at the regional level. The potential to address the issue in the WTO, either in the GATS or in multilateral competition policy discussions, will also be examined.

LINER SHIPPING – 130 YEARS OF INTERNATIONAL CARTELS

Liner shipping refers to containerised shipping services that are provided on a regularly scheduled basis to pre-determined ports. It is distinct from bulk shipping of non-containerised raw materials, such as oil, grain, coal and cement, provided on demand by individual shippers on non-scheduled routes. While bulk shipping is believed to be a fairly competitive market (WTO 1998), liner shipping has involved price-fixing and capacity-allocating arrangements for more than 130 years. In the 1870s fast steamships replaced the less efficient sailing ships, leading to cutthroat competition in transatlantic trade and increasing the costs of entering the market. In order to stop destructive price competition, liner operators entered into formal agreements – known as the conference system – that set common prices and allocated capacity.

Because of this history, liner conferences have been exempted from antitrust provisions and scrutiny in most parts of the world. In Japan, Australia and the European Union, the shipping industry is included in the list of block exemptions (exemptions apply to the entire industry) in national antitrust laws. In Canada shipping conferences were given immunity from the national competition law under the Shipping Conferences Exemption Act 1987. The attempt on the part of shippers to insert a sunset clause or a review provision into the legislation failed.

In the United States the exemption for liner conferences was specified in the 1916 Shipping Act. Until recently freight rates charged by conference members needed to be approved by the Federal Maritime Commission (FMC), the sector's regulatory body, and made public. Any discounts that were not specified in the schedules submitted to the FMC were subject to a fine, putting the regulatory body in the odd position of preventing price discounting. This particular scheme was devised to prevent conference members from offering preferential rates to larger shippers with greater bargaining power, with the thought that this would disadvantage smaller shippers. However, it is not clear whether the underlying intention was to protect the shippers or the shipping liners.

The antitrust exemptions granted to shipping conferences have been highly controversial and have come under constant criticism. The international shipping liners have put forward the following arguments to support cartels:

- Uncoordinated capacity allocation across different routes can lead to low capacity and high costs, or the reduction of services. Conferences ensure optimal capacity allocation, lower costs and more regular and predictable services.
- Unbalanced trade flows on certain routes may lead to excess capacity on the returning leg,[2] which can be very costly. Because conferences can ensure capacity is available, price fluctuations are lessened in the face of demand and supply imbalances.
- Intense competition will result in a highly concentrated market. By allowing carriers to earn a compensatory rate of return on their investment, conferences can ensure the sustainability of a less concentrated market.

Shipping conferences, and other similar agreements among liners, are widespread (Box 8.1). There are approximately 150 liner conferences operating throughout the world, with memberships of between two and forty separate shipping lines (OECD 2002). Other types of agreements and arrangements are even more prevalent. Available data indicate that the market share of liner conferences is approximately 60 per cent of the container capacity in the major trades. However, their market shares may be much higher on heavy routes, such as those between the United States and Asia.

These arrangements are continuously under review in OECD member countries. Although no countries have moved to eliminate the exemptions that shipping liners have in antitrust legislation, various measures have been taken to weaken the collusive power of shipping liners, particularly in the United States. The US Shipping Act of 1984 allowed liner conference members to offer discounted rates as long as these rates were made public and other carriers were notified in advance.[3]

Although this did lead to reductions in price, according to Clyde and Reitzes (1994), the public notification and advance notification requirements were obstacles to an independent and flexible pricing policy. In a move aimed at weakening the power of the conferences, the 1998 Ocean Shipping Reform Act removed these requirements and allowed individual carriers to enter into confidential contracts with individual shippers. Most agreements are now privately negotiated. According to the OECD, only 10 per cent of US–Europe traffic is negotiated strictly under the terms of a conference (OECD 2002).

The Ocean Shipping Reform Act also stipulates that conferences must be open, allowing carriers to enter or exit at any time without penalty as long as advance notice is provided (normally ten days before the intended action).

Box 8.1 Other forms of liner shipping arrangements

Capacity stabilisation and discussion agreements

Stabilisation agreements attempt to control freight rates and regulate capacity through a binding agreement covering all or most operators of the trade in the region. Such arrangements can be made among conference members or between conference members and non-conference members. Discussion agreements are similar arrangements but are non-binding. It should be noted that agreements between conference and non-conference liners are treated differently across countries. In Australia, Japan, New Zealand, Norway and the United States, such agreements are also exempted from antitrust laws. In the European Union, such agreements do not benefit from the block exemption and are closely scrutinised by competition authorities.

Consortiums

Consortiums are arrangements between liner companies aimed primarily at rationalising container shipping services in order to benefit jointly from economies of scale. Unlike conferences, consortiums do not involve the setting of uniform or common freight rates. Again, the treatment of such consortiums differs across countries. In Australia, Canada, Japan, New Zealand and the United States, such agreements are also exempted from antitrust laws. In the European Union, a consortium with a market share below a threshold level may benefit from the group exemption.

Strategic global alliances

These agreements are aimed at achieving operational integration in order to benefit from economies of scale. These cover the employment and utilisation of vessels, joint vessel route assignments, itineraries, sailing schedules, the type of vessels to be employed, additions and withdrawal of capacity, port rotations, use of joint terminals, pooling of containers and establishment of container stations, vessel feeder routes and coordination of inland services where permitted. An agreement may also entail restrictions on use of third-party carriers without prior consent of members and may include penalties for a breach of contract.

Examples of conferences/agreements
Transpacific Stabilisation Agreement
Philippines Europe Conference
Far Eastern Freight Conference
Far East/South Asia – Middle East Conference
Europe Indonesian Freight Conference
Japan/Philippines Freight Conference
Mediterranean/Far East Conference

Source: OECD (2002: 24–6).

Despite the weakening in the strength of conferences as a result of regulatory reform and the entry of lower-cost shipping liners, particularly from China, South Korea, Singapore and Taiwan, the shipping industry is still far from competitive. Pricing through bilateral negotiations between liners and shippers is opaque and potentially discriminatory. Moreover, the various ancillary charges that are often applied, such as terminal handling charges and adjustment factors for fuel and currency fluctuations, are designed to transfer risks to shippers without a clear formula and without supervision from a regulatory body.

The rationales put up by shipping liners are currently being questioned, however. For example, the OECD has found that better service and lower prices are more effectively achieved through a decline in conference power rather than through price-fixing and capacity-allocating arrangements (OECD 2002). It recommended that the antitrust exemptions for price fixing and rate discussions be removed. Similarly, a study for the World Bank found private anticompetitive practices to be the main obstacle impeding international shipping trade (Fink et al. 2001). The study proposes that current round of WTO services negotiations should seek to discipline such practices.

There has been considerable consolidation in the liner shipping sector in recent years. Several mergers have taken place including Maersk (Denmark) with Sealand (US) and P&O (UK) with NedLloyd (Netherlands). Neptune Orient Lines (Singapore) has taken over the American President Line (US) and Han Jin (South Korea) has taken over DSR-Senator Linie (Germany), which earlier took over the American shipping liner Senator. In 2001 the top twenty liner operators accounted for 72 per cent of world container capacity in terms of TEUs (twenty-foot equivalent units), while the five largest operators accounted for 34 per cent of capacity (Figure 8.1). The top five liners are Maersk Sealand (Denmark), P&O NedLloyd (UK), Mediterranean Shipping Co. (Switzerland), American President Line (Singapore) and Evergreen (Taiwan). Japan, South Korea and China also have several top twenty shipping liners. Since the 1980s many US shipping liners have been sold to foreign companies and now none of the top twenty liners is controlled by a US company.

The increase in concentration in the shipping industry can be attributed to the substantial increase in the average size of vessels in order to exploit economies of scale. With increasingly larger capacity, greater networks are required and hub-and-spoke structures (such as those found in the airline industry) are becoming more common. It is likely that mergers, consortia and alliances will continue in this industry.

THE SHIPPING LINER INDUSTRY IN ASEAN

As Asian countries continue to recover from the economic crisis in mid-1997 they have relied heavily on their ability to export. However, exporters and importers relying on shipping liners to transport goods are fully exposed to collusive practices that are beyond the reach of domestic competition law and policy. What options do ASEAN governments have to minimise such exposure?

In the past governments have sought to foster domestic shipping operators in the hope of avoiding the powerful foreign liners and saving precious foreign exchange.[4] Various tax incentives and subsidies have been offered to support domestic industries, and state-owned shipping operators have been established with the hope of spurring private investment in the future.

An alternative strategy has been to form national or regional shippers' associations to counter the formidable strength of the shipping liners. However, these associations have found it difficult to coordinate large number of shippers in order to apply pressure on the liner conferences.

Another option is to have the issue addressed through the WTO. The two channels by which concerns can be addressed are through the maritime sector negotiations in the GATS and through the competition policy agenda being discussed in the Working Group on the Interaction between Trade and Competition Policy.

These options are not mutually exclusive, and governments may choose to move forward on a number of fronts.

Government policy to promote local shipping industries

If governments wish to promote a domestic shipping industry, they must either concentrate on building a national shipping liner or encourage foreign shipping liners to register locally in the hope that technological transfer will create the conditions for a local industry to emerge.

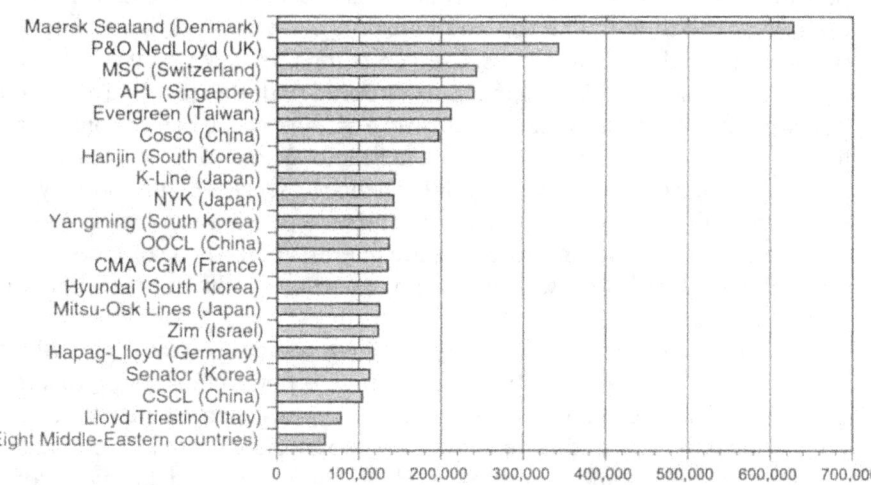

Figure 8.1 Top twenty liner operators (TEUs)

Source: Thai Farmers Research Centre (2001).

National shipping liners have been supported by tax incentives and, less commonly, subsidies for private investment in shipping.

The government of Thailand insists on having a national shipping line in order to save on foreign exchange spent on sea transportation. The Thai Maritime Navigation Company (TMNC), a state-owned enterprise, has a captive market. By law government agencies must buy shipping services from the TMNC unless its price is more than 10 per cent higher than that of the lowest bidder. In practice, bidding is rare and the TMNC usually gets the job. The TMNC itself does not own a vessel and buys space on foreign liners, which defeats the purpose of having a local shipping company to lessen dependence on foreign carriers.

Similarly, the Malaysian government adopted a cabotage policy[5] and offers financial and fiscal incentives for the establishment and expansion of a national fleet. It also set up a 2 billion ringgit (US$500 million) fund to develop the national shipping industry. The Philippines passed Republic Act No. 7471 (An Act to Promote the Development of Philippine Overseas Shipping), giving income tax and import duty exemptions to companies involved in shipping or the provision of spare parts to vessels.

It has become extremely difficult for governments to support a domestic shipping company, as shipping is not only capital intensive, but also knowledge and network intensive. The business has become very complex. According to the OECD (2002), the average size of vessels has increased significantly, which means that maintaining high capacity utilisation will become a significant challenge. The scale and scope of operations have also expanded. Numerous mergers have been occurring among liners, and this trend is ongoing. As large shippers such as Walmart have become more sophisticated and demanding, liners have had to become involved in logistics and land transport to ensure punctual door-to-door delivery. Many liners have become multi-modal transport operators with their own local land transport networks. It is no easy task to become one of the top fifty liners. Even US companies have left this extremely complex industry and US shippers deal instead with the cartels. This is why policy in the United States has shifted away from supporting international cartels to pushing for regulatory reform in the maritime sector.

Developing countries have very little chance of success in this industry. It is thus time for the Thai government to forget about supporting a domestic shipping liner and focus instead on protecting the interests of its own shippers, which are not as well endowed with bargaining power as Walmart and other large multinationals.

Shipping liners often choose to register in developing countries in order to take advantage of cheaper labour costs. There is fierce competition to attract international shipping liners – every country wants a share of the income and employment the liners bring, and compete to offer tax incentives. Competition is so strong that some countries, such as Singapore and Malaysia, offer permanently low corporate taxation rates as well as an array of exemptions from import duties, value-added tax, income tax for shipping crews, and so on (Table 8.1).

Government assistance to international shipping liners may be in vain since a liner can choose to register anywhere in the world. This is known as deflagging, where the link between the ship and the country of ownership is severed. A shipping liner registered in Thailand may shift to Singapore in order to enjoy the corporate income tax exemptions offered by the government of Singapore, for example.

The brutal competition for shipping registry has been to the benefit of shipping liners at the expense of the host countries. The competition has not only eroded the tax that could be collected from these liners, but the ability of countries to impose conditions aimed at technological transfer. These include conditions on local private sector equity, management participation and the employment of local workers. As can be seen in Table 8.2, Singapore imposes no equity or employment restrictions on shipping liners that choose to register in Singapore. Moreover, Singapore allows liners to flag their ships from anywhere in the world. In Thailand there are regulations requiring registered ships to undergo local inspections. This is known as a 'closed registry' as opposed to an 'open registry' where no requirements are imposed.

Competing for the registry of foreign shipping companies is a no-win game for any country. The footloose shipping liners will always find a better deal elsewhere, while all the host country is likely to gain is a few unskilled jobs on the ships.

National and regional shippers' councils

Prices are always negotiable in the shipping business. The more bargaining power that local shippers have, the lower the charges will be. There have been incidents in Hong Kong where shippers have united to refuse to pay terminal handling charges for craning and fork lifting, and liners have agreed to absorb half of the charges. In comparison Thai shippers pay much higher terminal handling charges.

To the author's knowledge, the Thai Frozen Food Association has been the only trade association in Thailand that has been able to unite in order to counter the market power of liners. The association was able to obtain preferential freight rates and bargained with the liners to waive the terminal handling charges. Unfortunately, other attempts to follow the success of the frozen food group failed, mainly because large players in the industry were unwilling to sacrifice their competitive edge over smaller players that had less bargaining strength and faced even higher freight rates. The liners divide shippers by offering different rebates for shippers of various sizes. Larger shippers are content with the deal they have secured, and are unwilling to help smaller shippers that compete with them in the market. Without the large shippers, smaller shippers can never hope to build up enough bargaining power to counter the liners.

With such obstacles in coordination even at the national level, there is little hope for a regional arrangement. At the regional level, the Federation of ASEAN

Table 8.1 Tax exemptions offered to registered liner shipping companies in the ASEAN5

	Import tax	Corpor. income tax	Personal income tax	Other tax
Thailand	Exempt import duty from Board of Investment (BOI) for ship up to 1,000 gross tons.	Exempt for 8 years.	Exempt for crews who work in a Thai ship that operates internationally. Facilitate speedier VAT refund.	Exempt tax on ship leasing. Exempt income tax on proceeds from sales of used company. Exempt income tax on the portion of income put aside for planned purchase of ships:
Singapore	Exempt.	Exempt.	Exempt tax on dividends from shares in liner shipping companies registered in Singapore. Exempt income tax for crews who work on a Singaporean ship that operates internationally on condition that most work is outside Singapore.	Exempt tax on the value added of a ship when it is sold. Exempt tax on ship rentals if ships are leased from domestic company, with a special rate applying when the ship is leased from overseas. Exempt corporate income tax. Exempt VAT on proceeds generated from asset sales. Exempt tax on freight for a company based in Singapore.
Malaysia	Exempt.	Exempt.	Exempt tax on dividend from holding shares in liner shipping company registered in Malaysia. Exempt for crews who work in a Malaysian ship that operates internationally.	Exempt tax on the value added of a ship when it is sold. Exempt tax on ship rentals if ships are leased from domestic company. Exempt corporate income tax. Exempt tax on freight for a company based in Malaysia. Allow accelerated depreciation of 60 per cent for the first year and 40 per cent for the second year.
Indonesia	Exempt customs tax and commercial tax for machines and tools imported from other countries.	None.	Exempt for crews who work in an Indonesian ship with special rate between Rp47.88 and Rp191.52 US$/year depending on responsibility and number of family member.	n.a.
Philippines	Exempt import duty for BOI member. Exempt duty and import tax for machines and tools used in ship maintenance in a dock registered with the Maritime Industry Authority.	None.	Exempt for crews with special rate of 5–10 per cent of revenue.	n.a.

Note: n.a. means not available.
Source: Thailand Development Research Institute (2000: 284–5).

Table 8.2 Conditions placed on foreign liners registering in the ASEAN5

	Type of business	Foreign equity	Employment
Thailand	Must be a limited company or a public limited company established under Thai law.	Foreign equity must be not more than 49 per cent of registered equity. Number of foreign shareholders must be less than half the total shareholders. These conditions do not apply to branch offices.	Up to half the crew must be Thai citizens.
Singapore	Must be a limited company or a public limited company established under Singaporean law.	No restrictions.	No restrictions.
Malaysia	Must be a company established under Malaysian law. Head office must be in Malaysia. Majority of management must be in Malaysia.	The majority of directors on the board and shareholders must be Malaysians.	n.a.
Indonesia	Must be a company established under Indonesian law. Size of ship must be no less than 20 cubic metres or 7 gross tons.	Foreign equity must be no more than 49 per cent of registered equity.	n.a.
Philippines	Must be a company or an association established under Philippine law. Size of ship must be more than 15 gross tons.	Foreign equity must be no more than 40 per cent of registered equity.	n.a.

Note: n.a. means not available.
Source: Thailand Development Research Institute (2000: 283).

Shippers Council (FASC) tries to address the problem of cartels, and urges member governments to pass regulations, but there is little that members from such diverse backgrounds can do. Nevertheless, the federation does have a voice that shipping liners and governments will have to take into consideration.

REGULATION OF INTERNATIONAL SHIPPING LINERS

Although international shipping liners are beyond the reach of domestic antitrust regulations, it is still possible to regulate certain aspects of their services, although not their freight rates, since that could easily lead to market distortions. Moreover, unreasonable rates may prompt liners to terminate services altogether. To balance better the negotiating power between domestic shippers and international shipping companies, the government could pass regulations that require international liners to consult the national shippers' council or association before any price increase is enacted.

In Thailand a Maritime Bill was drafted that stipulates that adequate notice of a rate increase must be given to the local regulatory agency and that shipping liners must negotiate with shippers before any increase. The Bill proposed that liners intending to increase freight rates must give ninety days' notice to the Office of Maritime Promotion Commission and outline the reasons supporting the increase. If the state does not object within fifteen days, the new rates can be enforced. If the two parties fail to reach an agreement, an arbitration committee made up of impartial outsiders would be formed and its decision would be final. In 2001 a new government came into power and did not push the Bill further. Malaysia is considering a similar law.

Legislation to prevent abrupt increases in rates has been adopted by many other countries, including Japan, Australia and South Korea. In Hong Kong the government has intervened to force a ten-month freeze on terminal handling charges. Such additional charges are not regulated by the Federal Maritime Commission and there has been little transparency and accountability in setting these charges.

SHIPPING CARTELS AND THE WTO

Maritime transport has always been a relatively liberalised service. The exclusive agreements that exist between 'national flag carriers' on international air transport routes do not exist in shipping services. There are also no restrictions on the frequency and capacity of ships calling at the ports. The fierce competition for the registry of international liners, as discussed earlier, has ended many policy restrictions on foreign equity, employment of foreign nationals, and even technical and safety standards. The only remaining restrictions involve cabotage policy, which often only applies to domestic shipping services, and the exclusivity of national flags on ships carrying government cargoes. The issues the shipping industry faces are more concerned with fair trade than with free trade.

The principle that there should be fair competition in services can be found in Article IX of the GATS. The article has little substance. Members are required only to provide non-confidential information and take part in consultations concerning alleged restrictive practices on the request of the affected country. So far this provision has been used only once by the United States, which brought a case against Belgium over the access of Ameritech, an American telecom firm, to a licence to publish commercial directories.

Although the provisions in the general GATS obligations may be weak, sector-specific commitments, such as those in the telecommunications sector, have included competitive safeguards. The Reference Paper on Telecommunications

Services[6] contains a commitment by members to prevent suppliers unilaterally or collectively engaging in or sustaining anticompetitive practices. But this particular provision is designed to guarantee foreign access to local markets, rather than establish international competition rules.

The competition policy agenda being discussed in the WTO Working Group on the Interaction between Trade and Competition Policy focuses exclusively on three issues, one of which is international cartels. The discussion below provides more details about the channels to address concerns about shipping cartels through the WTO.

GATS negotiations

The 1994 Uruguay Round Agreement incorporated schedules of members' commitments in maritime transport, and contained an annex to the GATS on negotiations in maritime transport and a ministerial decision to prolong maritime transport negotiations until 30 June 1996. A Negotiating Group on Maritime Transport Services was established and made the decision to further suspend negotiations until the Doha Round. The failure to reach an agreement resulted from the refusal of the United States to negotiate, on the grounds that commitments offered by other countries were insignificant to achieve real change in the industry. However, the thirty-two members (counting the European Union as one member) that participated in the negotiations agreed to abstain from imposing any additional restrictions. With the failure of the Doha Round negotiations in Cancun in September 2003, and no immediate prospect of relaunching discussions, maritime transport has remained off the table.

Thus far the maritime sector negotiations have concentrated narrowly on market access issues. There is a need to deal with anticompetitive practices of the maritime cartels. Large economies such as the United States, the European Union and Japan have sufficient bargaining power to stem the power of the conferences and protect the interests of their shippers, despite the extra-territoriality problems involved. Smaller states that are in a weaker position and have limited enforcement capacity may need to rely on international rules to enforce competition disciplines in the sector.

It would be in the interests of ASEAN nations, along with other developing countries, to demand that block exemptions provided for shipping cartels be removed from national competition laws. And, in case competition laws are intentionally not enforced, affected foreign interests should be able to challenge the anticompetitive practices of liners in the courts of the countries whose citizens own or control these shipping lines. This type of provision is found in the WTO rules on intellectual property and government procurement (Mattoo and Subramanian 1997). Developing countries should make this issue a prerequisite for entering into negotiations over maritime services in the Doha Round.

The competition policy agenda

Trade and competition policy is considered one of the Singapore issues; that is, one of the issues that were raised during the WTO Ministerial Conference in Singapore in December 1996.[7] The ministers decided at the conference to set up the Working Group on the Interaction between Trade and Competition Policy to consider various competition policy issues and concerns raised by members. The working group will not negotiate new rules or commitments. The ministers made it clear that no decision had been reached on whether negotiations would take place in the future, and stated that discussions could not develop into negotiations without a clear consensus.

Developing countries are apprehensive about the competition policy agenda as they suspect that the issue will be more about market access than ensuring fair trade. Since most developed countries have well-established competition laws, developing countries fear the agenda is about ensuring access to markets that do not have such laws. They believe that the differences in the member countries' competition laws, policies and institutions are so large that negotiations will not be feasible. This suggests that capacity building is necessary to narrow these gaps and allow negotiation in the Doha Round. The Doha Ministerial Declaration specified key issues to be addressed before the Fifth Ministerial Conference in November 2003 (Box 8.2).

Following the declaration, the working group identified three issues to be discussed in separate meetings in 2002: (1) technical assistance and capacity building; (2) international hardcore[8] cartels and multilateral cooperation; and (3) core principles in the enforcement of competition law. The discussion on cartels will include shipping cartels, as well as other manufacturing cartels. The main issues of concern include the definition of a hardcore cartel, the implications for domestic competition laws and policy, and the scope of cooperation in fighting these cartels.

It is interesting that paragraph 25 of the Doha Declaration states that cooperation should be voluntary rather than mandatory. This appears to be contrary to the principles of the WTO, which is known for its binding commitments, unlike forums such as APEC.[9]

ASEAN countries and other developing countries should join to propose an international trade rule that prohibits hardcore cartels, much like other fair-trade rules on dumping, subsidies and the violation of intellectual property rights. This suggestion is likely to meet with strong resistance from major industrialised countries that have an interest in protecting their own multinational shipping lines. This is, however, would be the most effective means of stamping out cartels.

An interim strategy would be to stick to the existing framework and demand mandatory obligations to provide assistance in law enforcement, requiring competition authorities of the countries where the cartel companies are based to supply non-confidential information on request. Failure to do so would subject them to a dispute resolution mechanism. This proposal was put forward by

> *Box 8.2* Doha Declaration
>
> *Interaction between Trade and Competition Policy*
>
> 23. Recognising the case for a multilateral framework to enhance the contribution of competition policy to international trade and development, and the need for enhanced technical assistance and capacity-building in this area as referred to in paragraph 24, we agree that negotiations will take place after the Fifth Session of the Ministerial Conference on the basis of a decision to be taken, by explicit consensus, at that Session on modalities of negotiations.
>
> 24. We recognise the needs of developing and least-developed countries for enhanced support for technical assistance and capacity building in this area, including policy analysis and development so that they may better evaluate the implications of closer multilateral cooperation for their development policies and objectives, and human and institutional development. To this end, we shall work in cooperation with other relevant intergovernmental organisations, including UNCTAD, and through appropriate regional and bilateral channels, to provide strengthened and adequately resourced assistance to respond to these needs.
>
> 25. In the period until the Fifth Session, further work in the Working Group on the Interaction between Trade and Competition Policy will focus on the clarification of: core principles, including transparency, non-discrimination and procedural fairness, and provisions on hardcore cartels; modalities for voluntary cooperation; and support for progressive reinforcement of competition institutions in developing countries through capacity building. Full account shall be taken of the needs of developing and least-developed country participants and appropriate flexibility provided to address them.
>
> *Note*: Paragraph 25 outlines the key issues to be addressed before the Fifth Ministerial Conference in November 2003.

Thailand in the second working group meeting in June 2002, but was strongly opposed by both the United States and the European Union. Other developing countries, in particular those without a competition law or a competition authority, were not supportive for fear of being bogged down by requests from developed countries. In this regard, many details still need to be worked out.

CONCLUSION

Liner shipping is complex, requiring massive investment in a large fleet, a good land transport network and expertise in logistics. Big liners are getting even bigger, while smaller ones seem to be disappearing from the picture. If countries lack the capability to run a successful domestic liner, they have little chance of becoming competitive at the international level and will only be able to survive under the protection of government subsidies and privileges.

Governments should focus on protecting their shippers from potential abuses of market power by international shipping cartels. Governments may consider passing regulations that require liners to notify and consult shippers before any rate increase. At the same time, they should push for having the issue addressed in the WTO, either in the maritime services negotiations or in competition policy discussions. Although the WTO's Doha Development Agenda is about developing countries, the blatant anticompetitive practices by liner conferences in developed countries have been sustained at the expense of shippers from developing countries with little bargaining strength. It is time that serious effort is made to establish fair competition as opposed to free competition at the multilateral level.

NOTES

The author would like to thank Khun Paiboon Ponsuwanna, president of the Frozen Foods Association and secretary general of the Thai National Shippers Council, for providing useful and insightful information on the shipping liner industry and practices.

1. The figure for developed countries is significantly lower at 4.2 per cent, reflecting more efficient transportation and the larger volumes and higher value of goods shipped.
2. For example, after the financial crisis that began in July 1997, Thailand's imports dropped significantly, while exports benefited from the weaker baht. As a result, there was a shortage in the supply of outbound shipping capacity, while the inbound capacity was excessive. This has led to a large increase in shipping costs for exporters and a decline in costs for importers.
3. Previously, a conference member could not offer discounts to shippers unless specified in the agreement.
4. The trade deficit for shipping that appears in the balance of payments accounts often understates the extent of foreign exchange loss. To avoid administration Thai businesses prefer f.o.b. arrangements when exporting and c.i.f. arrangements when importing.
5. Cabotage is a legal arrangement that restricts shipping rights to domestic companies.
6. The paper is available at <www.itu.int/newsarchive/press/WTPF98/WTO Referencepaper.html>.
7. Other issues were trade and investment, government procurement and trade facilitation.
8. The definition of a hardcore cartel is not yet conclusive. The OECD's definition in its 'Recommendation concerning Effective Action Against Hardcore Cartels' in 1998 includes price and quantity fixing, bid rigging and market allocation (see_http://webdomino1.oecd.org/horizontal/oecdacts.nsf/).
9. It worth noting that trade and investment obligations are to be binding. Making investment obligations binding but competition disciplines voluntary raises the question of whether the interests of host countries and foreign investors are properly balanced. That is, does this imply that foreign investors have the right to access domestic markets and pursue anticompetitive practices without any recourse?

REFERENCES

Clyde, Paul and James Reitzes (1994) 'The effectiveness of collusion under antitrust immunity: the case of liner shipping conferences', Bureau of Economics Staff Report, Washington DC: Fair Trade Commission.
Containerisation International (1998), *Containerisation Yearbook 1998*, London: Emap Business Publications.
Fink, Carsten, Aaditya Mattoo and Ileana Cristina Neagu (2001) *Trade in International Maritime Services: How Much Does Policy Matter?*, New York: The World Bank.
Mattoo, A. and A. Subramanian (1997) 'Multilateral rules on competition policy: a possible way forward', *Journal of World Trade* 31(55): 95–115.
Organisation for Economic Cooperation and Development (OECD) (2002) 'Competition policy in liner shipping: final report', DSTI/DOT(2002)2, Paris: OECD.
Thai Farmers Research Centre (2001) 'National liners: how to become self-reliant in freight transport', Krasaetat 7(1080), 19 July, Bangkok: Kasikorn Bank.
Thailand Development Research Institute (2000) 'Revision of domestic laws in ASEAN countries to support regional cooperation and trade liberalisation' (in Thai), Bangkok: TDRI.
World Trade Organisation (WTO) (1998) 'Maritime transport services: background note by the secretariat', S/C/W/62, Geneva: WTO.

9 The insurance industry

Melanie S. Milo

INTRODUCTION

The insurance industry has an important function in an economy. By offering financial security products to individuals and businesses, it can provide extensive coverage at reasonable cost of a wide range of economic activities and spread the risk of loss throughout the economy. It can also play a major role in overall economic activity through its financial intermediation function (Skipper and Klein 1999). In developing countries where bank deposits are the main method of saving, insurance, particularly life insurance, can further increase savings because the public finds it a more familiar and accessible route than the money market, for instance.

Furthermore, the 1997 Asian financial crisis highlighted the danger of firms' heavy reliance on bank financing and led to the conclusion that Asian countries should develop capital markets to provide alternative sources of financing. Given the dominance of commercial banking in Asia, the recommendation is that banks should foster the development of corporate bond markets and pursue a complementary role (Shirai 2001; Yoshitomi and Shirai 2001). The insurance industry can also help foster the development of capital markets.

In developing countries the banking sector has typically been the focus of financial sector policy, development and reform. More recently, the focus has somewhat shifted to the development of capital markets. In contrast, the insurance industry has remained largely underdeveloped.

This chapter looks at how competition in Asian insurance markets has been affected by market structures and regulatory regimes. It surveys the market structure and performance of insurance industries in the ASEAN5 economies of Indonesia, Malaysia, the Philippines, Singapore and Thailand. Market access alone is not enough to ensure vigorous, fair competition. The regulatory framework in these countries is also an important determinant of the structure and competitiveness of the industry, particularly public policy toward entry and the role of the industry regulator. Finally, the role of competition policy in regulatory frameworks is discussed.

MARKET STRUCTURE AND PERFORMANCE

Structure

The insurance industry includes primary insurers, reinsurers, and agency and brokerage firms. Primary insurance companies fall into two main categories: life and nonlife (general) insurers. Table 9.1 shows that there are fairly large numbers of insurance companies, especially nonlife insurers, in the five ASEAN economies. The number of reinsurance companies in Singapore is also quite large. The increase in the number of insurers in the 1990s was a response to the deregulation of entry, including foreign entry, into these markets.

Although the insurance industry in the ASEAN5 countries is principally made up of domestic private firms, there are many foreign-controlled and foreign-owned companies in the sector (Table 9.2). Foreign participation in the insurance industry, particularly the life insurance sector, was significant even before the deregulation of foreign entry in the 1990s. In fact, foreign insurers played a major role during the formative years of the industry, before market access restrictions were imposed in the 1960s. Table 9.3 shows that foreign firms dominate the share of total life insurance premiums in Malaysia, the Philippines and Singapore. In nonlife insurance, foreign firms are dominant only in the Singapore market.

The nonlife insurance sector is highly fragmented in the ASEAN5 countries, while the life insurance sector is significantly more concentrated (Table 9.4).

Table 9.1 Number of insurance companies by type of business in the ASEAN5

Country (as of)	Life	Nonlife	Composite	Rein-surance	Total	As of 1994 Life	Non-life
Indonesia (July 2001)	62	105	0	4	171	49	92
Malaysia (2002)	7	28	9	10	54	5	40
Philippines (2001)	40	1,110	3	4	157	25	98
Singapore (2002)	6	44	7	36	93[a]	8	44
Thailand (2001)	25	78	0[b]	1	104	12	62

Notes
a In addition, Singapore has around 50 captive insurance companies, including life, nonlife and composite insurers.
b Composite insurers were required to break up life and nonlife business into separate companies by April 2000.

Sources: The Indonesian Embassy, Philippines; Bank Negara Malaysia (2003); Insurance Commission, Philippines; Monetary Authority of Singapore; Ministry of Commerce (2001), Thailand; Swiss Re, *sigma* 6/1996.

Table 9.2 Number of insurance companies by type of ownership in the ASEAN5

Country (as of)	State-owned companies[a]	National private companies[b]	Foreign-controlled companies[c]	Branches and agencies of foreign companies	Total
Indonesia (July 2001)	4	122	45[d]	0	171
Malaysia (1997)	1	45	7	14[e]	67
Philippines (2001)	0	125	25	7	157
Singapore (2002)	0	17	24	52	93
Thailand (2001)	0	98	0	6	104

Notes
a State-owned companies are defined as companies where the majority (50% or more) of the controlling power belongs to the state.
b National private companies are defined as companies where the majority (50% or more) of the controlling power belongs to national entities excluding state-owned companies.
c Foreign-controlled companies are defined as companies where the majority (50% or more) of the controlling power does not belong to national entities excluding branches and agencies of foreign companies.
d Joint ventures.
e Branches of foreign insurance companies were required to be locally incorporated by 1998.

Sources: The Indonesian Embassy, Philippines; Insurance Commission, Philippines; Monetary Authority of Singapore; Ministry of Commerce (2001), Thailand; OECD (1999a).

The share of the five largest life insurance companies in gross direct premiums ranged from 66 per cent in Indonesia to over 90 per cent in Singapore and Thailand in 1999. In contrast, the share of the five largest nonlife insurance companies in gross direct premiums was less than 40 per cent. Given the greater number of nonlife insurance companies, this is still a significant degree of concentration. Table 9.4 also lists the Herfindahl index for these countries. This is a more precise way of measuring industry concentration, and shows that concentration is very high in the life insurance sectors of the ASEAN5, particularly in Singapore and Thailand. As in the banking sectors in these economies, the structure of their insurance industries is oligopolistic. However, concentration is not deemed a particular problem in the insurance sector, especially in life insurance, and is quite common in developed countries.

By themselves, these numbers do not mean much. The issue with respect to market structure is whether it is a market outcome or the result of government regulation. The fact that there are many firms in an industry does not mean that the market is competitive. The question is whether it is contestable. The presence of foreign insurers also does not automatically prove that the market is advanced in terms of product development. Although a high level of industry concentration

Table 9.3 Foreign participation in the insurance industry in the ASEAN5, 1999

Country share	Number of foreign nonlife insurers			Number of foreign life insurers			Foreign % of total premiums	
	Domestic (majority) foreign-owned companies	Joint ventures[a]	Foreign branches	Domestic (majority) foreign-owned companies	Joint ventures[a]	Foreign branches	Nonlife	Life
Indonesia	0	24	0	0	22	0	29%	46%
Malaysia	8	0	2	4	0	1	14%	65%
Philippines	8	0	6	19	0	0	19%	58%
Singapore	11	0	19	4	0	3	57%	55%
Thailand[b]	1	0	5	0	0	1	8%	49%

Notes
a Joint ventures with foreign shares of 49 per cent or above are included. This is to cover markets where majority foreign equity is not allowed although the foreign partner typically takes over operational control.
b For Thailand, a broader definition is sometimes attempted to capture insurers with effective management control exercised by foreign shareholders. This approach would yield a foreign share of more than 15 per cent in the nonlife insurance sector.
Sources: Swiss Re, *sigma* 5/1999 and 4/2001.

Table 9.4 Degree of concentration in the insurance industry in the ASEAN5, 1999

	No. of companies[a]		Share of top 5 firms[b]		Herfindahl index[b,c]	
	Life	Nonlife	Life	Nonlife	Life	Non-life
Indonesia	62	107	66.2%	34.3%	1,317	381
Malaysia	18	53	72.6%	30.3%	1,495	352
Philippines	40	110	76.0%	31.6%	1,615	335
Singapore	14	50	91.2%	32.6%	2,380	391
Thailand	25	73	90.2%	37.4%	2,975	462

Notes
a Indicates all locally registered insurers.
b In terms of gross direct premiums.
c The Herfindahl index is calculated by squaring the percentage of market share of each firm in the industry and then adding up those squares. The maximum score is 10,000, indicating a monopoly. A value above 1,800 indicates that a single insurer or a group of large insurers can exercise some monopoly power.
Source: Swiss Re, *sigma* 4/2001.

is not necessarily bad, it can be a potential source of monopoly power. Thus, there is a need to monitor the concentration process even in a deregulated environment to detect any further strengthening of the oligopolistic group and to ensure that it does not lead to a misuse of market power.

In the absence of government restrictions, insurance markets are structurally competitive in most cases. Low entry and exit barriers, and limited economies of scale and scope, prevent significant market power being gained by a small number of insurers. Even in highly concentrated markets, the constant threat of new entry can impose competitive discipline. If insurers gain significant market power, it is usually because of government restrictions over entry and competition (Skipper and Klein 1999). Thus, government policy or regulation is a significant factor affecting the state of competition in the industry, and ultimately the type, quality and price of the products offered to consumers and businesses.

Performance

Insurance markets can be classified into three levels of development: fully mature, transitional and incipient. Of the ASEAN5 only Singapore is classified as a transitional market. The insurance markets of Indonesia, Malaysia, the Philippines and Thailand are classified as incipient markets. But there are differences among this group. Malaysia has a more developed insurance market and is closer to the Singapore market, while Indonesia, the Philippines and Thailand are at a similar level of development.

Key indicators of insurance consumption include insurance density and insurance penetration.

Insurance density, defined as the value of premiums per capita, represents the average spent on insurance by each person and shows the depth of insurance coverage in an economy. A high insurance density implies that the insurance market is highly developed.

Insurance penetration, defined as the ratio of insurance premiums to GDP, measures the importance of insurance activity relative to the size of the economy. Insurance penetration is a rough indicator of growth potential. Individuals are likely to purchase more insurance as GDP per capita rises, with the caveat that the demand for insurance is low at both low and high levels of per capita GDP. In the former case, this is because the level of wealth can only provide for basic needs. And in the latter case, a saturation point is likely to have been reached, with most insurable interests already insured. Thus, the demand for insurance grows only marginally faster than wealth in both cases. In contrast, in transitional markets the demand for insurance is posited to grow significantly faster than wealth. As income rises above a certain minimum, people begin to accumulate personal assets, including insurance. The highest potential for growth is therefore in transitional markets (Chu 2001).

It should also be noted that insurance penetration is not a perfect measure of consumption. Because the volume of premiums is a product of quantity and price, a higher premium volume may reflect a higher quantity of premiums purchased, a higher price of premiums or other factors such as mortality and the desire to save. In addition a lack of competition or costly and inefficient regulation may increase the price of insurance but not insurance consumption (Beck and Webb 2002).

Figure 9.1 compares insurance density in the ASEAN5 countries between 1994 and 2000. There was a significant growth in insurance premiums per capita, particularly life insurance premiums, in Singapore and Malaysia prior to the 1997 Asian crisis. Insurance density had also been rising in Thailand before the crisis, but at a slower pace, while growth in Indonesia and the Philippines was stagnant over the entire period.

A similar pattern can be detected looking at the level of life insurance penetration in the ASEAN5. As a percentage of GDP, insurance premiums had been rising in Singapore and Malaysia before the Asian crisis hit, but growth was much flatter in Indonesia, the Philippines and Thailand. In contrast nonlife insurance penetration barely rose in any of the ASEAN5 economies.

Figure 9.3 shows the significant difference in market development between mature markets such as the United States and Japan, transitional markets such as Singapore, Taiwan, Hong Kong and South Korea, and the incipient markets in Southeast and South Asia. Japan, which is the only mature market in Asia, and the United States have very high levels of insurance density and insurance penetration. On the other hand, transitional markets still have considerable room to grow, and incipient markets are even further behind.

The prospects for further growth in the industry seem good. When looking at the growth in premium volumes, the ASEAN5 insurance markets registered significantly faster growth in the 1990s than world life and nonlife markets,

Figure 9.1 Insurance density: premiums per capita in the ASEAN5, 1994–2000 (US$)

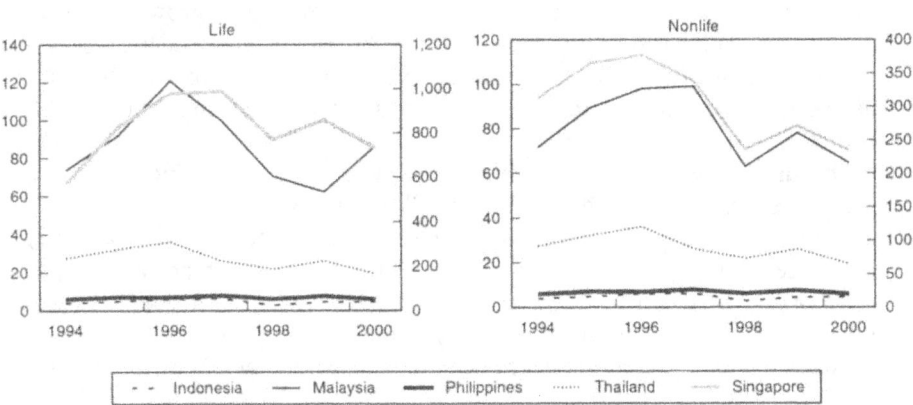

Note: Singapore is plotted on the right-hand scale.
Source: Swiss Re, *sigma* (various years).

Figure 9.2 Insurance penetration: premiums as per cent of GDP in the ASEAN5, 1994–2000

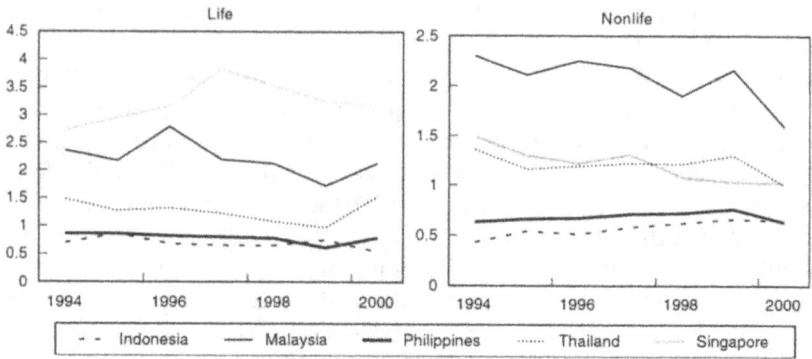

Source: Swiss Re, *sigma* (various years).

especially in the years prior to the Asian crisis. Between 1994 and 1996, the volume of total insurance premiums grew at an average annual rate of 28 per cent in Singapore and Malaysia, 17 per cent in Indonesia, 16 per cent in Thailand and 14 per cent in the Philippines (Figure 9.4). Growth in life insurance premiums was stronger than in nonlife insurance premiums. A sharp contraction in growth occurred in 1997 as a result of the Asian crisis, although there has since been some recovery, particularly in the life insurance sector. Overall, however, the ASEAN5 represents less than 2 per cent of the world market.

The rapid growth of the insurance industry in the ASEAN5 in recent years augurs well for the further development of the sector, and for its impact on capital markets and overall economic growth. In particular, the development of life insurance is far more likely to add to long-term capital growth than the activities of nonlife insurers and banks. Since the policies they sell are typically long term, life insurance firms can also lend funds on a long-term basis. It should also be noted that the insurance industry has been developing under a fairly restrictive regulatory framework.

The underdeveloped state of the industry, particularly in Indonesia, the Philippines and Thailand, has been primarily attributed to low levels of income and, hence, low demand. But consumer demand is not the only factor affecting insurance consumption. Beck and Webb (2002) argue that important supply-side factors also influence the availability and price of insurance, including varying levels of urbanisation, monetary stability, bureaucratic quality, the rule of law, corruption and banking sector development. In particular, a well-functioning

Figure 9.3 Insurance density and insurance penetration in the United States and Asia, 2000

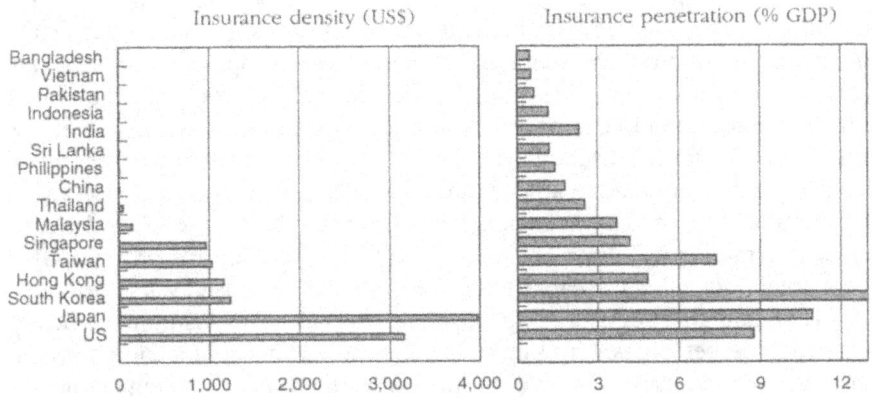

Note: In the incipient markets, insurance density ranged from US$1.40 in Bangladesh to US$151 in Malaysia. Figures for Indonesia, the Philippines and Thailand were US$9, US$14 and US$49, respectively.
Source: Swiss Re, *sigma* 6/2001.

Figure 9.4 Life and nonlife insurance premium volumes in the ASEAN5, 1994–2000 (US$ million)

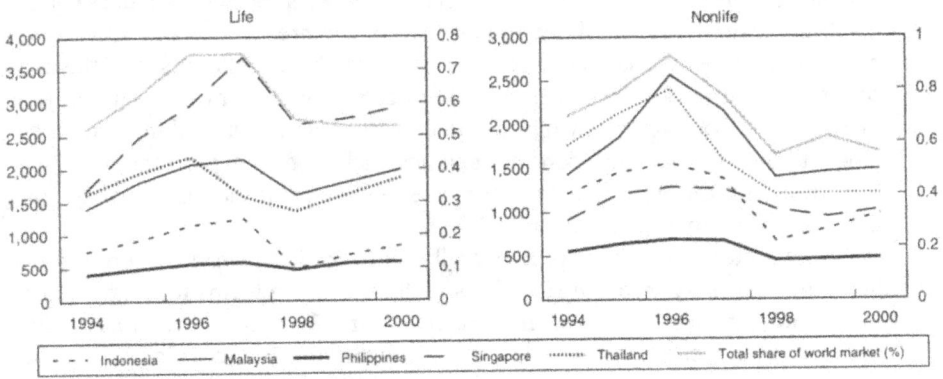

Note: Country data are plotted on the left-hand scale, while the ASEAN5's share of the world market is plotted on the right-hand scale.
Source: Swiss Re, *sigma* (various years).

banking system can raise life insurance consumption by increasing overall confidence in financial institutions and providing an efficient payments system. An efficient financial system, marked by the absence of distortionary policies, can also help insurers invest efficiently and thus provide more cost-effective insurance. A country's institutional framework or development is another key factor behind a dynamic insurance market, including efficient government bureaucracies and judiciaries. According to Ripoll (1996), insurance markets with fair and rigorous insurance legislation and strong regulatory bodies enjoy an important comparative advantage. Jenkins and Nuttall (2001) also argue that a favourable regulatory and tax structure for the industry is a key driver of insurance market development, in addition to an adequate and growing GDP per capita (indicating the capacity of consumers to purchase insurance).

Historically, the regulatory approach applied to Asia's insurance industry restricted market forces. It was thought necessary to limit competition between insurers through restrictions on entry, pricing, methods of calculating premiums, design of products, terms and conditions, and allowable investments. Not surprisingly, such a regulatory approach had adverse effects on industry structure and performance. Table 9.5 summarises the characteristics of the insurance industry in the four incipient markets.

Overall, the focus of financial sector policy and reform in the ASEAN5 has been on the banking sector, and the insurance sector has remained largely underdeveloped. Thus, the insurance industry is significantly smaller than the banking sector in these countries, particularly in Indonesia, the Philippines and Thailand (Table 9.6).

Commercial banks continue to dominate most developing countries' financial systems, with insurance companies and pension funds typically accounting for insignificant shares of total financial assets. Underdeveloped contractual savings institutions are the result of low income levels, the presence of pay-as-you-go public pension systems, the imposition of repressive regulations, and the use of insurance and pension reserves to finance public sector deficits at below-market rates. Contractual savings institutions are more developed in economies where there are mandatory pension schemes, including Singapore and Malaysia. But again, another important factor is the regulation of the insurance sector, particularly life insurance (Vittas 1992).

This chapter now looks at the overall regulatory framework governing the insurance industry in the ASEAN5, as well as major reforms that have been undertaken and the factors that have driven them. The focus is on public policy on entry as a means of improving the competitiveness and efficiency of the insurance sector, and on the role of the industry regulator.

REGULATORY FRAMEWORKS

The insurance industry in Asia has a long history, beginning with the establishment of some American, British and European nonlife insurance companies before

Table 9.5 Insurance sectors in the four incipient ASEAN markets, 1997

	Characteristics of the insurance sector
Indonesia	Underdeveloped: 8 per cent of population covered by insurance. Numerous small firms with limited range of products. Lack of expertise in insurance. A total 80 per cent of risk is reinsured overseas.
Malaysia	No new licences since 1985. Auxiliary insurance services limited. Insurance companies required to place 80 per cent of assets domestically and 25 per cent in government bonds. Deposit insurance in the insurance sector.
Philippines	Subsectors strictly defined. Life market highly concentrated: two firms hold 60 per cent of market. Nonlife premium rates set by government. Insurance funds subject to investment restrictions. Market highly dependent on reinsurance.
Thailand	Underdeveloped: 7.5 per cent of population covered by life insurance. Life insurance market highly concentrated. Premium rates require government approval. Insurance funds subject to investment restrictions.

Source: Dobson and Jacquet (1998).

Table 9.6 Size of the financial sector in the ASEAN5 (per cent)

	Assets of deposit money banks/total financial assets			Assets of deposit money banks/ GDP			Assets of other financial institutions[a]/ GDP			Assets of insurance companies/ GDP		
	1994	1997	2001	1994	1997	2001	1994	1997	2001	1994	1997	2001
Indonesia	89	n.a.	n.a.	51	58	49	n.a.	n.a.	n.a.	4	5	n.a.
Malaysia	65	64	69	79	115	117	39	52	44	11	12	18
Philippines	65	81	84	36	65	56	7	6	4	5	6	6
Singapore	n.a.	n.a.	n.a.	93	110	137	13	13	9	16	20	39
Thailand	89	79	73	89	118	99	10	15	24	5	5	n.a.

Notes
a Excluding insurance companies.
n.a. means not available.

Sources: Database on Financial Structure and Economic Development, World Bank; OECD (1999b); Bank Negara Malaysia (2003); Insurance Commission, Philippines; Monetary Authority of Singapore.

and immediately after World War II. After the war, local businesses and family groups began to venture into the insurance industry. Historically, the regulatory approach was to restrict entry and competition (Emery 1970; Thomas 2000).

The period from the 1950s to the 1960s was a critical stage in the development of Asia's insurance industry. The rise of economic protectionism and nationalism at the time was carried over into the financial sector. Thus, market access and national treatment were denied or curtailed to foster the development of the domestic industry. Existing foreign insurers were permitted to continue under a grandfather clause, and eventually became among the largest insurers. With barriers to foreign entry in place, the number of domestic insurance companies mushroomed. But the presence of many small firms led to some instability, causing regulators to impose domestic entry restrictions and tightly regulate the industry. Restrictions on domestic entry were typically backed by arguments that markets were small and that the number of local and foreign insurers already in operation was more than adequate. Such closed-door policies prevented the entry of new players with new products, more efficient distribution channels or better marketing, and removed the impetus for incumbents to consolidate, innovate or develop new products and distribution channels, ultimately creating insurance markets that were inefficient and lacked innovation. Competition was further circumscribed through the strict regulation of policy types, prices and allowable investments. Overall, the presence of a large number of small, inadequately capitalised firms, particularly in the nonlife sector, has been a principal cause of inefficiencies.

While market penetration by foreign brokers and underwriters was contained or restricted, foreign reinsurers played a more important role in the development of the insurance industry in Asia. They became a source of technology transfer in terms of product development, technical underwriting and management training, and gave guidance on rate evaluation and the construction of tariffs. It has been suggested that foreign reinsurers enabled small, inefficient domestic companies to survive, even thrive (Thomas 2000). This structure was also a key source of inefficiency because it added an unnecessary layer to the underwriting chain.

In the 1980s and 1990s, many developed and developing countries began to undertake financial liberalisation programs to improve competitiveness and efficiency, particularly in the banking sector. Reform of the other financial sectors, including the insurance sector, followed later. The discussion below briefly outlines policy reforms undertaken by the ASEAN5 economies with a view to improving the efficiency and functioning of financial institutions and markets, including public policy on entry and the role of the industry regulator.

Indonesia

Financial liberalisation in Indonesia occurred in two stages. During the first stage, Pakjun, beginning in 1983, interest rates were deregulated and credit ceilings were replaced with reserve requirements. From 1985 banks were also allowed to engage in securities underwriting, brokerage and trading, although these activities had to be transferred to the banks' holding companies beginning in December 1991. In 1988 Pakto came into effect, promoting competition in the financial sector by allowing domestic and foreign entry, although the latter was allowed mainly through joint ventures with domestic partners. Previously, foreign participation was only allowed in the life insurance sector; from 1988, general insurance was also opened to foreign participation. Prudential regulations covering reporting requirements began to be imposed in 1991, and were tightened throughout the 1990s. However, compliance was not strictly enforced until 1997. Minimum paid-up capital requirements for banks and nonbanks were raised in 1988 and throughout the decade. Minimum capital adequacy requirements for banks and solvency margins for insurance companies were set, and legal lending limits were also introduced (Dobson and Jacquet 1998).

The Insurance Law was promulgated in 1992. At the time Indonesia had around 145 insurance companies. This rose to 171 by August 1997, mainly because of the increase in the number of foreign joint ventures from nineteen to forty. However, significantly higher minimum capital requirements were imposed on foreign companies. In 1998 the minimum paid-up capital requirements for domestic companies were Rp2 billion for life insurance companies and Rp3 billion for nonlife companies. The corresponding requirements for foreign companies were Rp15 billion and Rp4.5 billion. However, in early 1997, thirty-three insurance companies, of which nineteen were life insurers, were found to have failed solvency tests based on liquidity, risk management, profitability and legal requirements (Chou 1999).

Except for products not available in the Indonesian market, insurance products can only be supplied through a locally incorporated insurance company that can be either Indonesian or foreign owned. Foreign commercial presence can only be through a joint venture with an Indonesian firm or through participation in the capital of a listed company, which was limited to 80 per cent in a joint venture and 40 per cent in a listed company. The commitments Indonesia made under the Financial Services Agreement (FSA), which was brought into the General Agreement on Trade in Services (GATS), include the removal of ownership limits on foreign insurance companies and the binding of up to 100 per cent foreign ownership in domestic companies, as well as the removal of remaining discriminatory capital requirements (Rajan and Sen 2002).

The Directorate of Insurance under the Ministry of Finance is responsible for the general policy framework, supervision, regulation and licensing of all insurance companies. Following the Asian crisis, the focus of Bank Indonesia has been on amending and improving the banking supervision and regulation system to comply with international standards, and on restructuring troubled financial institutions. In May 1999 Indonesia enacted a new Central Bank Act that conferred upon Bank Indonesia the status and position of an independent state institution. An important provision of this Act is article 34, which provides for the unification of financial sector supervision. In particular, the banking supervision function is to be transferred from the central bank to an independent financial services supervisory institution, which was initially to be established before 31 December 2002.[1] Besides supervising the banking sector, this institution will also supervise companies in other financial sectors, including insurance, pension fund, securities, venture capital and other financial institutions that manage public funds (Bapepam 2000). Changing the structure of regulation was deemed necessary to eliminate gaps in regulatory coverage of a significant group of unsupervised financial institutions (i.e., finance companies, many of which were affiliated with commercial banks) that contributed to the crisis.

Among the ASEAN5, the insurance sector is the least developed in Indonesia (Figures 9.1 and 9.2), despite the fact that Indonesia has the largest number of insurance companies. The industry is dominated by small firms offering a narrow range of products. The larger insurance companies are mostly state owned or part of family-owned business groups. The low capital base is coupled with low retention rates – more than 70 per cent of risk is reinsured with foreign firms. Thus, insurance companies are mostly commission earners rather than risk takers or risk carriers, which also limits the role of the industry as source of long-term investment funds (*Asia Insurance Review* 2000; Dobson and Jacquet 1998). The top six life insurers in Indonesia, including one state-owned company and three joint ventures, accounted for around 64 per cent of gross premiums in 2001. Overall, joint ventures accounted for 48 per cent of the market for life insurance. In the nonlife sector, the share of the five largest companies was over 50 per cent of the volume of premiums in 2001. Joint ventures are deemed to have led to higher capacity and a more significant transfer of technology.

Malaysia

Financial sector reforms began in the mid-1980s following a financial crisis in the early 1980s. In particular, Bank Negara Malaysia made the ringgit freely convertible in 1986. It also abolished deposit rate controls and made lending rates more flexible. In 1991 the basic lending rate, akin to the US prime rate, was freed from direct administrative control and was instead computed on a monthly basis using a four-element formula. In 1989 Malaysia adopted the Banking and Financial Institutions Act, which expanded the roles of financial institutions to foster market development. For instance, commercial banks were allowed to diversify into stockbroking and to hold equity in other stockbroking firms and insurance companies, although a licence was required when diversifying into non-traditional areas. At the same time, prudential regulations were tightened and the legal framework was radically changed. In particular, the Act broadened central bank supervision to include all deposit-taking financial institutions, gave the central bank wide powers to pursue illegal deposit-taking institutions and to act quickly in emergencies. Prudential regulations covering deposit-taking financial institutions and insurance companies addressed issues of shareholder diversification, risk diversification, reserve requirements and foreign exchange exposure. Overall, Malaysia's financial services sector remains segmented and uncompetitive because domestic liberalisation is incomplete and both domestic and foreign entry are restricted (Dobson and Jacquet 1998).

In an effort to streamline financial sector supervision, responsibility for the insurance industry was handed to Bank Negara Malaysia in 1988. The Insurance Act of 1996, which was further amended in 1999, aimed to enhance the regulatory regime by strengthening insurers' financial positions, providing better protection to policyholders, and ensuring professionalism and sound insurance principles. Provisions dealt with: the licensing of insurers, insurance brokers, adjusters and reinsurers; the setting up of subsidiaries and offices; the establishment of an insurance fund; the direction and control of defaulting insurers; the management of licensees and the accounts of licensees; the examination, investigation and enforcement powers of the central bank; the winding-up and transfer of the business of licensees; and other matters relating to policies, insurance guarantee scheme funds, offences and other general provisions. The growth of the sector in the 1990s has been attributed to improved consumer confidence as a result of these measures to strengthen the domestic insurance industry.

Another area that needed reform was the fragmentation of the sector, particularly the nonlife or general insurance sector. A financial crisis in 1985–86 left a number of insurance companies unable to meet the minimum solvency requirements. Mergers were therefore encouraged and no new licences were issued. Bank Negara Malaysia provided various incentives to promote consolidation, including a liberal branching policy, regional expansion, alternative distribution channels and tax exemptions. In particular, it envisaged a core of ten to fifteen well-capitalised and well-managed insurers. It also increased minimum paid-up capital and solvency margin requirements, which proved effective in promoting mergers and acquisitions (Nair 2001). As a result, the number of nonlife insurance companies declined from around forty in 1994 to twenty-eight in 2002.

In March 2001 Bank Negara Malaysia launched the Financial Sector Masterplan, its ten-year road map for the country's banking and insurance sectors. The objective is to build an efficient, effective and stable financial sector, with strong domestic institutions serving as the core of the financial system. The plan, which is being implemented in phases, is extensive and includes specific recommendations to manage the transition. Regular reviews and assessments will be conducted. In the insurance industry, the initial phase involves building the capabilities of domestic insurers through various deregulatory measures, including promoting bancassurance (the distribution of insurance products by banks) and deregulating pricing. Phase two focuses on promoting consolidation and strengthening incentives for improved performance, and will raise minimum paid-up capital requirements and enhance prudential supervision. Stimulating innovation through progressive liberalisation is the theme of the third and final phase, during which restrictions on foreign entry will be liberalised. The challenge now is to operationalise these recommendations.

Malaysia's graduated and progressive liberalisation of the financial services sector is also reflected in its GATS–FSA commitments, which generally limited foreign commercial presence to joint ventures in which the maximum foreign equity permitted is 15 per cent by a single or grouped foreign interest, to an aggregate foreign interest of 30 per cent. Holdings of more than 30 per cent foreign equity may be allowed on a case-by-case basis. In the insurance industry, the entry of foreign insurers is allowed through investment in existing insurance companies, subject to an aggregate foreign shareholding limit of 30 per cent. For existing joint ventures, foreign shareholders that were the original owners of the companies are allowed to own up to 51 per cent of the total shares. For the insurance sector as a whole, foreign equity ownership of up to 51 per cent is permitted and at least 30 per cent of equity must be owned by Bumiputra (indigenous Malays) (Rajan and Sen 2002).

In Malaysia the insurance industry is quite developed and product development is relatively advanced. For instance, the introduction of new annuity and investment-linked products in 2000 spurred the growth of life insurance. The Malaysian general insurance sector also has a high retention rate. Malaysia has also established the Insurance Guarantee Fund, which is financed by levies charged to all general insurers. More generally, Bank Negara Malaysia has been actively involved in developing the insurance industry since it took over the supervision of the industry. In particular, it encouraged the sector to play a more prominent role in capital markets (Dobson and Jacquet 1998).

Philippines [2]

The Philippines formally embarked on a financial liberalisation program in the early 1980s, beginning with the gradual liberalisation of interest rates from 1981 to 1983 and the easing of restrictions on the range of operations that financial institutions were allowed to conduct in domestic markets, including the introduction of universal banking in 1980. But soon after financial liberalisation began, the financial system underwent a series of crises because of a combination of factors, which included an unstable macroeconomy, weak prudential regulation and supervision, concentrated lending and insider abuse of banks. Financial reforms resumed in 1986, and focused on accomplishing prudential bank management. Banking reforms implemented in the 1990s included the deregulation of entry restrictions on new domestic banks and bank branches in 1993, which were further eased in 1995, and the partial liberalisation of the entry of foreign banks in 1994. The government also moved to reduce its direct participation in the banking system by privatising five of the six banks that it took over during the financial crises in the 1980s. However, entry restrictions on banks were again imposed as a result of the Asian crisis.

There was also an effort to expand the coverage of financial sector reforms in the second half of the 1990s. These included moves to develop equity markets and liberalise entry into the private insurance industry. A ban on the entry of new domestic and foreign insurance companies had been in place since 1966, although existing foreign companies were allowed to continue operating. Foreign participation in the industry was limited to 40 per cent equity, and only in the nonlife insurance sector to help improve its weak capitalisation. In 1992 the insurance industry was opened to new domestic entrants, which were allowed to form joint ventures with foreign investors. The restriction on foreign equity in the life insurance sector was also removed, although the maximum 40 per cent limit on foreign equity remained. The repeal of the Uniform Currency Law, which required all transactions to be conducted in the national currency, allowed the issuance of insurance products denominated in foreign currency.

In 1994 the entry of new foreign insurance and reinsurance companies was partially liberalised, as part of the government's move to liberalise, deregulate and privatise critical economic sectors and activities, including finance. This was in line with the decision to join the GATS and later the World Trade Organisation (WTO). A foreign insurance or reinsurance company or intermediary was allowed entry under only one of the following modes: (1) ownership of the voting stock of an existing domestic insurance or reinsurance company incorporated in the Philippines; (2) investment in a new insurance or reinsurance company or intermediary incorporated in the Philippines; or (3) establishment of a branch, but not for an intermediary. To qualify for entry, companies had to belong to the top 200 foreign insurance companies, reinsurance companies or intermediaries in the world or among the top ten in their country of origin, and had to have been in business for at least ten years. A foreign insurance or reinsurance company that would operate as a branch, or where foreign equity in the company or intermediary was more than 40 per cent, was allowed entry only for two years from the time the policy came into effect. During this period the number of foreign insurance or reinsurance companies (including intermediaries) allowed entry was five each, although this could be increased to ten on the recommendation of the Department of Finance and the approval of the president. Composite licences were not able to be issued. Significantly higher minimum paid-up capital requirements were set for new companies. In March 1996 Republic Act 8179 was enacted, which deleted the Negative 'C' List from the Foreign Investment Act and allowed up to 100 per cent foreign equity in key industries, including insurance.

In contrast to the change in the policy on entry, other regulations remain stringent and outdated. Furthermore, the regulatory framework does not take into account the differences between classes of insurance. It is notable that only the Philippines has not updated its insurance code among the ASEAN5 economies. Changes to the Insurance Code of 1978 have been few. Historically, the regulatory framework governing the insurance industry was marked by conservatism and risk aversion. Although this achieved overall financial soundness, regulations were overly cautious and constrained the growth and development of the industry. The Insurance Code requirements on investment policies and practices were particularly restrictive, and resulted in insurance companies making very conservative investment choices. Restrictions on the portfolio of assets that insurance companies could hold included: limits on investments in stocks, bonds and other certificates of indebtedness; real estate investments; investments in a single enterprise; and investments in foreign currency. These restrictions, coupled with the required security deposits, meant that a high proportion of the industry's portfolio was put into short-term assets and government paper (World Bank 1992).

The insurance industry is the second largest financial sector in the Philippines. But it is also underdeveloped and has lagged behind in product development and innovation. The industry is also highly dependent on reinsurance. The nonlife insurance sector in particular is characterised by a large number of small, family-owned firms that are inadequately capitalised and operationally weak. Thus, significant amounts of risk premium are ceded offshore. This structure has been identified as a key source of inefficiency in the subsector because it adds an unnecessary layer to the underwriting chain. On the other hand, the life insurance sector is deemed as adequately capitalised, albeit overcrowded. Although the insurance industry is largely privately owned, it also includes five government insurance corporations: the Government Service Insurance System, Social Security System, the Philippine Crop Insurance Corporation, the Philippine Deposit Insurance Corporation, and the Home Mortgage and Guarantee Fund. These government corporations are governed by their respective charters and do not fall under the authority of the Insurance Commission. In particular, the Social Security System and the Government Service Insurance System provide compulsory social security for employees in the private and public sectors, respectively, and have consistently been twice as large as the entire private insurance industry in terms of assets.

In the Philippines another important impact of restrictive regulation in the industry was regulatory arbitrage. A parallel industry – the preneed industry – has grown significantly under a regulatory environment that is less restrictive than that faced by the life and nonlife insurance sectors (World Bank 1992). The preneed industry covers the provision of future services or payments for health, education, pension or funeral needs. Because preneed plans are classified as securities, the industry fell under the jurisdiction of the Securities and Exchange Commission (and the Department of Health for Health Maintenance Organisations), which was more liberal than the Insurance Commission. In 2000 the total assets of the private insurance industry amounted to approximately 212 billion pesos, while the total assets of the preneed industry amounted to around 148 billion pesos.

Singapore

Singapore has become a sophisticated regional financial centre because the Singapore government has focused on creating favourable conditions for domestic and foreign financial institutions to service nonresidents. Overall, the government's policies provide a moderate regulatory environment. However, domestic financial intermediation is fairly heavily regulated, and thus remains costly (Dobson and Jacquet 1998). For instance, no new direct general and life insurers have been admitted since 1984 and 1990, respectively. The only exceptions were direct general insurers underwriting specialised businesses that were deemed as beyond the expertise or capacity of existing insurers. In contrast, Singapore has an open admission policy for reinsurers and captive insurers. Thus, many of the world's top reinsurers operate in Singapore.

The rationale for the closed-door policy toward direct insurers has been the same as in the other ASEAN5 economies – to prevent excessive competition, given the small size of the domestic market and the adequate number of local and foreign insurers already in operation. However, it has been also recognised that the policy has had adverse effects on the industry. Although a few local insurers have done well in Singapore and Malaysia, none has become a significant regional player in line with Singapore's aim to become a world-class financial centre. Thus, creating a more competitive environment was considered necessary to raise standards to match international best practice and turn Singapore into a leading centre for insurance services in the Asia Pacific. Freeing entry and ownership was seen as a necessary step toward achieving these aims. In March 2000 Singapore liberalised entry into its direct insurance sector, lifted the 49 per cent limit on foreign ownership of local insurers and adopted an open admission policy for insurance brokers (MAS 2000). The entry of new insurers will be controlled to minimise the risk that greater competition will lead to unsound practices. In addition, corporate governance, market conduct, management practices and disclosure requirements will be strengthened to international best-practice standards to protect policyholders' interests. The Monetary Authority of Singapore's supervision of the industry is geared toward 'minimal control with responsibility' (OECD 1999b), and regulations are constantly assessed and upgraded to ensure they remain effective. Finally, a committee was formed to study and recommend changes to improve the efficiency, transparency and quality of the distribution of insurance products.

In contrast, Singapore did not address the issue of reforming and liberalising the domestic banking sector, which remains protected. The rationale for wanting Singapore banks to maintain a significant share of the market was that they perform a critical role in the conduct of monetary policy, the domestic payments system and the process of intermediation in the economy. But similar reforms are essential to the positioning of Singapore banks in the broader international competitive environment.

Singapore's financial sector is well developed because of an explicit strategy to turn the country into a major regional and global financial centre. Its reinsurance industry is particularly strong in the region. Singapore also has the largest captive market in Asia, with around 50 captive insurers. In 1987 the Monetary Authority of Singapore established the Policyowners' Protection Fund to cover policyholders whose insurance companies have become bankrupt. It is maintained by a fee imposed on registered insurers. Singapore also has an

Insurance Ombudsman Committee that handles policyholders' complaints and disputes. Finally, another key feature of the Singapore market is its compulsory pension scheme, the Central Provident Fund, which has led to a high rate of compulsory savings (Dobson and Jacquet 1998).

Thailand

Thailand began to liberalise its financial markets in the early 1990s. The main components of the reforms included: liberalisation of interest rates; easing of controls on foreign exchange transactions; widening the scope of business opportunities for financial institutions; developing and strengthening the system of prudential regulation and supervision; establishing an offshore banking system; and capital account liberalisation, particularly through financial institutions. The reforms resulted in tighter competition, especially between banks and finance companies, which led to imprudent management of assets and liabilities. Inadequate regulatory and supervisory frameworks, both for banks and even more so for finance companies, also contributed to the weakness of the financial system, which culminated in the financial crisis that then spread throughout East Asia in mid-1997 (Kawai and Takayasu 1999).

Under Thailand's 1997 International Monetary Fund (IMF) program, reforms planned for the financial sector included: the adoption of international loan classification and provisioning standards, the introduction of a deposit insurance system, the implementation of new bankruptcy laws, and the commitment to remove restrictions on foreign equity ownership in banks and finance companies over the following ten years. Similar to Indonesia and South Korea, Thailand negotiated a series of financial sector reforms as part of a support program that also included reforming the institutional structure of financial regulation. But unlike South Korea and Indonesia, Thailand did not seek to establish an integrated regulator. Instead it drafted a new Financial Institutions Act that will give the Bank of Thailand the sole responsibility for supervising financial institutions (as opposed to sharing responsibility with the Ministry of Finance under current laws) and will pave the way for universal banking in Thailand. It will also empower the Bank of Thailand to supervise and monitor financial subsidiaries and conglomerates on a consolidated basis, and will specify steps for prompt corrective action and exit procedures for unviable financial institutions. The Act specifically aims to eliminate redundancies and discrepancies between different laws applicable to different types of financial institutions. Thailand has also drafted a new Bank of Thailand Act to strengthen the independence and accountability of the central bank, and to limit its objectives to maintaining price stability and safeguarding the stability of the financial system.

The regulatory body in charge of overseeing the insurance sector is the Department of Insurance under the Ministry of Commerce. The Insurance Act was revised in 1992 to strengthen supervisory measures and establish an insurance arbiter. Overall, regulations remain stringent and outdated. In particular, foreign ownership is highly restricted. Most insurance companies are local, with only one foreign life and five foreign nonlife branches in existence in 2001. But as in the other markets in the region, the foreign share in total life premiums was almost half. Although the 1992 revision of the Insurance Act allowed the Minister of Commerce to grant licences to foreign companies without obtaining cabinet approval, it was not government policy to do so until 1995. The insurance market in Thailand shares similar characteristics to the markets in Indonesia and the Philippines. In addition to still fairly low income levels, the lack of personnel trained in actuarial science has been identified as an impediment to growth (Dobson and Jacquet 1998).

Thailand undertook to liberalise the insurance industry in three stages beginning in 1997. In the first stage, 25 per cent of foreign equity participation in domestic insurance companies was allowed. Twenty-five new insurance licences – twelve in life insurance and thirteen in nonlife insurance – were also granted. In the second stage, foreign equity participation is expected to be raised to 49 per cent of registered share capital. In the third stage, foreign equity will be allowed beyond the 49 per cent limit once appropriate legal institutions have been in place for five years (Rajan and Sen 2002).

In early 2001 the Bank of Thailand announced that it will come up with a master plan to increase the competitiveness of financial institutions, improve public access to financial services, ensure financial system sustainability, and correct remaining problems in the financial sector. However, the focus will be on commercial banks and other financial institutions under its supervision. It is envisaged that the plan will provide a common framework for policymaking among the other supervisory authorities in Thailand.

In summary, the regulatory framework has been an important determinant of the structure and performance of the insurance sector in the ASEAN5, particularly state entry barriers. On the other hand, greater market access was facilitated by the Financial Services Agreement, which was deemed an important milestone in the evolution toward competitive financial markets. Although commitments made under the FSA were very modest and essentially formalised the status quo, the FSA laid the legal foundation for market access (Skipper and Klein 1999; Dobson and Jacquet 1998). There were also unilateral liberalisation efforts, such as in Singapore and the Philippines.

The critical role of the industry regulator was highlighted in the cases of Malaysia and Singapore, which also recognised the importance to the financial system of developing and strengthening insurance markets, albeit within a fairly restrictive regulatory framework. It is worth noting that insurance regulation and supervision in both Singapore and Malaysia are conducted by their respective central banks. In contrast, industry regulators in Indonesia, the Philippines and Thailand fall under the Ministry of Finance, Department of Finance and Ministry of Commerce, respectively. In the Philippines, it has been noted that the Department of Finance's role is poorly defined and weak, especially with respect to its oversight functions (World Bank 1992).[3] The same could be said of Indonesia and Thailand. Overall, central banks have been found to exercise stronger financial sector oversight than other financial sector regulators or supervisors. This is not surprising considering that the need for strong and independent central banks has been well established (Das and Quintyn 2002).

Table 9.7 gives a summary of recent insurance regulation in the ASEAN5. Overall, the incipient insurance markets in the ASEAN5 continue to be highly regulated and protected. Reform of the insurance industry is still in the initial stages and more market-oriented reforms are needed. For Indonesia, the Philippines and Thailand, the primary task is to strengthen the regulatory framework, including the institutional framework, in parallel with market-oriented reforms. As such, these countries can learn a lot from the way reforms have been implemented in banking sectors and in the insurance sectors of Malaysia and Singapore, especially with respect to prudential regulation and supervision.

COMPETITION POLICY IN THE INSURANCE INDUSTRY

In most markets, enhancing competition typically involves the removal or easing of state-imposed regulations that inhibit the workings of the market. In the financial sector, it is recognised that some form of regulation is necessary to protect the reputation and soundness of the financial system. Because asymmetric information and systemic risks are inherent in the financial sector, it remains closely regulated and supervised in most economies (Grimes 1999).

One common key lesson and policy prescription is that adequate prudential and regulatory provisions are essential to ensure the soundness of banking and insurance industries and the protection of consumers. In particular, prudential regulation and supervision should focus on solvency oversight, disclosure and consumer information, and market monitoring. Thus, while prudential regulations can be anticompetitive, some degree of prudential regulation can also promote competitive forces (Grimes 1999).

The strengthening of the regulatory and supervisory framework should occur in parallel with market-access and other market-oriented reforms, particularly competition and liberalisation measures, to improve the efficiency of the insurance industry (Kawai 1997). Market access alone is not enough to ensure vigorous, fair competition. The insurance regulatory regime also has to be sound so that relaxing such constraints on competition will serve to enhance efficiency and innovation (Skipper and Klein 1999). This also requires a regulatory and supervisory body that is capable of carrying out these tasks. A supportive attitude toward strengthening market elements and intensifying competition in the financial sector is considered as part of the scope of competition policy (Broker 1989).

Developed countries continue to heavily regulate their insurance sectors. However, the Organisation for Economic Cooperation and Development (OECD) has detected a shift in these countries from policy interventions designed to restrict competition, to deregulation of such restrictions and a refocusing of regulation on prudential controls and consumer protection issues. There has also been a focusing of regulation on consumer product lines (OECD 1998).

That is, better regulation does not necessarily call for the institution of more or stronger rules, just a different kind of rules.

Regulations that restrict market entry are among those that have the most direct impact on competition.[4] Such restrictions are typically imposed for public safety or efficiency reasons, including preventing overinvestment or overcrowding in certain markets. But primary importance is often placed on the elimination or reduction of government barriers to market entry to enhance the contestability of markets and the competitive process (Grimes 1999). Thus, the overarching theme of the competition principles identified by the Pacific Economic Cooperation Council (PECC) was 'the openness of markets to contest from all sources of supply', acknowledging that the ultimate goal of competition policy is 'to protect (or at least provide "minimum distortion" to) the competitive process, not to protect competitors/producers' (PECC 1998, in Grimes 1999: 4).

On the other hand, open entry into the insurance sector (and the financial sector in general) is not practised even in the most liberalised and deregulated financial sectors, for prudential and consumer protection purposes. That is, entry is typically subject to strict licensing processes. Although licensing requirements are technically entry barriers, such entry restrictions are necessary to ensure the financial soundness and the technical and managerial capabilities of insurance companies. But in some developing countries, entry is not just regulated but banned, particularly the entry of foreign insurers. Others apply an economic needs test or require local equity participation (Skipper and Klein 1999). When the licensing process is not transparent, entry can become discretionary and the prudential purpose is ultimately negated. Such restrictions are typically applied to protect and promote the domestic industry. But even if it is deemed worthwhile to purposely restrict competition to pursue wider social objectives, a national competition policy can then require the government to justify its interventions and restrictions in the market. That is, another aspect of competition policy would be to make such government interventions and restrictions transparent, and open to public scrutiny and assessment of their effectiveness (Cabalu et al. 1999).

However, there will be further pressure to bring down state entry barriers, particularly under the GATS–FSA framework. In fact, it has been noted that a major proponent of the extension of US trade policy to services was its financial services industry, led by the insurance sector (McCulloch 1990, in Dobson and Jacquet 1998). There are also some clear benefits of such a move, especially in incipient markets where regulation has served to protect industry players at the expense of consumers. It is worth emphasising that governments should be concerned about total welfare and not just producer welfare. For Indonesia, the Philippines and Thailand, it would be useful to draw up a master plan for the entire financial sector (similar to those of Malaysia and Singapore), which places domestic objectives and strategies, and externally generated/directed deregulatory reforms, in a consistent and coherent framework that includes clear targets, indicators and timeframes. Some policymakers are understandably

Table 9.7 Insurance regulation in the ASEAN5

Country	Insurance law and supervisory body	Licensing requirements	Supervisory requirements	Market access for foreign insurers[a]
Indonesia	Law No. 2 (1992) concerning Insurance Business and Various Amendments. Ministry of Finance decrees. Director of Insurance under the MOF.	Minimum capital for a new insurance company is Rp100 bn.	No government-set tariffs but self-regulation via the Insurance Association. A risk-based capital (RBC) system was implemented in 2000. The RBC ratio (adjusted capital to required capital funds) will be increased in stages to 120% by the end of 2004.	Only in the form of joint ventures. The foreign partner can increase its equity share beyond the previous 80% limit provided the capital of the Indonesian partner is maintained. WTO commitment: 100% foreign ownership of insurance subsidiaries but no branches.
Malaysia	Insurance Act 1996. Insurance Regulation Department under Bank Negara Malaysia (BNM).	Minimum paid-up capital of RM100 mn effective 30 June 2001.	Motor and fire business subject to rate and form control. Insurers are not allowed to carry both life and nonlife business. BNM has issued various incentives and guidelines to promote mergers and acquisitions.	WTO commitment: 51% ownership limit on existing foreign companies; 30% limit if foreign insurers wish to acquire a stake in an existing locally incorporated company; no branches.
Philippines	Insurance Code 1978. Insurance Commission under the Department of Finance.	Minimum paid-up capital of P75 mn for new local insurers, plus a contributed surplus fund of P25 mn. Minimum paid-up capital for (partially) foreign-owned insurers of P250 mn, plus a contributed surplus fund of P50 mn, where foreign equity is 60% or more; P150 mn, plus a contributed surplus fund of P50 mn, where foreign equity is between 40% and 60%; and P75 mn, plus a contributed surplus fund of P25 mn, where foreign equity is 40% or less.	Tariffs applicable for motor and surety lines. Margin of solvency for nonlife insurers is a sum no less than P500,000 or 10% of net premiums written in the previous year, whichever is higher. For life insurers, the solvency margin is 0.2% of the preceding calendar year's in-force sums assured	Branches, locally incorporated companies and joint ventures are allowed. WTO commitment: foreign companies can take up to a 51% stake in new and existing domestic insurers; subsidiaries allowed but no branches.

Singapore	Insurance Act (Ch. 142) 1967 with subsequent amendments, Insurance Intermediaries Act 1999. The Insurance Department, as part of the Financial Supervision Group within the Monetary Authority of Singapore (MAS).	Minimum paid-up capital of S$25 mn for all insurers. Certain deposit requirements with MAS.	No rate control, but form approval required. For nonlife insurers, the Singapore Insurance Fund (Offshore Insurance Fund[b]) solvency margin is the greater of S$5 mn (S$1 mn), 50% (20%) of net premium income in the preceding accounting period, or 50% (20%) of loss reserves in the preceding accounting period. For life companies, the fund's solvency margin is based either on policy reserves or the sum insured.	No foreign ownership limitations.
Thailand	Non-Life and Life Insurance Act 1992. Department of Insurance under the Ministry of Commerce.	Newly established nonlife companies should have not less than Bt300 mn paid-up capital, and Bt500 mn for life insurers.[c] There are proposals to raise the capital requirements of existing companies, but the decision has been put on hold.	Fire and motor business subject to tariffs. Tariff rates are also applicable to natural hazards like earthquakes, windstorm, floods and bush fires. For nonlife insurers, the solvency margin is 10% of the preceding year's written premiums, net of reinsurance and subject to a minimum surplus of assets over liabilities of Bt30 mn. For life insurers, a capital fund should be maintained of not less than 2% of all reserves, or not less than Bt30 mn.	Thailand has subscribed to a three-stage liberalisation process, raising foreign ownership in steps to 25%, 49% and 100%. The current regime allows foreigners a 25% equity stake in existing domestic companies or higher if foreign insurers acquire shares from existing foreign investors in a Thai insurance company (although government approval is still required). WTO commitment: 25% foreign ownership allowed.

Notes

a WTO commitments are included as some countries' current market access regimes are more liberal than their commitments. This means the host country can restrict market access to the level that it has committed, which implies some uncertainty for foreign insurers.

b Insurers are required to set up separate funds for Singapore insurance business (Singapore Insurance Fund) and offshore insurance business (Offshore Insurance Fund). There are separate solvency margin requirements for each fund and for the insurance company as a whole.

c Application of financial regulations is not retroactive.

Source: Swiss Re, *sigma* 4/2001.

sceptical of the benefits of financial liberalisation, in the light of the financial crises of the 1990s. A balance needs to be struck between the potential costs and potential benefits of allowing greater competition. In particular, the possible adverse effects from enhancing competition through lowering the barriers to entry can be addressed by properly applying prudential regulation.

Identifying the appropriate level and form of intervention is a serious challenge for governments. Regulatory efficiency affects overall economic performance. Inefficiency results in costs to the community through higher taxes and charges, poor service, uncompetitive pricing, or slower economic growth. In order to control costs and ensure effectiveness, regulation has to be placed within a consistent framework. To do this, it is necessary to establish clearly what needs to be regulated and why, as well as to define the principles for effective and efficient regulation (Wallis et al. 1997). A corollary to this would be the identification of the appropriate regulatory structure. The development and application of a national competition policy is a necessary and useful step in this direction, and enhancing the role of competition in regulation may be one guiding principle.[5]

Ultimately, developing the insurance sector and deepening the reform process will rest on a clear understanding and appreciation of, and strong commitment to, competitive insurance markets as being in the national interest.

NOTES

The author would like to acknowledge the excellent research assistance of Ms Alellie Sobreviñas. The usual caveat applies.

1. The date was later moved to January 2004.
2. This section draws on Milo (2000).
3. The issue of institutional structure for financial sector regulation is discussed more fully in Milo (2002).
4. Aside from direct entry restrictions, there are other policy-induced barriers to entry such as fiscal incentives and credit subsidies, as well as structural (e.g., scale economies) and behavioural (e.g., predatory pricing) entry barriers. Barriers to entry serve to limit the number of producers or sellers, and thus stifle or restrict competition. In particular, they are factors that allow incumbent firms to raise and maintain prices above costs without fear that new firms will enter the market (Medalla 2000).
5. For instance, Skipper and Klein (1999) propose a set of procompetitive principles in the design of insurance regulation that is adequate, impartial, minimally intrusive and transparent, as the basis for the creation of competitive insurance markets in the public interest.

REFERENCES

Asia Insurance Review (2000) 'A strong hard look at the Indonesian market', November.
Bank Negara Malaysia (2003) *The 2002 Insurance Annual Report*, Kuala Lumpur: Bank Negara Malaysia, April.

Bapepam (2000) *Indonesian Capital Market Blueprint 2000–2004*, Jakarta: Capital Market Executive Agency (Bapepam).
Beck, T. and I. Webb (2002) 'Determinants of life insurance consumption across countries', Working Paper 2792, Washington DC: World Bank and International Insurance Foundation.
Broker, G. (1989) *Competition in Banking*, Paris: Organisation for Economic Cooperation and Development.
Cabalu, H., N. Doss, I. Firns, T. Jefferson, P. Kenyon, P. Koshy, L.K. Lim and K. Brown (1999) 'A policy framework for competition policy in the Philippines', draft report submitted to the Philippine Tariff Commission, Quezon City.
Chou, C. (1999) 'Indonesian banks: survival of the fittest', in *Rising to the Challenge in Asia: A Study of Financial Markets, Vol. 6 (Indonesia)*, Manila: Asian Development Bank.
Chu, J.F. (2001) 'The makings of imminent insurance markets in Asia', *Best's Review*, April.
Das, U.S. and M. Quintyn (2002) 'Crisis prevention and crisis management: the role of regulatory governance', IMF Working Paper 02/163, Washington DC: International Monetary Fund.
Dobson, W. and P. Jacquet (1998) *Financial Services Liberalization in the WTO*, Washington DC: Institute for International Economics.
Emery, R.F. (1970) *The Financial Institutions of Southeast Asia: A Country-by-Country Study*, New York: Praeger Publishers.
Grimes, A. (1999) 'Competition policy: application to financial services', paper presented at Pacific Economic Cooperation Council Trade Policy Forum, Auckland, June.
Jenkins, T. and P. Nuttall (2001) 'Insurance company valuation in the M&A context', *Insurance Digest (Asia Pacific edition)*, August: 10–13.
Kawai, Y. (1997) 'The reform of regulatory and supervisory systems in transition insurance markets', in *Insurance Regulation and Supervision in Economies in Transition: Second East–West Conference on Insurance Systems in Economies in Transition*, Paris: OECD.
Kawai, M. and K. Takayasu (1999) 'The economic crisis and banking sector restructuring in Thailand', in *Rising to the Challenge in Asia: A Study of Financial Markets, Vol. 11 (Thailand)*, Manila: Asian Development Bank.
Medalla, E. (2000) 'Issues in competition policy and elements of a rational competition policy for the Philippines: an overview paper', PASCN Discussion Paper No. 2000-08, Makati City: Philippine APEC Study Centre Network.
Milo, M.S. (2000) 'Analysis of the state of competition and market structure of the banking and insurance sectors', PASCN Discussion Paper No. 2000-11, Makati City: Philippine APEC Study Centre Network.
—— (2002) 'Financial services integration and consolidated supervision: some issues to consider for the Philippines', PIDS Discussion Paper No. 2002-22, Makati City: Philippine Institute for Development Studies.
Ministry of Commerce (2001) *Annual Insurance Report of Thailand 2001*, Bangkok: Ministry of Commerce, Royal Government of Thailand.
Monetary Authority of Singapore (MAS) (2000) 'Liberalization of the insurance industry', Press Release, Monetary Authority of Singapore, 20 March.
Nair, S. (2001) 'Country profile: the Malaysian insurance industry', *Asia Insurance Digest*, December.
Organisation for Economic Cooperation and Development (OECD) (1998) *Competition and Related Regulation Issues in the Insurance Industry*, Paris: OECD.

—— (1999a) *Insurance Regulation and Supervision in OECD Countries, Asian Economies and CEEC and NIS Countries*, Paris: OECD.

—— (1999b) *Insurance Regulation and Supervision in Asia*, Paris: OECD.

Rajan, R.S. and R. Sen (2002) 'Liberalization of international trade in services in Southeast Asia: Indonesia, Malaysia, Philippines and Thailand', Discussion Paper No. 0217, Adelaide: Centre for International Economic Studies, Adelaide University.

Ripoll, J. (1996) 'Domestic insurance markets in developing countries: is there any life after GATS?', Discussion Paper No. 117, Geneva: United Nations Conference on Trade and Development.

Shirai, S. (2001) 'Searching for new regulatory frameworks for the intermediate financial market structure in post-crisis Asia', Research Paper Series No. 24, Tokyo: Asian Development Bank Institute.

Skipper, H. and R. Klein (1999) 'Insurance regulation in the public interest: the path towards solvent, competitive markets', Atlanta: Centre for Risk Management and Insurance Research, Georgia State University.

Thomas, R. (2000) 'An active regional player's perspective of the insurance industry in Asia – its past, present and future', *Asia Insurance Review*, December.

Vittas, C. (1992) 'Policy issues in financial regulation', Policy Research Working Papers No. 910, Washington DC: World Bank.

Wallis, S., B. Beerworth, J. Carmichael, I. Harper and L. Nicholls (1997) *Financial System Inquiry Final Report*, Canberra: Commonwealth of Australia.

World Bank (1992) *Philippines Capital Market Study (in 2 volumes, Vol. 1: Main Report; Vol. 2: Contractual Savings Sector)*, Washington DC: The World Bank.

Yoshitomi, M. and Shirai, S. (2001) 'Designing a financial market structure in postcrisis Asia – how to develop corporate bond markets', Research Paper Series No.15, Tokyo: Asian Development Bank Institute.

10 The interaction between contract and competition law

Lewis Evans and Neil Quigley

INTRODUCTION

This chapter provides some economic perspectives on the interaction between contract law and competition (antitrust) law. It surveys relevant aspects of the literature and provides some specific examples of the theory and development of contract enforcement institutions; the vertical contractual relationships between firms at different levels in the production and supply chain; and the role of contracts in enabling specialised investments to take place by limiting opportunism, spreading risks and assigning property rights. It considers the lessons that developing countries may draw from this literature as they consider the sequencing of reforms relating to contract and competition law, and the economic implications of the commitment of resources to developing Western-style legal frameworks in each area of law.

Most contractual relationships raise questions about the balance between the efficiency gains from ex ante specification of rights and entitlements, and the potential reduction in social welfare that may come from the exclusion of other parties from the relationship and the resources committed to it. By focusing only on the detriment side of the welfare ledger, especially where the resources committed or the market shares of the contracting parties are large in the context of the relevant markets, enforcement of competition law may sometimes reduce welfare by overturning or undermining contracts that have large efficiency benefits but nonetheless may have some lesser anticompetitive detriment. Furthermore, setting aside contracts that have been in existence for a significant term, for reasons of anticompetitiveness arising from circumstances unforeseen at the time of contracting, imposes external costs on the wider economy.

This chapter considers the role of contracts, the need for their enforcement and the intersection of contract law with competition law. It looks at vertical integration, contracts and spot markets as substitute vertical control instruments for firms. A discussion of the economics literature describes how contracts can affect competition and how competition law can distort managerial choice between contracts and vertical integration. Long-term contracting offers benefits in terms of economic efficiency but can restrict competition. This chapter looks at how long-term contracts are dealt with by Australian and New Zealand competition law, particularly the authorisation procedures. Then two New Zealand examples (the Kapuni and Telecom/Clear cases) where contract law and competition law have interacted are examined in detail. The chapter concludes by arguing that the balance between contract and competition law in Western economies may not be correct, that competition law in these economies may be inhibiting the use of some types of efficient contractual relationships, and that to maximise economic efficiency developing economies should focus on the development of a framework for the enforcement of contracts first and consider competition law as a second priority.

CONTRACTS AND ENFORCEMENT

The ability to write and enforce contracts promotes economic efficiency and enhances social welfare. In particular, long-term contracts of the type required to underpin large investments or facilitate access to network industries are important for driving dynamic efficiency.

Contracts necessarily impose restrictions on the actions of parties through the terms and conditions of the contract. From an economic perspective, contracts enable certain market arrangements to be put in place and certain investments to occur that otherwise would not be possible, by providing a degree of certainty about the obligations and conduct of the parties to the contract. They do this by:

- limiting the potential for opportunistic behaviour;
- reducing the transaction costs of organising economic activity (by holistically addressing a range of issues simultaneously and providing a means of enforcement);
- assigning property rights; and
- allocating risks between the parties to the contract.

Contracts are forward-looking arrangements that parties believe will maximise their net benefits ex ante in the presence of uncertainty about the future state of the world. One or more parties to a contract may take a different view ex post and perhaps seek to either have the contract renegotiated, or have the contract invalidated through legal channels, or may unilaterally breach the contract. One legal avenue is to claim that the contract is in breach of competition law.[1]

Competition law tends to view contracts and other restrictions on the behaviour of economic entities with some suspicion. This is especially the case with the example of exclusive contracts that cement vertical relationships between firms, and relationship-specific contracts that are long term in nature. Contracts found to be in breach of the law may be declared void, and be unenforceable. The whole contract may be affected, or in some cases, the provisions tainted by illegality may be severed, preserving the enforceability of the other provisions.[2]

Where contracts cannot be enforced ex post and the associated property rights under the contract are reassigned or invalidated, the certainty required to underpin future investments is undermined and this may have implications for a party's willingness to commit to investments requiring enforceable contracts in the future. If the enforceability of contracts is reduced they will be used less often or be more costly to put in place in the future. Either way, investment is reduced and society is worse off.

For contracts to be effective it is important that they are enforceable. As Evans and Quigley (2000: 81) state: 'From the perspective of economics, all provisions of legal contracts should be enforced irrespective of the ex post facto distribution of gains associated with completion of the contract, and the maxim is applicable to all market situations.' Yet if a contract is declared void because it has been found to be anticompetitive and illegal under competition law, the welfare objectives of competition law and contract law may come into conflict, especially if the judiciary focuses on the ex post distribution of gains from the contract in assessing its efficiency. As Trebilcock (1986: 403) noted:

> In emphasizing these ex post allocations of gains and losses to parties immediately implicated in the contractual relationship, the judicial process tends to become preoccupied with short-run distributive justice issues as between these parties and to discount long-run efficiency implications of given decisions for the welfare of these classes of parties in the future.

THEORY AND HISTORY OF CONTRACT ENFORCEABILITY [3]

The role of competition law in economies as they develop their contract enforcement institutions has received little attention from researchers. It is noteworthy that earlier institutions such as trade associations that facilitated transactions and trade before the rule-of-law institutions of state were developed would be constrained by modern competition law. These institutions had to be monopolistic because they were addressing an externality and had invested time and money into forging credible reputations. There may have been some scale economies in operation as well. The monopolistic elements, of necessity, evolved to include sanctioned trade practices and information exchanges that modern competition law seeks to regulate. For example, in the 1930s trade association membership in the United Kingdom entailed being party to a contract that typically promulgated a range of trade practices. The associations enforced such practices as minimum retail prices by sanctions that included fines for a breach. Many of these practices are per se offences under modern competition law. Furthermore, there is now very limited ability to induce contract enforcement by penalties under the rule of law, even if they are written into the contract.[4]

The development of the rule of law operated by the state has forced out earlier contract enforcement institutions. While contract enforcement is strengthened through the state institution of the rule of law, this institution also provides a credible way of regulating general commerce by means of competition law. Through both the actions of statutory-based regulatory watchdogs and parties seeking to modify contracts, contractual uncertainty is enhanced by competition law.

From an alternative perspective, consider the common argument that economically efficient trade requires the reliable enforcement of exchange agreements. This assertion is backed up by opinion surveys of traders, which reveal that contract enforceability varies widely across countries and that this results in less trade (Anderson and Marcouiller 2002). Given this result, why do countries not develop institutions that facilitate contract enforcement and thereby enhance trade and its concomitant benefits? There are various possible explanations. One explanation is that the social hierarchy in some economies provides the ruling elite power over a quiescent judiciary. This explanation is not entirely satisfactory in an open economy, since the ruling elite would benefit from the taxes and business opportunities that trade would bring. A competing explanation is a lack of strong institutions, represented by an absence of skills, organisational frameworks, and professional norms and ethos. Neither is this explanation entirely satisfactory. Many less-developed countries operate free trade zones that are likely to be extendable to international trade more generally. Finally, there may also be incentives for traders to prefer less-than-perfect contract enforcement.

Anderson and Young (2000) examine the implications of different institutional stages of development and the incentives for these to evolve over time. They consider the entire set of traders differentiated by their exposure to contract breach and their bargaining strength when a breach occurs. Traders incur ex ante costs of exchange, and agreements reached before these costs are incurred would be upheld by the rule of law. Absent the rule of law, traders that had incurred costs would be 'held up' as the other party sought better terms. In an anarchic situation – defined as one where prior agreements cannot be enforced and agreements are settled on the balance of power to compel – suppose sellers can force very advantageous terms when dealing with buyers. In this situation, few buyers would incur trading costs or contemplate transactions, more sellers would be attracted to the transactions and hence the probability of matching sellers and buyers would be lower than if hold-ups were not so likely. The sellers' favourable terms of exchange will therefore be dissipated by the lower probability of transactions. The welfare of all sellers may be improved by binding all parties to agreements under a 'rule of law' that impartially enforces agreements and thereby reduces hold-ups.[5]

Anderson and Young (2000) speculate that within geographically and politically fragmented Europe early development of the rule of law, largely independent of the power structure, facilitated inter-country trade in a way that was not necessary in China, which, although geographically diverse, had a unified jurisdiction. Foreign trade being of negligible importance, order in China was obtained by means of an efficient extensive bureaucracy. Over the past twenty years, as China has sought to foster international commerce, there have been significant attempts to institute the rule of law.

The public institutions and social mores required for the rule of law took a long time to develop in Europe. In the interim a variety of institutions evolved to enable transactions within and across jurisdictions. These included monopolistic trading organisations such as guilds and associations.[6] They were necessarily monopolistic in that they facilitated trade by internalising the negative externality that attended individual pursuit of hold-ups under anarchy, and had well-established identities, interests and reputations that enabled them to commit credibly to not holding up individual traders no matter their jurisdiction origin. Anderson and Young point out that the sunk costs – including investment in reputation – of setting up such a monopoly had this effect. Government sanctions provided commitment at a lower cost in some circumstances. However, monopolistic traders may resist the development of the rule of law in order to preserve their monopoly rents.[7] They suggest that while a trading coalition may dispel hold-up issues by supporting the formation of a countervailing coalition,[8] the rule of law can be obstructed by vested interests when each side of the market is dominated by a trading coalition.[9]

In a second paper, Anderson and Young (2002) argue the rule of law may not always be in individual traders' short-term interests and that this may inhibit the development of requisite institutions. The core element to this story is the general equilibrium interaction of contract breachers and their victims ex ante and ex post of the event. Their building block is traders that negotiate contracts before incurring the sunk cost of entry. After this cost is paid shocks affect traders' outside options. An ex ante desirable contract may, ex post, prove undesirable. Contracts will be enforced with some probability – changes to which represent changes to contract enforcement. The victims and defaulters may both turn to a spot market, in which case their sunk costs remain sunk and are irrelevant to the result of bilateral bargaining. Because not all traders transact in the contract or in spot markets there is a transactions inefficiency.

Traders who hold the more powerful position in a transaction may impose an externality on weaker traders by reducing the probability of matching, as described in Anderson and Young (2000). An increase in enforcement increases the probability of matching by attracting a greater number of weaker traders, but at the cost of the expected return to the stronger traders, as it impedes their ability to repudiate trades after a bad deal. Anderson and Young (2002) find that there are stable and unstable equilibria and that the effect of changes in enforcement depends on the distribution of shocks. An increase in enforcement can, in equilibrium, increase the rate of contract breach. The decrease in contracts honoured can hurt traders on both sides of the transaction. Their model implies that for stronger traders:

1) complete execution is worse than a set of high but incomplete levels of execution, and/or
2) no execution is better than a set of low levels of incomplete execution, even though,
3) complete execution is better than zero execution, and between these two situations, the profits of a monopsonist (monopolist) would fall as the price falls (rises).

They argue that where buyers or sellers could veto changes in enforcement, as in international trade, they may do so. Countries such as China, India and Russia that appear to have the institutional functionality to enforce contracts may choose not to do so. As (1)–(3) suggest, small improvements in enforcement for a low-enforcement economy may lead it to be worse off than no improvement, although the large improvements propounded by international agencies may leave it better off. The analysis is also applicable to domestic markets where strong traders have greater individual bargaining power and dictate institutional development. They suggest that international trade has driven China's modernisation yet unreliable contract enforcement has been a standard complaint of its trading partners. It may be that China's WTO membership represents a commitment to improve contract enforcement to a significant extent.

In examining the basis for strengthened contract enforcement, this chapter has not invoked the cost–benefit calculus that might attend enforcement appraisal. It would be unusual in economics if the polar outcome of perfect enforcement were to maximise welfare when costs are considered. Nevertheless, in the models considered, a very high level of consistent enforcement is welfare enhancing.

CONTRACTS, SPOT MARKETS AND VERTICAL INTEGRATION

Firms can choose to organise themselves vertically using a variety of mechanisms. These can be thought of as existing along a continuum. At one end are simple spot market transactions. Moving along the continuum, the transactions may still occur through a market, but the governing contracts may be longer term and involve various restraints on the actions of the parties to the contract. At the other end of the spectrum, transactions may be arranged within the firm – in other words, the firm may vertically integrate – either backward (to include suppliers) or forward (to include customers). The choice of whether or not to establish a vertical relationship externally through markets or internally within the firm is a cost–benefit judgement facing each firm depending on its particular market circumstances.

In the tradition of Coase, the most influential explanation of the choice of integration instrument is that it is driven by a desire to minimise the transaction costs associated with controlling principal–agent problems (Coase 1937).[10] Whether the firm chooses spot markets, long-term contracts or vertical integration will depend on the relative costs and benefits of each option. They are substitutes – but not always perfect substitutes. A firm will choose the vertical control instrument that delivers the highest net benefit.[11]

For example, the service quality of a retail firm might affect the demand for an upstream firm's products. The upstream firm accordingly has an incentive to control the downstream firm's quality decisions. The simplest way to do this may be to specify the desired level of quality in a contract. However, because quality may be difficult to specify, observe and verify in a contract, it may be void for uncertainty, or even if enforceable, may not be particularly effective at motivating the downstream firm. Vertical integration might 'internalise' this externality and prove the cheapest way to overcome the problem. In other cases, the use of vertical restraints (e.g., tying arrangements, exclusive dealing, exclusive territories, resale price maintenance) written into contracts may prove the best way to 'incentivise' the downstream agent to operate in the best interests of the upstream principal.

A related explanation for the use of contracts is the potential for asset-specific hold-ups. This occurs where goods or investments are highly specialised to a particular task or relationship between two or more firms.[12] Examples might include a gas pipeline being built from a particular gas field to supply a retail network in a particular town, or the purchase of container cranes by a port to service certain types of ships.

After the investment has been made and (due to its specificity) largely sunk, one party to the transaction may behave opportunistically ex post (e.g., hold up by threatening not to use the infrastructure or seeking to do so at a price lower than agreed before it was built). Mitigating this risk through spot markets, or short-term arrangements, is very difficult, or at best, costly. Vertical integration may prove the most efficient means of overcoming opportunism and the risk of hold-ups in such circumstances.

Long-term contracts that are struck ex ante can mitigate hold-up and spread the risks and benefits of an investment between buyers and sellers, provided contracts are enforceable. In effect, contracts assign 'property rights' over the benefits and costs of the venture before investments are made and costs are sunk. If long-term contracts cannot be struck, or are unenforceable, such investments may not take place and a particular market may not come into being. As Goolsbee (2000) has pointed out, the welfare cost of forgone investment can be very high as it can result in a 'missing market' in which the total of producer and consumer surplus is forgone.

Long-term contracts can also help protect relationship-specific assets from opportunistic behaviour, and encourage investment in high-risk projects and network industries.

COMPETITION LAW, CONTRACTS AND VERTICAL RESTRAINTS

While entering into contracts can be efficient and deliver improvements in social welfare, contracts can also be entered into for anticompetitive purposes.

In particular, long-term contracts can be used as a barrier to entry by foreclosing the opportunity for new entrants to get access to customers or to key inputs.

Perhaps the best way to think about this is to consider a monopolist producer of an intermediate good. This good is combined with other inputs (e.g., sales assistance, advertising, a shop front) downstream by a number of retail firms for ultimate sale to the public. The downstream retail market is competitive.

In this situation, Aghion and Bolton (1987) have shown that the adoption of exclusive dealing contracts between the upstream monopolist and downstream retailers will be rational and will raise entry barriers. Where retailers break contracts by dealing with a new entrant, they are liable to pay liquidated damages to the monopolist. Liquidated damages clauses raise the costs of entry. This is because a new entrant looking to gain a foothold in the intermediate goods market will need to sign up a good number of the retailers presently contracted to the monopolist. To do this, the new entrant will need to offer to pay the damages owed to the monopolist by each of the retailers that breach their exclusive dealing contract by dealing with the new entrant. This increases the cost of entering the market – a sort of entry fee related to the level of liquidated damages (Aghion and Bolton 1987: 388–401).[13]

While these contracts may be privately optimal for the incumbent monopolist and individual retailers, they are socially suboptimal. It is also collectively suboptimal for the retailers taken as a whole, but this externality is not factored into the decisions of individual retailers. Welfare costs of exclusive contracts are imposed in terms of higher prices, or diminished service and quality, by preventing the entry of new players altogether or by delaying it (until the contracts expire). Imposing legal barriers to entry through foreclosure may harm the level of dynamic efficiency and innovation, reducing social welfare over time.

A recent paper by Mathewson and Winter (1997) has shown that, under certain conditions, the use of tying arrangements by an upstream monopolist can achieve a similar result to the use of exclusive contracts. This occurs where the tying is for the purchase of a given patented (monopolistic) good across two time periods (i.e., the period under patent and the period after expiry). This drives the choice of contract length toward longer-term contracts covering both periods, so as to foreclose entry of any new (competitive) players in the post-patent period (Mathewson and Winter 1997: 577).

The above suggests that competition law has a legitimate role in curtailing certain types of anticompetitive contracts (especially exclusive arrangements) and vertical restraints between wholesalers and retailers. However, it is important to remember that contracts and other vertical arrangements can deliver efficiency benefits to society as well as competition detriment. Even contracts that harm competition may be welfare enhancing overall if the efficiency gains achieved outweigh the competitive harm. The policy implications are ambiguous.[14]

The various ways in which contracts are treated under competition law (and by antitrust authorities) can have profound ramifications for the choice of integration instrument employed by firms. As noted earlier, these can encompass spot markets, contracts or vertical integration.

The asymmetry imposed on the managerial decisions of firms by antitrust legislation can be modelled using the same example of a monopolist producing an intermediate good and a competitive downstream retail market. In addition, think of three forward integration strategies available to the monopolist, which under certain assumptions will have the same efficiency-enhancing effects in downstream markets:

1) using tying arrangements to control the downstream production mix;
2) integrating forward by acquiring the downstream retailers; and
3) integrating forward by organic (internal) expansion.

Efficiency may not be enhanced if competition law biases firms in favour of vertical integration by restricting the enforceability of vertical contractual arrangements on the basis of concerns about their anticompetitive effects.

LONG-TERM CONTRACTS, SPECIFIC INVESTMENTS AND AUTHORISATION

Goddard (1997) considers three key reasons why firms might want to enter into long-term contractual relationships:

1) to achieve a reduction of contracting costs;
2) to achieve the efficient allocation of risk over time; and
3) where there is a need to make specialised investments in order to be in a position to perform under the contract. (Goddard 1997: 424)

The first rationale is straightforward. It is self-evident that entering into a single long-term contract will reduce the transaction costs from re-negotiating and entering into a multitude of shorter contracts. The risk allocation function of long-term contracts is common to the rationale for entering into shorter-term contracts. However, risk allocation through contracting over a longer period may pose additional complexity in terms of the incentives to breach the contract and in the application of competition law. As noted above, highly specific investments raise major principal–agent problems that long-term contracts can help to alleviate. The second and third rationales are more complex and have the potential to cause a conflict with competition policy.

Long-term contracts may be adopted purely for the purpose of allocating specific risks to those parties that are in a better position to bear that particular risk. For example, under energy supply contracts the energy producer may agree to lock in the price of the output for the duration of the contract, while the buyer may agree to acquire their total fuel requirements or some specified minimum quantities from that supplier (e.g., as in 'take or pay' clauses) (Goddard

1997: 425–6). This type of contract may also be used in the supply of highly specialised inputs, where both the seller and buyer are exposed to opportunistic behaviour (Carlton and Goddard 2002: 19). Long-term contracts are also common in network industries where ownership of essential infrastructure (upstream) may be in the hands of a vertically integrated incumbent. New entrants seeking to gain access to the network in order to compete against the incumbent in downstream markets may prefer to enter into longer-term contracts in order to provide greater certainty for their entry decision.

In the case of specialised investments, a party to a trade may be required to make a large, specialised (and largely sunk) investment[15] in order to be in a position to perform under a contract. The cost of that investment will need to be recouped over a long time horizon in the context of a specific trade relationship with the other party to the contract. Following the making of such a specific investment, and in the absence of a long-term contract, the other party to the trade relationship may refuse to pay the initially agreed price or to meet other conditions upon which the investment was undertaken (e.g., the level of use or minimum purchase requirements). As noted above, this behaviour is known in the economics literature as asset-specific hold-up.

As an example, imagine that a port company is required to invest in specialised infrastructure in order to handle the goods of a specific exporter or importer. Following the port company making the specific and sunk investment (and in the absence of a long-term contract), the exporter/importer, knowing that the asset is specific, may refuse to pay the previously agreed price, insisting on a lower charge, applying a take-it-or-leave-it approach. As a consequence, the port owner would then need to incur additional transaction costs in pursuing litigation based on estoppel or in renegotiating the terms of use of the infrastructure.[16]

Where the investment involved is considerable and the asset specific,[17] a long-term contracting arrangement may be required ex ante in order for the investing party (i.e., the port company) to be certain to recoup the total cost of the investment over time, and therefore to commit to the investment. Were a shorter contract to be used, the opportunity for hold-up by the exporter/importer would again arise at the expiration of the initial contract. Provided that they are enforceable ex post, the use of long-term contracts (or vertical integration) limits this type of opportunism, spreading the risks associated with investment in specific assets, and promoting economic efficiency.

The above example demonstrates that there are various efficiency-enhancing reasons for parties to enter into long-term contracts. However, owing to their nature in restricting the freedom of parties to differing degrees, certain clauses in these contracts will, by necessity, restrict competition (Tonking 1998: 23). Long-term contracts can be potentially more problematic than short-term contracts under competition law because they restrict the economic freedom of the parties for significant periods. Tonking (1998: 15) states: 'it is the element of exclusivity over a term which raises substantive issues of competitive concern, not least because supply and demand may vary during the term of the contract, and may not be predictable'.

In addition to raising competition policy concerns, a longer term in a contract may also increase the incentives for a disadvantaged party to seek to set aside the contract ex post. These incentives are expected to increase with the length of term, as the magnitude of losses suffered from honouring the contract are larger (Evans and Quigley 2000: 89–90).

Evans and Quigley (2000) describe the detrimental effects associated with the ability of a contracted party to challenge the validity of a long-term contract under New Zealand's competition law, stating that such opportunistic behaviour results in an increase in the costs of signing long-term contracts, possibly resulting in parties being unwilling to sign efficient long-term contractual agreements. It may also result in a shortening of the length of contracts below that which is optimal (reducing the incentive for a party to challenge the contract under competition law), and possibly reduce the extent to which a party invests in information relating to the contract, resulting in less-efficient contracts which are more likely to be challenged. The overall consequence is likely to be a reduction in dynamic efficiency by reducing the level of certainty required for investment in specific assets, and a reduction in the overall gains from trade between erstwhile contracting parties.

Australian and New Zealand competition law can easily catch welfare-enhancing contracts, undermining the certainty associated with long-term contracting. In New Zealand challenges under competition law to the enforceability of contracts can come under two main sections of the competition legislation – the Commerce Act 1986. These are section 27 (anticompetitive agreements) and section 36 (misuse of unilateral market power), especially under effects tests[18] (Evans and Quigley 2000: 90–2; Carlton and Goddard 2002: 33–72). However, the authorisation provisions (Part V of the Commerce Act) are available to provide ex ante clearance of potentially anticompetitive long-term contracts provided they have offsetting benefits to the public. The problem is that in both Australia and New Zealand the authorisation provisions have at times come into play once contracts have been in existence for a considerable period, and then it is very hard to say ex post whether the length of the contract and restrictive (and potentially anticompetitive) clauses are justified/appropriate in terms of the public interest.

Two New Zealand cases provide illustrations of when the validity of long-term contracts has been challenged on anticompetitive grounds. The cases deal with two different types of long-term contracts: where specialised investment is required for a party to be in a position to perform the contract (in the case of gas field exploitation) and where long-term contracting facilitates access to essential infrastructure (in the case of telecommunications).

NEW ZEALAND EXAMPLES

The following cases concern the gas and telecommunications industries, where considerable investment in long-term production infrastructure is extremely important. In the Kapuni case, a long-term contract was entered into in order to allocate the risk involved in making considerable specialised infrastructure investment. In the case of Telecom/Clear, a long-term contract was entered into in order for a competitor to gain access to an essential infrastructure facility. In both cases, the validity of the long-term contract was challenged during the term of the contract.

Kapuni

The Kapuni gas case concerned the enforceability of a long-term (exclusive) requirements contract for the supply of gas. The exclusive supply contract was entered into in order for the parties to make specialised investment in gas production infrastructure before the supply contract came into effect. Under the contract the owner of the gas field agreed to supply all of the gas produced from the field to one party to the exclusion of all others. The court recognised the benefits from these types of long-term contracts:

> 'Output' and 'Requirements' contracts are recognized as having various benefits for new entrants to a market where large capital investments are required as well as existing participants in a market where economies of scale may result from such contracts ... However, the exclusive dealing characteristics of such arrangements may run foul of competition laws. (Tonking 1998: 19)

The validity of the contract was challenged by the owner of the gas field, under sections 27 and 36 of the Commerce Act, more than twenty years after the contract was entered into. The concerns related to the combined effect of two long-term contracts that tied up the entire supply from the only two significant gas fields in New Zealand to two related companies.

Specifically, the exclusive buyer at the Kapuni field, Kapuni Gas Contracts Ltd (KGCL), was wholly owned by a company that held a significant interest (33 per cent) in NGC, a company entitled to supply of residual oil from the Maui field.[19] The Kapuni agreements were entered into before the Maui agreements. The gas field owner claimed that the existence of the Kapuni long-term contract in combination with the Maui long-term contract was in breach of the Competition Act because it conferred market power upon NGC in the wholesale and retail reticulated gas markets, substantially lessening competition in these markets.

The court found that the combined effect of the Kapuni and Maui contracts was to substantially lessen competition in the reticulated gas market in breach of section 27 of the Commerce Act. In making its finding, the court stated:

> Here we have a long-term contract in a wholesale market, effectively totally foreclosed to competition, which has run for 29 years. We are asked by the

defendants to find that, because it concerns a dedicated field, we should not strike it down, even though it might run for another 20 years ...We do not believe that the exploration and efficiency arguments are sufficient to overcome the foreclosure of competition which arises from the [buyer's] unconstrained market power. (Tonking 1998: 19)

The New Zealand High Court did explicitly take into account the economic benefits of the long-term supply contract, in terms of its impact on 'exploration and efficiency', in assessing whether a breach had occurred, weighing it against the anticompetitive detriment. The court had accepted expert evidence to the effect that gas exploration would be adversely affected if long-term contracts could be held to be unenforceable ex post (Tonking 1998). Further, the court hypothesised that had it been asked at an earlier stage to authorise the contract that it may have done so. However, the court opted for a highly interventionist remedy, varying the Kapuni gas contract to release half of the total gas production of the field to a competing party.

Telecom New Zealand vs Clear

This case concerned a long-term contract entered into between the owner of the telecommunications network infrastructure in New Zealand, Telecom Corporation of New Zealand (Telecom), and a new entrant to the industry, Clear Telecommunications Ltd (Clear).[20]

Clear sought access to Telecom's network in order to compete with Telecom for the provision of certain telecommunications services. Following a long-running dispute between the parties about the terms on which Clear could have access to part of Telecom's network, an interconnection fee agreement was reached. Under the agreed pricing regime, Clear would pay no access fee to Telecom for use of the network but would pay a constant charge per minute for network usage. The usage charge would remain constant throughout the five-year term of the contract. Subsequent to entering into the contract, Telecom expanded its offering of a new off-peak charging regime for services to households, a service for which Clear was competing. The adoption of this regime made it difficult for Clear to match Telecom's prices for this service. Clear attempted to renegotiate the pricing terms with Telecom, which refused. Clear reacted by refusing to pay Telecom the agreed interconnection fee under the long-term contract and resorting to the Competition Act in seeking to have the contract overturned.[21]

In challenging the enforceability of the contract under competition law, Clear alleged that Telecom held a position of dominance in the market for interconnection services, and that its charges under the interconnection agreement had the effect of diminishing competition and were a breach of sections 27 and 36 of the Commerce Act.[22]

Telecom attempted to have the claims struck out on the grounds that the parties had contracted out of the Commerce Act in settling their interconnection disputes within a private contract. The High Court held that it was not possible to contract out of the Commerce Act, making it clear that private contracts cannot take precedence over the application of competition laws.[23]

By entering into an interconnection agreement with no connection fee and a fixed usage charge, Clear avoided the risk associated with obtaining a certain level of scale,[24] but accepted the risks associated with its inability to obtain volume discounts and to differentiate pricing between peak and off-peak calls. Clear exposed itself to the risk that Telecom might adopt a pricing strategy that made the volume-based interconnection fee disadvantageous, but it must be assumed that it did so having calculated the costs and benefits associated with different strategies in contract negotiation (Evans and Quigley 2000: 84).

One interpretation of Clear's strategy was that it accepted an interconnection contract that minimised its exposure to a lump-sum access payment on the assumption that it would be able to challenge the contract under competition law if competition in the market evolved in a way that made the contract disadvantageous. The fact that the entrant (Clear) has the option to appeal to competition law, but that the incumbent in the market does not, is an illustration of the asymmetric effects of competition law. These effects may have implications both for the price at which the incumbent is prepared to enter such contracts and for the efficiency of the contracting process more generally. This dispute thus illustrates the way in which competition law may undermine the enforceability and efficiency of contracting.

CONCLUSION – STRIKING THE APPROPRIATE BALANCE BETWEEN CONTRACT AND COMPETITION LAW

Given the need to strike some balance between certainty in contracting (through the proper enforcement of binding contracts) and the role of competition law (in striking down agreements that harm competition), there is a potential for conflict in terms of maximising social welfare. Since it is not open to contracting parties to opt out of the application of competition law, there is no obvious mechanism by which contracting parties can avoid the costs that result from uncertainty about the enforceability of contracts. Precedents in New Zealand mean that there is some degree of uncertainty for parties as to the ultimate enforceability of the contract going forward. As the case studies above suggest, New Zealand's competition law can easily catch welfare-enhancing contracts (Kapuni). In addition, parties to a contract may seek to use competition law in an opportunistic or strategic way once a contract is in place (Telecom/Clear).

It seems that the right balance between contract and competition law is yet to be reached. What is required is some means to increase the degree of certainty in the future enforcement of contracts, particularly long-term contracts where the contract has been entered into in order to provide assurances surrounding a specific investment. An ex ante clearance approach similar to that currently applied to mergers is one possible solution.[25] This process should not just be open to contracts that yield public benefits, as per the present authorisation procedures, but it should also apply to contracts where the benefits are largely private but the various clauses of the contract may be open to challenge on competition grounds.

Furthermore, with or without an ex ante clearance process, the courts should be very reluctant to set aside long-term contracts that have been in place for a considerable period. This is especially true where the basis for doing so rests on changed circumstances that were unforeseen at the time of the original contracting process or on the opportunistic behaviour of one of the parties to the contract. Such intervention imposes significant external costs on the economy, and is inconsistent with economic efficiency. Large investment projects often require enforceable contracts, and perceptions of enforceability are harmed when contracts are being overturned or struck down. Such decisions undermine contract law and put investment and efficiency at risk.

The implications of this analysis for developing countries is that their first priority should be to promote mechanisms that will reduce uncertainty about the enforceability of contracts. In Western societies mechanisms that were important in promoting contractual enforcement in the past would be illegal under modern competition law. This suggests, equally, that a balance between the evolution of Western-style competition law and a tolerance of traditional institutions that may promote contractual enforcement will be part of an efficient reform path for developing economies. Competition law should have a lower priority, both because of the ambiguous welfare implications of aspects of competition law and because of its intolerance of institutions that reduce competition in some dimensions but have a net positive impact on economic welfare because they promote the enforceability of contracts.

NOTES

1. On this issue, see Evans and Quigley (2000: 79–94).
2. Section 89 of New Zealand's Commerce Act deals with the issue of severance providing that 'the fact that a contract contains a provision which was entered into in breach of section 27, or giving effect to which would breach section 27, does not affect the enforceability of any other provision of the contract'. As noted by Evans and Quigley (2000: 86–7), it may be inefficient to set aside only part of the bundle of obligations agreed to under a contract.
3. This section relies heavily on Anderson and Young (2002).
4. Under the 'doctrine of penalties', courts generally find that parties may be compensated *restitutio in integrum* for non-performance of a contract but that penalties need not be paid. For a discussion of the doctrine and its policy underpinnings, see Lanyon (1996). The doctrine is not economically justifiable because it reduces the set of feasible contracts. This point and the application of the doctrine to multilateral contracts are discussed in Arnold (2001: 611–43).
5. Anderson and Young (2002) derive a condition that ensures this outcome. The condition relates to the costs and benefits of trade and to the elasticities relating to traders and price margins. They argue that the condition is quite general and admits the possibility that it is in the interest of the social elite and may be driven by the demand for trade with foreigners.
6. These included guilds and coalitions of merchants. For an analysis of contract enforcement by reputation in those times, see Grief et al. (1994: 745–76).

7 The finding by Classens et al. (2000) of strong negative correlations between the shareholdings of the fifteen largest families and indices of judicial efficiency and the rule of law in modern East Asian countries suggests that this is a serious problem.
8 Anderson and Young (2002) argue that this was the modus operandi of the East India Companies of Britain and the Netherlands. Tracy (1991) reports that they frequently sought exclusive trading agreements with local princes who held some military power. Anderson and Young also argue that bilateral arrangements reduced search costs.
9 Grief et al. (1994) also argue that medieval rulers in Europe may have encouraged coalitions of foreign merchants to credibly secure their trading rights.
10 A principal–agent relationship is one where one entity (the agent) acts on behalf of another (the principal). If the incentives of the agent are not (perfectly) aligned with those of the principal, and if the principal cannot perfectly monitor the agent, the opportunity arises for the agent to behave in a manner that may be counter to the principal's interests. This behaviour is described in the economics literature as moral hazard.
11 The seminal work in this area is Coase (1937). More recently, see for example, Perry (1989) and Tirole (1988).
12 This form of principal–agent problem is well treated in Holmstrom and Roberts (1998: 73–94). See also Goddard (1997: 423–58).
13 The Aghion and Bolton (1987) model is predicated on the incumbent monopolist not having perfect information regarding the efficiency of potential entrants; consequently, the level of damages may not be set high enough to prevent entry. Still, if entry does occur, the contract enables the incumbent to extract (all or part of) the surplus of any entrant that does come in. In order to 'bribe' retailers to sign up, the incumbent will need to share some of the gains with them.
14 A formal treatment of the ambiguous welfare implications arising from the phenomenon of exclusive dealing has recently been provided by Bernheim and Whinston (1998: 64–103). They conclude that even where the use of exclusive dealing contracts is anticompetitive, a ban on exclusive dealing practices may have negative welfare consequences because it may encourage more inefficient forms of exclusion that are less explicit.
15 The term specialised investment refers here to when there is not otherwise a market for the goods or services that are the subject of the contract, and where the investment is sunk, in terms of being largely unrecoverable.
16 Estoppel is a legal principle that applies in contract law to prevent a party from denying that a contract actually exists, even where, according to the rules of contract, one does not technically exist. A party will be stopped from denying that a contract exists where they have made statements/representations as to the fact that a contract does or will exist and, as a result, induced the other party to change their position (e.g., make a significant investment in specific infrastructure) on the faith of that representation.
17 According to Williamson (1983: 519–40), there are four types of asset specificity: site, physical asset, human asset and dedicated asset specificity.
18 For example, section 27(2) of the Commerce Act essentially prohibits contracts that substantially lessen competition or may have the effect of substantially lessening competition.
19 Fletcher Challenge Ltd owned 33 per cent of the shares of NGC and wholly owned KGCL. KGCL had an agreement to on-sell the gas from the Kapuni field to various petrochemical companies and to NGC, which was entitled to all gas that was not consumed by the petrochemical companies. The gas produced at

the Maui field was dedicated under a long-term contract to three parties, one of which was NGC.
20 This is a high-level summary based on the review of the case in Evans and Quigley (2000).
21 As Dammery (1999: 246–57) states, 'the courts in New Zealand have taken the view that pending a decision on the substantive question of legality under the Commerce Act, a contract provision that is plausibly claimed to be in breach of the Act, even by a party to the contract, cannot be enforced' (cited in Evans and Quigley 2000: 79). This may increase the incentives of a party to a contract to challenge its validity under competition law, especially in the cases concerning withholding of payments under a contract.
22 Telecom New Zealand Limited vs Clear Communications Limited (Court of Appeal, CA 206/97, 9 December 1997, unreported).
23 High Court, CL 20/97, 18 July 1997, unreported.
24 A more detailed analysis of the risks under different classes of two-part tariff interconnection agreements is given in Evans and Quigley (2000: 84–6).
25 On the elements of such an ex ante approach, see Tonking (1998: 27–30); and Evans and Quigley (2000: 92–3).

REFERENCES

Aghion, P. and P. Bolton (1987) 'Contracts as a barrier to entry', *American Economic Review* 77.

Anderson, James E. and Douglas Marcouiller (2002) 'Trade, insecurity and home bias: an empirical investigation', *Review of Economics and Statistics* 84(2).

Anderson, James E. and Leslie Young (2000) 'Trade implies law: the power of the weak', NBER Working Paper 7702, Cambridge: National Bureau of Economic Research.

—— (2002) 'Imperfect contract enforcement', NBER Working Paper 8847, Cambridge: National Bureau of Economic Research.

Arnold, Terence (2001) 'Governance in the New Zealand electricity market: a law and economics perspective on enforcing obligations in a market based on a multi-lateral contract', *The Antitrust Bulletin* 3: 611–43.

Bernheim, D.B. and M.D. Whinston (1998) 'Exclusive dealing', *Journal of Political Economy* 106: 64–103.

Carlton, D. and D. Goddard (2002) 'Contracts that lessen competition – what is section 27 for, and how has it been used?', in Mark N. Berry and Lewis T. Evans *Competition Law at the Turn of the Century – A New Zealand Perspective*, Wellington: Victoria University Press.

Classens, Stijn, Simeon Djankov and Larry H.P. Lang (2000) 'East Asian corporations heroes or villains?', World Bank Discussion Paper 409, referred to in James E. Anderson and Leslie Young (2002) 'Imperfect contract enforcement', NBER Working Paper 8847, Cambridge: National Bureau of Economic Research.

Coase, R.H. (1937) 'The nature of the firm', *Economica* 4: 386–495.

Dammery, R. (1999) 'Section 46 of the Trade Practices Act: the need for prospective certainty', *Competition and Consumer Law Journal* 6: 246–57.

Evans, L.T. and N.C. Quigley (2000) 'Contracting, incentives for breach, and the impact of competition law', *World Competition* 23: 79–94.

Goddard, D. (1997) 'Long-term contracts: a law and economics perspective', *New Zealand Law Review* IV.

Goolsbee, Austan (2000) 'The value of broad band and the deadweight loss of taxing new technology', University of Chicago Graduate School of Business Working Paper, Chicago: University of Chicago.

Grief, Avner, Paul Milgrom and Barry Weingast (1994) 'Coordination, commitment and enforcement: the case of the merchant guild', *Journal of Political Economy* 102(4): 745–76.
Holmstrom, B. and J. Roberts (1998) 'The boundaries of the firm revisited', *Journal of Economic Perspectives* 12: 73–94.
Lanyon, Elizabeth V. (1996) 'Equity and the doctrine of penalties', *Journal of Contract Law* 9(3): 234–58.
Mathewson, F. and R. Winter (1997) 'Tying as a response to demand uncertainty', *RAND Journal of Economics* 28: 566–83.
Perry, M.K. (1989) 'Vertical integration: determinants and effects', in R. Schmalensee and R.D. Willig (eds) *Handbook of Industrial Organization, Volume I*, The Netherlands: Elsevier Science Publishers.
Tirole, J. (1988) *The Theory of Industrial Organization*, Cambridge: MIT Press.
Tonking, A.I. (1998), 'Long-term contracts: when are they anticompetitive?', *Competition and Consumer Law Journal* 6.
Tracy, James D. (1991) 'Introduction', in James D. Tracy (ed.) *The Political Economy of Merchant Empires*, Cambridge: Cambridge University Press.
Trebilcock, M.J. (1986) *The Common Law of Restraint of Trade: A Legal and Economic Analysis*, Toronto: Carswell Company.
Williamson, O. (1983) 'Credible commitments: using hostages to support exchange', *American Economic Review* 73: 519–40.

11 Regional cooperation in competition policy

David K. Round

INTRODUCTION

Until two or three decades ago, competition and consumer protection policies were the preserve of major developed economies like the United States, the United Kingdom and some European countries. Now competition issues are on the top of many an international agenda as globalisation spreads and as the operations of the World Trade Organisation (WTO), the World Bank, the Asia Pacific Economic Cooperation (APEC) forum and other organisations have brought about a realisation that regulatory reform – and in many economies the creation for the first time of regulatory instruments for competition and consumer protection – is an imperative.[1]

Most of the economies of East Asia have been slow to adopt an uncompromising policy stance in favour of competition and consumer protection, despite increasingly embracing market forces as the ultimate regulator of economic activity. Comprehensive laws do exist in some economies, but mostly these are very recent, as in Malaysia and Indonesia, for example, or they have been used with limited effect, as in Korea. If any effective controls have been put into place, they are more likely to have been of a specific and targeted nature. Yet sector-specific regulation is subject to many problems – capture, bureaucratic failure, or inconsistent treatment of similar firms or practices or industries. The best long-run solution will always be to promote competition in order to achieve efficient market outcomes.

A culture for competition and consumer protection, and for the innovation, efficiency and choice that accompany the competitive process, has been lacking in many economies. Not all stakeholders in the competitive process have been treated equally by governments. Consumers, in particular, have been relatively ignored and business organisations have been accommodated through soft intervention designed to reduce market failure. Yet consumers, and fair and efficient businesses, stand to reap significant welfare gains if markets are committed to competition, either willingly or internally by government policies, or externally by competitive pressures transmitted through globalising firms and crumbling trade barriers.

For the East Asian region there are four possible approaches to competition and consumer protection:

- laissez-faire, with market forces left untouched by government intervention;
- independent action by each nation, following its own privately optimal path (in terms of content, targets and speed of implementation);
- a harmonised approach, where each economy takes account of events in neighbouring economies, and through consensus follows a relatively common path on as many issues as possible, including policy development, content, legislation, administration, education, enforcement and review;
- while keeping an eye on markets for non-traded goods and services, work with the forces of globalisation to import into each economy the attitudes and strategies associated with firms that have operated in developed economies with long traditions of competition and consumer protection policies.

The third strategy is likely to be the best long-run approach for the region, as the pursuit of a unified, but not necessarily unitary, policy and enforcement stance will provide not only the flexibility to handle specific problems in each economy, but also will promote a convergence to a set of broadly agreed goals, standards, prohibitions and methods that will provide a transparent regulatory framework, as well as incentives for businesses and consumers to get the most out of market processes, thus enhancing private and social welfare.

The realisation is slowly growing in East Asia that competition and consumers must reign. But old habits die hard. The path to more competitive markets will be strewn with obstacles and challenges. The faster these problems are overcome, the quicker will society eliminate the deadweight losses of anticompetitive behaviour. And if, in the process, the forces of globalisation can be enjoined to tackle simultaneously but from different directions the problems leading to these losses, East Asian markets will be able to deliver higher levels of performance for the net benefit of all stakeholders – consumers, small firms, large firms, bureaucrats and governments.

This chapter looks at how national and regional cultures for competition can be developed. There are strong policy arguments in favour of the regional harmonisation of competition and consumer protection initiatives and enforcement philosophies. There are also several barriers that stand in the way of such regional harmonisation. The chapter considers how regional cooperation might be put into effect, and assesses how globalising companies might provide an added impetus to national and regional efforts to enhance domestic competitive mechanisms. It suggests that the time is ripe for a leader – a particular government, or an individual, or a group – to take on the mantle of developing a truly regional approach to the promotion of competition and consumer protection.

DEVELOPING NATIONAL AND REGIONAL CULTURES FOR COMPETITION

The current attitude to competition

There are many stakeholders in the competitive process, of which the regulatory environment is an essential component. The positive theory of regulation treats the quantity and type of regulation provided as a political and bureaucratic response (the supply) to the narrow interests of pressure groups (the demand from businesses and consumers). Those who can best organise, or organise more cheaply, or who have the greatest private incentive to do so, will benefit. In East Asia, as elsewhere, this is usually the business community, which gains at the expense of consumers.

The business sector in most developing economies is not especially noted for displaying strong pro-consumer sentiments. Buyers lack knowledge, misinformation abounds, search costs are high, and generally there exists a gross imbalance of bargaining power, often assisted by the traditional methods of doing business, and a reluctance by buyers to lose face by complaining if a deal turns out to be against their interests. Individual economies may have a good reputation for being internationally competitive, but this can mask a notable lack of competition in domestic markets. For example, Chen and Lin (2002) have argued, with respect to Hong Kong:

> Laissez faire has been treated with great respect, and market forces have been regarded as the best way of allocating resources ... It is also generally believed that the Hong Kong economy is highly competitive. While Hong Kong is truly competitive in international markets in terms of exports and the ability to attract foreign investment, this competitiveness does not mean, nor does it ensure, that competition exists among firms in domestic markets. In service sectors where import substitution is not applicable, monopolistic markets can still exist in open economies ... There was, in fact, never a level-playing field in many of the non-tradable sectors in Hong Kong ... For a long time, the Hong Kong government never considered the lack of competition in some sectors to be a problem. It was believed that monopolists had important purposes to serve. The public has various misconceptions about the role of antitrust ... in particular, tending to confuse free competition (laissez faire) with fair or perfect competition, and international competitiveness with competition among domestic firms. Both the government and the public believe that antitrust is necessarily a government interventionist policy resulting in distortion of the functions of a free market system. Thus, it is not surprising that it has been difficult to develop a competition law under Hong Kong's laissez-faireism policy. (Chen and Lin 2002: 145–6)

Experience in other East Asian economies also shows how difficult it is to promote competition, even when competition laws are passed. Political, legal, economic and institutional factors have all conspired to retard the evolution of a culture for competition. Business interest groups have resisted strongly any attacks on their monopoly rents, power and position in society. A more proactive lead is needed from governments in individual economies as well as at the regional level. Comprehensive laws to promote competition are needed, as is a commitment to fearless regulatory pursuit of these goals. The effective privatisation of state-owned enterprises must be put high on the agenda. Entry barriers to markets must be tackled and lowered. Consumers must be educated to demand competitive market outcomes. Jurisprudence must be built up.

A culture for competition

The culture for competition being advocated in this chapter is a behavioural, not a structural, one. Rivalrous, non-coercive, non-collusive attitudes and conduct are what make a market perform well. Market structure, measured by the market shares of firms and concentration ratios, is not necessarily a good indicator of performance. Entry barriers are far more determinative of market outcomes, but these too are much better analysed in terms of strategic entry-deterring phenomena. Structural barriers to entry are usually either exogenously determined beyond the control of the market, or are the result of government decisions as in the case of exclusive licences to operate. Size per se may not be a bad thing for competition, at least for small firms seeking to make acquisitions in order to become more efficient, although the large size of existing firms in developing economies may be of concern if they are inefficient and have become used to dominating their markets, and if they regard themselves as national champions that should not be hindered by procompetitive rules.

In a laboratory, a culture can be easily grown in a dish. Its whole environment can be controlled to get the desired result. It is much harder to grow a culture for competition. Many factors impinge on this culture, which unfortunately cannot be controlled under laboratory conditions. In particular, the stock of entrenched market power and its links to governments provide the hostile environment on to which the culture for competition must be grafted. Just as the treatment of severe burns to the body might necessitate several lengthy and painful skin grafts, any attempt to attach the spirit of competitive rivalry on to the cultural, social and political corpus of long-standing market power will not achieve an instant fix. The process must be an iterative one, proceeding slowly after each fresh initiative and waiting for it to develop effectively before moving on to the next treatment. Done properly, multiple skin grafts can leave little evidence of scarring. So too with developing a culture for competition and consumer protection – in the long run the damage will have been repaired, the trauma of the process will fade, and market health will be restored.

There can be no quick fix, given the entrenched pro-business attitudes. The damages caused by a lack of competition in the past are forever sunk, and are accumulating rapidly. But future losses can be forestalled if the conditions for competition are carefully nurtured. It means a break with tradition, but the gains from competition are a non-zero-sum game. Markets will work more efficiently. Consumers will be better off. Firms that are prepared to engage in good, hard, but fair rivalry will prosper.

Competition policy brings about concentrated perceived losses to a narrow section of business interests (but only for some, as the competitive process can be used to good effect by efficient, innovative firms). In terms of developing a culture for competition and consumer protection, the winners (buyers) will usually be poorly organised and widely dispersed politically, geographically and economically. Consumer support will suffer from free-rider problems and dispersed focus, as well as a lack of knowledge on how and where to argue for the cause. Consumers need to be educated to be insistent in their demands for a competitive culture by firms, governments, bureaucrats and the enforcers to become widespread in society. The losers – those who previously enjoyed the ripe fruits of market power, either directly or indirectly – will typically be concentrated and focused in their opposition to the new policy, and able easily to fund their discontent and influence the degree to which the policy is implemented.

Buyers' and sellers' attitudes to competition will thus initially be diametrically opposed, but over time they should begin to converge, as in the principle of minimum differentiation. Buyers will gain knowledge and confidence and some sellers will see the strategic advantages of acting in a competitive manner. This convergence of interests, values and cultures can be a slow and painful process within any one economy. At the regional level, the process of developing a joint competitive culture becomes even more difficult. Not only does it have to contend with within-economy heterogeneity, but it must also face the even greater difficulties of overcoming between-economy differences in history, culture, attitudes, goals, expectations, infrastructures, acceptable remedies and political structures. But a regional culture of cooperating on trade issues has been developed, albeit over time, and in principle there is no reason why the same result cannot be achieved (hopefully, though, faster) on issues relating to competition and consumer protection.

Regional convergence between governments on competition and consumer protection policies could be much harder to achieve, at least in the detail, than domestic acceptance of the need for these policies. But the detail will come with experience. Commitment to principles is needed first. The Pacific Economic Cooperation Council (PECC) principles published in 1999, since picked up by APEC in its Principles to Enhance Competition and Regulatory Reform, provide the basic foundation on which to build lasting commitments to competitive principles and markets. As the APEC economic leaders declared, 'These principles provide a core part of the framework for strengthening our markets which will better integrate individual and collective actions by APEC economies' (APEC 1999).

There should be no disagreement that markets work best in the long run when competitive principles govern the outcomes. If broad agreement could be established by even just two or three economies at the regional level, this could induce other governments to pursue domestic competition policies, if only because domestic firms not used to competitive pressures may find it much harder to compete in regional markets where competition policies have been effective and where buyers are better informed and more demanding that their requirements be met by firms, whether domestic or foreign.

WINNERS AND LOSERS

In any process of change there will always be winners and losers. There will be significant adjustment, search and learning costs associated with developing the culture, and many problems will be encountered. Producers believe that market forces should prevail and thus will feel betrayed, and the political consequences might be that their traditional close links with ruling parties could be damaged. The close association between businesses and governments has made it difficult for consumers to achieve legislative support designed to protect them from misuses of market power, fraudulent and misleading behaviour by sellers, and unconscionable conduct generally. There exists widespread concern that small and medium-sized businesses could be unduly hindered by procompetition legislation, especially if it has a strong focus on consumer protection. A new culture must be developed.

Economic agents will need to be more flexible and adaptable than before, and to learn how to cooperate with others in a much wider operating and institutional environment. Mistakes will be made. Learning by doing will be necessary for firms when working under new institutional conditions, and buyers will need to acquaint themselves with problems of information gathering and evaluation, and the associated costs, as well as with making optimal choices under uncertainty. Tensions will inevitably arise in sorting out the appropriate trade-offs to be offered while still retaining domestic political, economic and social harmony.

But these costs, albeit initially appearing large, will ultimately translate into a much greater final amount if the misuse of market power is tolerated for a longer period of time. The deadweight losses of monopoly are sunk. Short-term adjustment costs may be high, but long-term social gains could easily outweigh them. The quicker is the competition policy and enforcement response, the faster will these future deadweight losses be eliminated. And if, in the process, the forces of globalisation can be enjoined to tackle simultaneously, but through different directions, the problems leading to these losses, East Asian markets could deliver higher levels of performance for the net benefit of all stakeholders, and especially consumers, in the regional economy.

The benefits from embracing a competitive culture are likely to be so high that the winners could in theory compensate the losers (this is an equity argument rather than an efficiency one, as by definition consumers will gain and only socially inefficient firms will suffer in the process) and there would still be a credit balance left at the end of the accounting process. In practice, of course, such a process does not happen, as there is no simple mechanism to achieve this redistribution.

When a developing economy initiates a competition policy, state-owned enterprises and their employees may find it difficult to cope with the new expectations that they will now face, particularly the efficiencies and responsiveness to the forces of supply and demand that are required to succeed in a competitive market. If this new institutional framework is accompanied by privatisation, the difficulties will be compounded.

Bureaucrats will be more accountable under a competitive culture, which must be accompanied by transparency and objectivity in the administration and enforcement of the laws. What they propose, and act on, will be a matter for the public record. If enforcement is through legal processes, judges will need not to feel pressured to rule in favour of those clinging to their market power. If enforcement is through administrative review, a balanced and commercially and politically unaligned tribunal is needed. Provision must be made, under either system, for independent review of first-instance decisions. Such processes are expensive to operate.

Similar comments apply to politicians and ministers – those who make, refine and respond to the law and its operation in the market place. Politicians have traditionally feared that laws to promote competition and consumer protection will damage their political support and harm the health of the economy. A culture for competition may eliminate traditional power bases; it may conflict with other ministerial interests or responsibilities; it may demand that new alliances are formed and new sympathies are developed. When consumers start to experience the benefits that the competitive process can deliver to them, however, they are likely to create a groundswell of support for those who delivered them these gains. Through a 'bottom up' process of change (where grassroots activism either forces a change in behaviour by firms or becomes a populist avalanche that cannot be ignored by a government), activism by consumers will likely gather pace as their education, information, experience and affluence expand in an increasingly democratic, competitive and technologically and socially progressive environment.

The intersection of trade and competition law

The gains from trade liberalisation are well known. They include more opportunities for businesses as a wider range of markets becomes available; a consequently greater level of productive efficiency and ensuing benefits for consumers; and ultimately, as domestic firms are forced to adjust to foreign competition, greater allocative efficiency both within and between economies as resources shift to their optimal usage patterns. These gains, however, are not free of adjustment problems and they are not symmetrical in their occurrence. While it is accepted that tariff and non-tariff barriers to trade decrease social welfare, and great strides are being taken to eliminate them, trade liberalisation means little to consumers if it is circumvented by within-economy agreements or by unchecked unilateral misuses of market power.

Trade and competition law can exist independently, but they will work much better if they operate together. Trade liberalisation can bring in new sources of competition, but its benefits must not be dissipated through a denial of domestic competitive freedoms. If governments try to protect national champions or their major supporters, or pursue strategic trade policies, attempts to build a favourable trading environment for the competition agencies of different economies to work in, or aspire to, will likely founder, or at the very least will take a long time to come to fruition. If trade liberalisation fails to make domestic markets more competitive, then competition policy should be brought to bear. But the latter should not be seen only as an adjunct or ex-post supplement to the former. It can be effective regardless of the degree of trade liberalisation. It must be recognised, however, that tension is always likely to exist between trade and competition issues and policies.

Epstein (2002) has pointed out that a major difference exists between competition and trade laws – they are two parallel universes. He argues that competition laws seek to regulate *private* actions that harm consumer welfare, and are 'largely based on domestic legal principles, intended to maximise economic efficiencies, and enforced by judicial branches of government not ensconced in the ever-revolving nuances, standards, and diplomacy of international trade issues aimed at market access' (Epstein 2002: 345). Competition laws are enforced in a largely adversarial context and usually result in a winner-take-all outcome. In contrast, trade laws seek to correct *public* actions that seek to protect domestic firms from foreign rivals, thereby opening markets up to outsiders. Trade laws have international foundations and are enforced through international organisations as a result of negotiated solutions, diplomacy and ongoing working relationships and review.[2]

A SHARED REGIONAL PHILOSOPHY ON COMPETITION POLICY AND ITS ENFORCEMENT

Competition law does not have to be an end in itself. Rather, it is part of a broad social contract that governments should negotiate with all stakeholders in the political, social and economic arenas. Just as it carries the burden of providing a kind of domestic 'superglue' to hold market processes together, the role it can play in increasing efficiency in regional markets has frequently been overlooked.

The adoption of domestic competition laws is a necessary but not sufficient step for developing economies that wish to protect themselves from domestic and international abuses of market power. A concerted, consistent and cooperative approach to competition and consumer protection is needed in and between all East Asian economies. A regional consensus would yield great long-term net social gains, where the only losers would be those seeking to deprive consumers of their natural rights to a fair deal, a competitive price, safety and the right to choose based on good information.

The origin of the word compete is the Latin word *competere*, in its early interpretation meaning to come together or strive together, only later meaning to contend for in a rivalrous manner. The suggestion here is that the nations (but not the firms) of East Asia should compete in the original sense of the word – to come together and strive jointly to develop a culture and practice of competition and consumer protection. As interdependence increases with trade, and national commercial borders become blurred, such cooperation would be a vast improvement on the melange of national laws that are now developing, and whose enforcement is yet to show any truly consistent pattern, either within or between economies. Agreement would be needed on many issues – the type and specific focus of the legislation; the detail and coverage of the laws as far as their proscriptive and prescriptive elements are concerned; the quantum and method of enforcement; the desirability of policy convergence; the need to minimise sectoral exemptions and generally to avoid government-induced problems; and how best to operationalise the commitment to competition.

The pursuit of a cooperative regional policy and enforcement stance requires the flexibility to handle economy-specific problems, and should promote a convergence to a broadly agreed set of goals, standards, prohibitions and methods that will provide a transparent regulatory framework and incentives for businesses and consumers to get the most out of market processes, thus enhancing private and social welfare. A harmonised approach would involve each economy taking account of what is happening in its neighbouring economies, and through consensus following a common path on as many issues as possible, including policy development, legislation, administration, education, enforcement, penalties and review. The keywords should be communication and convergence to a regional approach – a unified but not necessarily a unitary approach to the problem. The achievement of cross-economy standards is certainly possible, as will be discussed later. If governments fail to follow this joint path, they may find the increasing pressures of globalisation will overtake them and produce a converging market-based international outcome.

However, competition laws within economies will always reflect the underlying political, economic, legal and philosophical attitudes, history and cultures of those responsible for their creation, revision and enforcement. Just as each economy differs significantly from its neighbours, so too do beliefs in the efficacy of the competitive process and the degree to which it needs to be promoted or regulated, as well as on whose interests should be protected by the competitive process – consumers or firms (especially small firms),[3] and on the most appropriate policy instruments. Grappling with competition issues presents a major challenge for most East Asian economies. It is unreasonable to expect immediate or complete harmony in the fledgling competition and consumer protection laws of the developing economies of East Asia. But, unless these views and goals are co-coordinated, or balanced, or in some way distilled down into a reasonably unified set of parameters, then effective regional cooperation on competition and consumer protection will be highly unlikely.

Regional cooperation can be seen as a response to the demands coming from multiple global forces and growing interdependencies. Member economies can pool their strengths, build capacity, share their experiences and more effectively plan group welfare-enhancing policies. Through rationalisation, states can reap the benefits of free trade, and at the same time keep regional control over the whole process through cooperation and the coordination of decisions. Regional integration could begin with non-controversial issues and then grow into the more complex process of building policies, and then institutions. Substantial agreements on trade liberalisation have been reached internationally in the past few years, albeit after many years of work and false starts. The same thing will happen with competition and consumer protection legislation and enforcement. There may well be no current best-practice solution, but one should emerge with shared visions and experience over time.

Flexibility is clearly called for in the interpretation and implementation of any shared philosophy. But this is further down the track. What is needed first is the development and sharing of a common regional philosophy on the importance of putting in place at an early stage a broad-based, systematic approach to competition and consumer protection policies. A commitment to principles is needed. Too late a realisation and acceptance of this imperative will result in the hardening of existing attitudes that do not favour consumers, causing irretrievable damage and making future corrections more difficult to initiate.

BARRIERS TO REGIONAL HARMONISATION

Developing a regional consensus

Developing a regional consensus on competition and consumer protection is a bit like bringing a child into the world and then guiding its development. The first steps are baby steps, and then the child becomes mobile with a training aide or walker. There are falls along the way. The child learns by doing. It adjusts to its environment. Parents give advice and a helping hand. It is a costly process, bringing up a child. It will be no different bringing to fruition a responsible and mature regional competition policy. Unification will be difficult to achieve in goals, legislation and enforcement.

Cooperation is the keyword. A prerequisite for that is flexibility, and some degree of shared vision as to the goals. There has to be an entry fee to join this club. That price is a willingness to look beyond national boundaries for the good of all parties in the region (a club, after all, exists to enhance the welfare of all its members) and, as in any club, there has to be a minimum requirement for membership, which here is the acceptance of a commitment to some shared basic philosophy as to aims, undesirable conduct that needs to be eliminated, enforcement, penalties and review.

No economy should be forced to join the club, or be subject to its rules if they elect to keep their own company or that of another club, and all should be able to join on the same terms – to have competitive parity or an equality of opportunity to influence the debate. The club could too easily become the preserve of the incumbent elite if membership dues are set too high. But reciprocal rights should be negotiated with other clubs, to provide shelter and hospitality when away from home. Thus other economies should stand willing to provide intellectual and advisory support, but only on request.

None of this can be achieved without cost. Governments face many urgent macroeconomic and distributional issues that lay claim to time, policy development and resources. The appropriate operational instrument must be chosen for each policy target. There will be significant opportunity costs for governments and bureaucrats of the time spent planning, cooperating, researching, educating, legislating and implementing competition and consumer protection laws. Firms will need to ensure they are aware of the likely changes and are ready to deal with them.

Rivalries between economies within the region will have to be put aside. Information must be shared, and trust will be needed that information provided by one government will not be taken advantage of by another for its own national benefit. Any attempt to harmonise competition laws for the regional good will only be as successful as the level of shared commitment to enforce them. Short of the establishment of a single regional regulator, itself not an easy task, this may be difficult to achieve. Annual independent reviews of actions taken by different economies (perhaps by a regulator from an adjoining region, or by a panel of experts from a variety of professional, business and regulatory backgrounds), and especially of actions not taken, and why, will be of the utmost importance in ensuring that a regional consensus is developing.

Loss of control

Should there be competition for competition laws? If it means a race to the bottom by passing laws with few real teeth, then this is a type of ruinous competition that ultimately benefits no one and promotes the law of the commercial jungle. This is not socially desirable. If, on the other hand, it means a race to the top, and the gaining of a private first-mover advantage in providing a sensible institutional and regulatory environment within which businesses can legitimately seek to develop a sustained commercial advantage simply by meeting consumers' needs better than their rivals, regional social welfare may be maximised. Multinational firms like carefully articulated policy regimes that are predictable.

Nevertheless, room should be left for some local controls, at least in the short run, to provide for political acceptance and accountability. No government will be keen to be seen by its electorate as conceding control to a regional rival, especially control over the local business sector. At the same time, a free-riding problem will exist. Some governments may either not be convinced of the need to pursue a common approach, and will adopt a 'wait and see' attitude, or they may deliberately let the running and cost be taken by another regime, in order to enjoy the positive externalities that might flow from the actions taken by the innovating government. Such strategic behaviour needs to be avoided, or at least be carefully monitored.

Nationalism and national champions

An important issue that needs to be considered in getting agreement between economies is how to treat state-owned enterprises, or those that were once owned by the state but have recently been corporatised or privatised. It can be difficult enough to control them in the domestic economy, even in a developed economy,[4] let alone in economies like China and Taiwan where state-owned enterprises have dominated for so long. Each economy will have its own unique set of difficulties in dealing with these enterprises in transition,[5] and it will be a major domestic issue to find the optimal way to guide them into working under a competitive environment, a process that will take much time and good judgement. Regional harmony on this process may be difficult to achieve for some time.

In developing economies industrial policy goals often will reign supreme, certainly over competitive considerations. The economic health of 'competitors' will usually be of greater policy concern than the competitive process and the welfare of consumers. While some would argue that competition policy should come only after industry policy has achieved the desired level of sustainable growth, and domestic businesses have grown strong enough to produce sustained national benefits, others might say that this is akin to shutting the gate after the horse has bolted. There is little doubt that a tough competitive environment in domestic markets breeds businesses that are well equipped to survive in regional or global markets.

Neither a national champion nor a state-owned enterprise would have much incentive to operate efficiently or to act in the interests of consumers unless it is exposed to competition, either from local or foreign rivals. Trade liberalisation certainly has a procompetitive impact, but does not advance competition in markets for non-traded goods and services. Apart perhaps for limited transition exemptions, there should be no exceptions to a vigorous competition policy regime for any economic entity.

THE PRACTICAL DETAILS OF REGIONAL COOPERATION

Policy development

The economies of East Asia are now slowly embracing competition policies from a variety of backgrounds – from socialist to laissez-faire. This indicates independent recognition that a prophylactic is needed to prevent the worst outcomes from happening to these transitional economies, which are simultaneously facing the pressures of liberalised trading conditions. But each one has a differing set of ideas on the meaning of competition. The chaebols of Korea, the numerous duopolies of Hong Kong, and the keiretsu of Japan, with their interlocking vertical links, would be looked at unkindly by US and possibly other antitrust regimes.

Given the problems that developed economies have experienced with the introduction of competition and consumer protection laws, it is not realistic to put forward a single model as a guide for East Asia. It may not be feasible to introduce at one time a complete package; or, even if one is feasible, the resources required to implement it may be so great that only a small part of it will be pursued through regular enforcement. The regulatory burden must be kept in mind. Education for the development of the culture for competition may be a better short-run investment, although some practices such as price fixing, for which there exists almost universal condemnation of its effects, could be outlawed immediately. It is hard to believe that any developing economy could find a justification not to act against such conduct. The culture change will need to be significant:

> The right culture has to be created; attitudes have to change; laws must be debated, refined and designed to be mutually compatible; legislators have to be committed to competition; the bureaucracy has to be supportive; enforcers have to be found; judicial or other appeal mechanisms must be put in place; sound precedents need to be created; and, above all, businesses must realize and accept that they are operating under a new regulatory regime. (Round 2002: 110)

Currently there is considerable use of cooperative arrangements with respect to competition issues in many regional trade agreements (RTAs) around the world, including both between and across developed and developing economies. But these RTAs differ considerably in the extent to which they seek to coordinate substantive competition rules. The degree of coordination largely varies with the level of integration underlying the agreements and with the role given to supranational institutions to enforce the rules for competition – compare the close harmonisation of the EU with more general obligations to take action against anticompetitive behaviour in the North American Free Trade Agreement (NAFTA). As well as RTAs, there are several other kinds of agreements or instruments that are used internationally to deal with competition law and policy issues: bilateral cooperative agreements; multilateral agreements; mutual legal assistance treaties; agreements for cooperation on economic regulation; and friendship and commerce treaties. Their usefulness for the promotion of competition in East Asia merits detailed consideration. Currently, however, external pressures like those coming from the WTO and RTAs are not producing a fast enough response.

The Doha Ministerial Declaration in 2001 gave a fresh impetus to the role of the WTO in promoting a multilateral framework for the promotion of competition (WTO 2001, paragraphs 23–25). The Working Group on the Interaction between Trade and Competition Policy has been asked to clarify core principles, including transparency, ways of voluntary cooperation, and support for competition agencies in developing economies through capacity building. Given the previous fragmented and less-than-centralised approach to competition issues in the past by the WTO, not surprising given that its consideration of the trade and competition interface is quite new, this is a welcome if belated development.[6] There also exist other institutional settings in which competition issues are being discussed internationally, including the World Bank, the United Nations, the Organisation for Economic Cooperation and Development (OECD), the United Nations Conference on Trade and Development (UNCTAD) and, of course, PECC and APEC.

That the task is not an easy one was clearly recognised by PECC in 1999 when it presented its carefully researched Competition Principles, which were based on the competitive process being a coherent vehicle for sustained development and economic growth, especially in the face of globalising markets, and which were designed to provide non-binding policy framework principles for individual economies, not rules or prescriptions. The idea was that competition principles might promote a 'convergence of intentions not necessarily policy conformity' (Vautier 1999). It saw competition as playing a 'unifying role' in policy development, but warned that education was needed, and that major issues would arise in relation to sequencing issues, implementation problems, and also with respect to capacity building.

PECC established four core non-binding principles as a unified framework to guide coherent policy development in individual economies – comprehensiveness, transparency, accountability and non-discrimination in order to ensure competitive neutrality – and several second-level principles to uphold these core principles, including the nature and extent of other regulations needed to pursue regulatory objectives, and cooperation in policy direction. It was recognised that different stages of development and differing positions on policy sequencing, as well as differing institutional capacity levels, meant that different economies needed flexibility in timing and implementation. PECC noted that the competition framework had to cover market distortions related to actions by the state. It recognised that the optimal progression would be an incremental one, in which a policy framework for competition developed gradually after taking account of the numerous complex issues involving all of the stakeholders in the competitive process. Transition problems were explicitly recognised. However, it warned that this flexibility should not be used as an excuse for opting out or for an unduly slow take-up of the principles. Three years later, however, it appears that the advocacy for competition and the implementation of the principles has yet to accelerate in many economies.

Nevertheless, the August 2001 Competition Law and Policy options put forward by APEC for voluntary inclusion in individual economy action plans spelt out a welcome series of goals for the development and implementation of competition laws and policies and their enforcement, all to be applied consistently with the APEC Principles to Enhance Competition and Regulatory Reform. Among them are to protect the competitive process; to establish autonomous and independent competition authorities; to ensure due process and rights to appeal; to develop the necessary regulatory and administrative procedures to ensure timely and efficient enforcement actions; to increase education about the importance of sustaining the competitive process; and to encourage enforcement authorities to cooperate internationally. These are compelling and necessary options. However, the road ahead will be long and tortuous while the necessary culture is developed and matured.

Now that the broad principles have been established by PECC and APEC, the debate must begin in earnest on what should be done. This goes to legislation in each economy; to national and regional enforcement methods and agencies; and to finding ways to ensure consistency in decisions both within and between economies. It is time now to move away from general guidelines and to develop specific comprehensive competition policies for individual economies in East Asia and for the region as a whole.

Legislation and the form and extent of agreement

Two different approaches for regional harmony could be taken. First, an agreement could be made to accept an obligation to control certain types of anticompetitive behaviour, by the creation of domestic legislation if necessary (as in the NAFTA agreement between the United States, Canada and Mexico). Second, an agreement could be made to coordinate legislation either entirely or on certain practices. If this type of agreement were to be pursued in East Asia, not only should there be similar legislation on the substantive provisions, but there should also be some commonality in terms of enforcement priorities and techniques.[7] Strict timelines should be set for achieving these objectives and for getting the system operational.

In the European Union, the freeing of trade between member countries has resulted in a supranational competition regime, and some EU trade agreements have been made with non-member countries, although in these the extent of coordination depends on the level of economic integration involved in the agreement. Broad-based prohibitions on certain types of anticompetitive conduct have been written into subregional agreements in Africa, in the form of the Treaty Establishing the Common Market for Eastern and Southern Africa (COMESA). COMESA is considering the development and implementation of a regional competition policy to harmonise those already existing or to introduce one where none previously existed, in the context of progressing to a full customs union.[8] Australia and New Zealand have shown with their Closer Economic Relations Trade Agreement (CERTA) that harmonisation is possible in competition laws, especially in the context of predatory behaviour. A company with a substantial degree of power within Australia or New Zealand, or both, must not take advantage of that power for one of three proscribed anticompetitive purposes. A misuse of market power in any market in the two countries can be attacked by the competition agency of either economy.

Consultation and cooperation mechanisms must be developed in East Asia. A distinction has to be made between two situations: where there will be consultation and cooperation between national competition agencies; and where provision is made for extraterritorial jurisdiction,[9] or a supranational authority, or where a supranational body or committee can issue enforcement orders that are then implemented by the competition authorities of member economies. A system presided over by a supranational authority does not preclude various degrees of cooperation between the individual national agencies dealing with competition issues.

At least an agreement should be reached that the economies will consult on the effectiveness of their individual competition laws, and will cooperate on enforcement by way of mutual legal assistance, the exchange of information and consultation in general. On a wider scale, APEC provides the model here, with member economies having ongoing exchanges of views on competition issues. In the non-binding APEC Principles to Enhance Competition and Regulatory Reform, members have committed to introduce or maintain effective and transparent competition legislation and improve enforcement by way of disseminating best-practice methods. They have also pledged to hasten the adoption of competition laws and regimes among members that do not currently embrace these goals, as well as other issues designed generally to promote competition and expedite deregulation. However, much remains to be done on these issues, as has already been noted.

Administration and enforcement

The question of who will adjudicate on competition issues under a regional approach is an important one. At first instance, there are three possibilities – bureaucratic, administrative or judicial. Many issues need detailed consideration. Of high importance is the national composition of whatever panel is established. Will each participating economy have a member? Or will membership rotate? What should be the length of appointment? On what grounds will the chair of the panel be appointed? How will this appointment be made? What special authority will the chair have? To what body will the panel report? Careful attention needs to be paid to the review/appeal stage of the investigation process. Is it to be entirely judicial? What are the grounds on which appeals can be heard? How can the attitudes brought by judges from different legal systems (for example, common law versus administrative law) be recognised and harmonised? Should judicial procedures be adversarial or inquisitorial? A complex web of issues needs to be resolved.

It must also be decided whether this body, or some other group, will be responsible for providing advice to governments on the operation of the harmonised laws, and for making suggestions for changes in the laws and their enforcement. Careful review procedures will be essential.

Elements of a cooperative regional culture – what is the bare minimum?

The prospect of easily securing regional agreement on what to include and how to manage enforcement consistently is not particularly promising at this stage. Initially a minimum set of competitive standards could be proclaimed for all member economies. While agreement on what should be included might not be immediately forthcoming, prime candidates would be price-fixing, output-restricting agreements, and price and non-price predatory behaviour. Anything beyond that may in the short run be difficult for the courts or regulatory agencies in some economies to deal with, either consistently or on a one-off basis, for reasons of history, economic tradition and social culture.

A major issue that would need early attention is how to treat state-owned enterprises or other entities with special or exclusive rights. Extensive discussion will be needed on how these bodies will be controlled. As an illustration, the free trade agreement between Colombia, Mexico and Venezuela requires state-owned enterprises to follow commercial considerations in their own markets and not to use their monopoly status in such a way as to harm firms in non-monopolised markets in other member states. But getting agreement on such issues will not be easy in economies where state-owned enterprises have traditionally been unchecked by competitive market forces.

But even broader agreements are necessary to set the proper foundation for a regional approach. Should the chief goal be efficiency – both allocative and production – or should it be fairness in the form of distributional equity? Given that developed countries with long histories of competition policy have not necessarily seen eye to eye on these goals (for example, the United States has generally stressed the former while the European attitude has been more in favour of the latter), it should not be expected that ready regional agreement on goals, especially those imported from other nations, will be forthcoming.

The idea of an international competition policy and a global 'super-regulator' for competition and consumer protection issues is not new.[10] But to many observers, it conjures up visions of Don Quixote's impossible dream or a frontier that shimmers weakly on the horizon. Besides, developing economies need the flexibility to be able to use a wide range of policies to enhance their development, unconstrained by the dictates of an externally imposed (either regional or international) competition regime.

Who should take the lead?

A focal point is essential for the planning of a regional competition policy, but care is needed to ensure that one economy does not take over the agenda to the exclusion of the needs of other economies or of the region as a whole. In the absence of a clear and regionally acceptable lead being provided by one nation, the prime external candidates would appear to be APEC, with its already-signalled commitment to competition, or a body within the WTO, which in 1996 formed the Working Group on Interaction between Trade and Competition Policy, although to date, owing to the less-than-overwhelming enthusiasm for the concept, it has not resolved how a multilateral framework on competition policy might be developed. It depends on whether the goal is a truly regional unitary competition policy, or whether instead it is more fruitful to pursue a consensual, harmonised, one-step-at-a-time sequence of initiatives that in the end may seek similar goals but through different procedures and frameworks.

The beginnings – sharing information

Good regulation – both efficient and fair, and that rewards innovation – provides firms with a predictable working environment and reduces sovereign risk.[11] Governments should therefore seek to produce such a model set of regulations. Rather than a race to the bottom, in the long run the first-mover advantage will reward the government that takes the initiative with the respect and therefore the investment of regionalising and globalising firms that are good corporate citizens. Like the cream rising to the top of the milk, such a government will stand out and will provide the model for other governments to follow.

Recognition of these factors should lead to similar attitudes being expressed, and policies developed, by economies with respect to competition and consumer protection. In theory a competitive race to the top could occur. Such attitudes have been slow to develop, however, in East Asia. Convergence is acknowledged as a desirable goal, but practical embracement of it has yet to occur in any serious way. Meanwhile different economies will pay attention, to differing degrees, to their own problems. The efficient level of (joint) regulation in the region is still a long way off.

But a start should be made. Information sharing between national regulators or bureaucrats is relatively inexpensive, and it saves duplication of information-gathering activities. It could start with bilateral exchanges and subsequently move on to multilateral or regional sharing. Once common problems are identified and recognised, the next step – a discussion of common treatment of the problem – will be much easier. But there will need to be agreement on whether particular phenomena should be regulated, and here there may exist considerable differences between economies. Reaching a regional consensus on any issue is rarely easy. Flexibility and sensitivity is needed in convergence. But just as the antitrust laws of Australia and the United States differ, for example, we should not expect complete harmony in the fledgling competition and consumer protection laws of the economies of East Asia.

Medium-term possibilities

Over time some regional specialisation in regulatory function could emerge – while there might be no single supranational regional regulator, cross-economy regulatory authority for some sectors or behaviours could be vested in a transnational institution. This could achieve real scope and scale economies in regulation, would ensure the optimal concentration and efficient use of information, and would provide consistency in investigation procedures and decision making. Where these bodies would be located should be a mutual decision based on comparative advantage, as well as the record on regulatory performance in the home economy, and a demonstrated sympathy to the problems of other economies.

The type of regulatory agency

Within a given economy, a choice has to be made between sector-specific regulators, or one regulator with extensive coverage. Unless a convincing case can be made for having single-sector regulators,[12] having just one regulator to cover all competition and consumer protection issues is usually preferable.[13] There exists less chance of regulatory capture, and a greater likelihood of consistency in treatment across all industries and types of conduct. And that architecture, by itself, along with a reputation for sensitive, sensible and efficient regulation, could give the economy a distinctive competitive advantage in attracting globalising firms to enter and to invest on a significant scale, and giving domestic firms a greater degree of regulatory certainty and efficiency.[14]

From a transnational perspective, there exists a trade-off between having one regulator, with the possibility that it will lack sufficient knowledge of each economy it oversees, and the more detailed and focused economy-specific knowledge of individual regulators. A further issue is whether it is optimal to have a series of sector-specific supranational regulators, such as in energy, transport, finance, telecommunications, and so on, or whether more could be achieved if each economy had in place sector-specific regulators, but with an eye being kept on regional cooperation or at least following a broadly similar method and philosophy to that of other economies in the region. The system with one separate regulator for each economy is perhaps less open to capture, and may lead to competition between agencies to be seen as the leader in the region, providing an example for other economies to follow.

Such a competitive race might offer better outcomes and provide for a greater diversity of perspectives on treatments, compared with having a single mega-regulator for a region, which over time could lead to a better concluded view as to the optimal way to control any particular type of conduct. Only then might a supranational regulator be considered. Certainly, there can be no doubt that the regulatory needs of different economies in East Asia vary enormously at this stage of their development.

The impact of globalisation

The advent of globalisation has forced economies to recognise that trade and competition issues are not only important but are inseparable. They are not substitute products, but rather are close complements. Globalisation can be regarded as one of the 'gales of creative destruction' first identified by J.A. Schumpeter (Schumpeter 1942). If there is one fundamental characteristic of globalisation, it is the competition for growth. It is the race to be the best that drives firms into new products, new markets, new technologies, new countries, out of their comfort zones and into new cultures, new political circumstances, and to face new rivals and new competitive pressures. Globalisation and competition are inseparable bedfellows in the international economy.

The insistent forces of globalisation can help enrich domestic competitive processes by bringing the seeds of change into economies with a complacent competitive culture. These forces should be used by East Asian governments to assist in promoting competition and consumer protection. Globalising firms are more than likely to have been operating under competitive regimes in their home markets. They have learnt how to compete, and so are likely to bring positive attitudes to competition with them, forcing rivals in the host economies to change their ways. Significant benefits will flow to consumers. However, it is essential that globalising firms do not act in ways that achieve their own private ends without at the same time creating positive spillovers for the economy in which they choose to operate.

Many firms now operate in dozens of economies, and are subject to the local rules that govern market behaviour. While economic problems are increasingly becoming transnational, economic regulation, especially with respect to competition and consumer protection, is still largely national. Local regulators will, in most cases, seek to control the firm in a vacuum – that is, without taking any account of the firm's activities in any other economy, either neighbouring or more distant. Firms may well follow a global strategy, in which the particular economy concerned may play only a small role. That global strategy may or may not seek to achieve goals that are in harmony with the host economy's social objectives. Thus the local regulatory mechanism will seek to intervene in order to achieve some local optimum, which may not accord with either the firm's local or international private optimum, or with the supranational social optimum. But in a very real sense no single economy can successfully regulate a truly multinational conglomerate. It exists beyond national and even regional regulatory oversight.

This may not be a bad thing. Chicago-leaning economists will argue that, in the absence of entry barriers and with the right information available, when firms make their privately optimal choices, market performance will be enhanced. Resources will flow to where their social return is greatest. Buyers and sellers will be better off. Government intervention will result in less-than-optimal outcomes. The dynamics of globalisation can best be harnessed with few regulations on the international flow and disposition of goods and services, either within or between economies. The heavy burden of complying with regulation is minimised, and regulatory errors do not have to be endured. Interjurisdictional competition between economies to host the operations of these firms with mobile employees and capital would force governments to offer the optimum regulatory environment.

To those opposed to these free market forces, the process just described would result in an unseemly and socially unrewarding 'race to the bottom', as governments seek to provide light-handed regulation designed to attract globalising firms that ignore consumer welfare. Effective regulation is an absolute necessity, therefore, especially in developing economies.[15] It should be welcomed by globalising businesses that espouse consumer interests and work through the competitive process.

The Asian crisis has been instrumental in alerting its developing economies to the desirability of regulating globalising firms through both trade and competition policies, and of encouraging local enterprises to ratchet their conduct up to globally competitive levels. One consequence is the growing realisation that markets are now increasingly self-regulated through the international competitive process rather than entirely through direct government intervention.[16] But the impact of globalisation will not be so all-embracing or unambiguously positive for social welfare as to negate the need for regulatory oversight. Market failure will always be present. And in the face of increasing globalisation, care needs to be taken to ensure that large globalising corporations do not play one host economy off against another by claiming that they cannot work with two or more different regulatory regimes (which is in itself a bluff, as by engaging in globalisation they have already committed to working with at least two – in their home economy and in the foreign economy in which they wish to operate).

CONCLUSION

It is early days yet for the development of a culture for competition in East Asia. Competition and consumer protection policies are still generally in the initial stages of being drawn up and implemented. There is little case history to evaluate in many economies. While the resource costs of delayed opportunities to create competitive markets are irretrievable, they are not forever sunk, as the benefits of competitive behaviour flow as soon as it is put into operation. The longer it takes, however, to put competition policies into place, the more entrenched become anticompetitive attitudes and the harder and more expensive it will be to force their reassessment.

For a very short period it may be justifiable to argue that no regulation is better than ill-conceived or hasty regulation, but that argument runs thin after a commitment to a competitive culture has been promulgated. Meanwhile, businesses that seek to subvert the competitive process and convert consumer surplus into producer surplus will benefit from delays in the introduction of legislation and enforcement. Such enterprises understandably prefer to operate untrammelled by local regulators, or by a cohesive regional agenda designed to protect consumer welfare.

The experience of history tells us that market failure is too endemic and pervasive to be safely ignored. Disease spreads unless checked. Preventative medicine is more effective and certainly cheaper in the long run than post-event treatment of disease outbreaks. Anticompetitive behaviour and the misuse of market power are no different. A healthy procompetitive attitude is essential. Immunisation is a good social investment. Remedial procedures must be available to correct problems.

If cooperation is to occur, it is better if it starts before too many economies begin to set in concrete their own idiosyncratic legislation, institutions, enforcement mechanisms and penalties. Yet is it possible for a regional competition policy to be developed with a unified enforcement mechanism if member economies have had little experience of such things? A way must be found that creates a path for a gradual awakening of ideas and progression to the frontier.

There are several keywords to keep in mind when thinking about the development of competition policy in East Asia – issues, flexibility, information sharing, cooperation, culture, learning by doing, experience, harmonisation, globalisation and review. These apply equally to the promotion of competition and consumer protection within any given economy as they do to bilateral or regional policies. However, at the present time they hardly constitute a blueprint for convergence, let alone agreement. There exists considerable diversity between economies in attitudes, laws, history and enforcement priorities. While the absence of a competition law does not automatically mean that markets will not function in a socially efficient manner, neither does the presence of such legislation guarantee optimal performance in the face of unenthusiastic governments or bureaucracies. What is needed, in the broad sense, is a facilitator for free markets – a competition co-coordinator or clearing house that can promote, simplify and harmonise regional attitudes and procedures on competition.

Competition law and its enforcement cannot be separated from their historical, social and political contexts. An all-embracing push for competition is not called for at this time – some minimum set of rules needs to be developed as a result of regional consensus, with the aim subsequently being to introduce incremental changes as the need for them is jointly recognised. It can be difficult to appreciate the long-run benefits of competition when the short-run adjustment costs are so evident, especially if international competition threatens the development of domestic infant industries. But some incentive mechanism to encourage participation and progress is desirable.

The pursuit of a unified but not unitary policy would permit the flexibility needed for a gradual convergence in goals and methods, in terms of dealing with a policy concept that is relatively new in East Asia. A regional perspective is unlikely to be forthcoming until the players' domestic experience with the promotion of competitive markets has been positive. Convergence to a broad consensus to promote some kind of workable framework to promote regional competition should be an immediate policy goal for the economies of East Asia. But it must be a real commitment, not a series of vague hopes. The potential benefits are great, for economic integration, consumer welfare and the region's economic performance.

In the long run the goal should be to achieve a comprehensive and systematic framework that offers all firms the equal opportunity to succeed in any market they may choose to enter, and most importantly, that advances consumer sovereignty. While no regional advance is likely unless national sovereignty is also respected, it cannot be denied that the economic interests of all economies are increasingly being intertwined as a result of globalisation – domestic and foreign policy instruments are beginning to take on similar appearances, both within and between economies. Thus a global competition and consumer protection policy could in time emerge through the operations of international bodies like the WTO and the World Bank.

Economies should be free to choose the competition policy they think is best – but they must be alert to, and reminded of, the regional spillovers from their choice. At the very least there should be some consistency in national laws on the worst anticompetitive practices like price fixing. It is recognised that different economies will face different problems with respect to competition policy, depending on their particular stage of development.[17] Over time, consistency in treatment of any given type of behaviour is essential, especially if a regional mega-regulator is not established. Globalising firms need to know the conditions under which they are expected to operate – and the more common the operating environment is, the greater the private and public benefits from globalisation are likely to be.

The way to start is to find leaders committed to the cause. Agreements to cooperate in planning would be useful. The collection and sharing of information on perceived common problems would be an appropriate first step. Research into common problems could be sponsored. Consideration of what controls are necessary, and whether proven methods from developed countries can be adapted, or whether a unique regional jurisprudence is called for, would be essential starting points.

An East Asian commission on competition and consumer protection could be established and jointly funded by participating nations. It could be comprised only of representatives from economies newly embracing competition and consumer protection principles, or could involve also (either actively or in an advisory capacity) those regional economies with established policies and enforcement regimes. Governments could start referring issues to it for dispassionate evaluation. Research staff could be drawn from regional members and seconded from competition agencies in neighbouring regions. From this body recommendations and reports could emerge that would inform and guide the various economies to a general consensus on regional laws and enforcement options. Such a measured, cooperative and consultative process will minimise the chances of inter-economy differences standing in the way of progress and lessen the inevitable tensions that will occur.

In the absence of a unified regional agreement, formal or otherwise, on competition and consumer protection policies, there is little hope for the emergence of an efficient, integrated regional economy, even in the presence of trade liberalisation. The adoption of domestic and regional competition laws is a necessary (but not sufficient) step for developing economies that wish to protect themselves from both domestic and international abuses of market power. East Asia is fast approaching a major crossroad. It must not turn around and head back into the past laissez-faire attitude to markets, or to reliance on large private or state-owned enterprises to run markets. Neither should it take inefficient detours, or take another road to a less desirable destination. The road ahead may look daunting and there will be hazards along the way. But with careful attention, and by driving at acceptable speed limits and in accordance with local conditions, the goal will be reached and regional welfare will be enhanced for all travellers.

The question is not whether a regional approach to competition and consumer protection will be forthcoming, but when will it be achieved, with what goals, based on what models,[18] in what philosophical and legislative form, in consultation with what stakeholders, with what focus (both in practices and sectors), with what exceptions for economies whose stage of development makes them less likely to benefit from global competition, and with what mutually agreed enforcement techniques and priorities?[19] This is not the place or time to argue detail. What is needed now is the establishment of a common understanding on general principles of aspirations, method, coverage, content, investigation, adjudication, remedy and review.[20] There should be no precipitate rush forward, as hasty law is usually bad law. Commitment and policy adjustment will take time. But the longer it takes and the less regional harmony there is, the greater will be the accumulated sum of sunk social welfare losses that could have been avoided by the diligent and timely pursuit of stringent and comprehensive competition and consumer protection policies.

In China the process of privatisation is known as 'cutting off the milk supply'. The suggestion of this chapter is that East Asian economies should now modernise milk production, and re-engineer and adapt the whole supply system, so that society gets more milk and more cream, in the form of a more richly articulated and homogenised competition and consumer protection regime.

NOTES

Thanks are owed to Bhanu Bhatia for research assistance and to Christopher Findlay and Richard Pomfret for their comments and suggestions on the ideas presented in this chapter. The author was for many years an Associate Commissioner of the Trade Practices Commission and the Australian Competition and Consumer Commission, and currently serves as a member of the Australian Competition Tribunal and the Australian Communications Authority. The views expressed in this chapter are, of course, attributable only to the author.

1   For a symposium containing several papers on international competition policy see *Antitrust Bulletin* XLIII(1), Spring 1998.
2   An interesting policy issue is whether one or the other set of laws could be expanded to regulate both types of behaviour.
3   Simple economics tells us that it is not efficient to try and eliminate each instance of market failure. It is, of course, hugely socially efficient to eliminate forever the worst abuses of market power, fraud and deception, but as society progressively gets rid of these problems, the net social benefit of one more enforcement action declines. Ultimately, in a world of positive enforcement costs and imperfect information, a regulatory optimum will be reached beyond which it is not socially worthwhile to proceed. The optimum level of enforcement

will obviously vary from time to time, from practice to practice, from market to market, and from one economy to another.
4   As an example, the emergence of Telstra in Australia from a government-owned monopoly provider of telecommunications, into a fully competitive market, has not been an easy transition, either for the government, Telstra itself, or its new rivals.
5   For a discussion of some of the problems being encountered in China and Taiwan, see Yang (2002: 167–83) and Liu and Chu (2002: 129–43).
6   Of course, there have been piecemeal competition-related provisions in many WTO agreements, including, for example, in various GATT articles mainly related to antidumping provisions and state-owned enterprises; in GATS (General Agreement on Trade in Services) articles covering monopolies and services suppliers; and in the TRIPS (Trade-Related Aspects of Intellectual Property Rights) provisions against conduct that unreasonably restrains trade or adversely affects the transfer of technology. As well, WTO Trade Policy Reviews frequently deal with issues related to competition.
7   Proof that this can be achieved between economies at quite different stages of development and with different goals may be found in the recent Euro-Mediterranean Association Agreements.
8   For details, see Musonda (2000).
9   An example is the CERTA between Australia and New Zealand, whereby extraterritorial jurisdiction is exercised without an independent supranational authority by way of each country's courts and competition agencies having overlapping jurisdiction for actions involving the misuse of market power. The agencies consult with each other when necessary. In addition, a separate bilateral enforcement agreement permits each agency to provide to the other assistance in investigations, to exchange non-confidential information, and to engage in co-ordinated enforcement.
10 See, for example, Scherer (1994).
11 Of course, there will always exist in any regulatory regime the need to consider the possibilities for, and consequences of, two types of errors. Type 1 errors involve the classification of good conduct as being bad, and Type 2 errors occur when bad conduct is found to be socially acceptable. Opinions may well differ from time to time, economy to economy, and action to action as to which error is the more serious, either in the short run or the long run.
12 Sector-specific regulation that controls conduct by way of prescription or proscription is often justified on the grounds of protecting incomes in that sector, but there may be other policy options that can achieve that goal more efficiently, and that are less damaging to the competitive process.
13 In this case the panoramic view of the wood may distract one from the sight and the health of the individual trees, but in the former case the focus on each tree and its problems can lead to a failure to appreciate what is happening in the whole forest.
14 Kay (1993) argues that a firm can develop a sustainable competitive advantage by developing distinctive capabilities in architecture, reputation, innovation and strategic assets. It is but a small step to apply this method to regulation frameworks offered by various governments.
15 Of course, regulation is not acceptable if it is aimed at protecting local markets from foreign competition, by putting globalising firms through needless bureaucratic procedures.
16 A good example of this is shown in the way the Australian Competition and Consumer Commission assesses mergers for a breach of the Trade Practices

Act 1974, which prohibits mergers that are likely to result in a substantial lessening of competition in a market. It is the practice of the ACCC not to oppose mergers, even if they will result in a duopoly, if there is evidence of sustained and sustainable levels of import competition.
17 For an interesting discussion on these issues see Kurokochi (2000: 1–6).
18 For example, some aspects of the TRIPS model or of the GATS agreement could be used as guidelines in developing progressively a multilateral or regional model for the promotion of competitive markets.
19 Agreement on these two issues may be the hardest of all to achieve, for many reasons, including a narrow internal focus, and different perceptions as to occurrence and remedy.
20 This is hardly a new agenda. The PECC Competition Principles addressed many of these issues in 1999. Yet comparatively little progress has been made in resolving these issues, and in securing cooperation in policy direction.

REFERENCES

APEC Economic Leaders' Declaration (1999) 'The Auckland challenge', Auckland, New Zealand, 13 September, available at <www.apecsec.org.sg/>.

Chen, E. and P. Lin (2002) 'Competition policy under laissez-fairism: market power and its treatment in Hong Kong', *Review of Industrial Organization* 21, September.

Epstein, J. (2002) 'The other side of harmony: can trade and competition laws work together in the international marketplace?', *American University International Law Review* 17.

Kay, John (1993) *Foundations of Corporate Success*, New York: Oxford University Press.

Kurokochi, H. (2000) 'The relationship between economic development and competition policy', *ACCC Journal* 25, February.

Liu K.C. and Y.-P. Chu (2002) 'Market power in Chinese Taipei: laws, policies and treatments', *Review of Industrial Organization* 21, September.

Musonda, J. (2000) 'Enhanced technical assistance and cooperation: priorities for the effective implementation of competition policy in Africa – the case of COMESA', paper presented to the WTO Regional Workshop on Competition Policy, Economic Development and the Multilateral Trading System, Capetown, February.

Round, David K. (2002) 'Editorial introduction. Market power in East Asia: its origins, effects and treatments', *Review of Industrial Organization* 21, September.

Scherer, F.M. (1994) *Competition Policies for an Integrated World Economy*, Washington DC: The Brookings Institution.

Schumpeter, J.A. (1942) *Capitalism, Socialism and Democracy*, New York: Harper.

Vautier, K.M. (1999) 'PECC competition principles: for guiding the development of a competition-driven policy framework for APEC economies', Singapore: PECC, available at <http://www.pecc.org/publications.htm#trade>.

WTO Ministerial Declaration (2001) Ministerial Conference, fourth session, November 14, WT/MIN(01)/DEC/W/1.

Yang, J. (2002) 'Market power in China: manifestations, effects and legislation', *Review of Industrial Organization* 21, September.

Index

Page numbers in *italics* represent tables. Page numbers in **bold** represent figures. Page numbers followed by 'n' represent endnotes.

accountability 52, 59, 237
advertising 26
Aghion, P.: and Bolton, P. 220
Air Do 166n
Air Philippines 157
airline industry 3, 145–69; airfreight shipments *149*; APEC 163–4; ASEAN 163; bilateral air services agreements (ASAs) 145; cabotage rights 146; cargo shipments 148; characteristics 147–51; Chicago Convention 165n; club approach (plurilateral) 161–2, 165; computer reservation system 145; deregulation 159; domestic deregulation (US) 147, 150; Government Procurement Agreement (GPA) 159; 'hub-and-spoke' networks 150; interlining 150; predatory pricing 149, 150; Taipei–Hong Kong route 158; US bilateral open skies initiatives 160–1; WTO Doha Round 158–60
allocative efficiency 4
Anderson, J.E.: and Young, L. 217
Anderson, R. 2
Ansett 152, 153
anticompetitive behaviour 6
anticompetitive policy: borderline 50
Antimonopoly Law: Japan 15
antitrust law 8, 9
antitrust suits (US) 25
APEC 9, 163–4, 235; competition policy *10–11*; Principles to Enhance Competition and Regulatory Reform 244, 246
Aquino, C. 89
ASEAN: Framework Agreement on Services (AFAS) 163; shipping liner industry 174–7
ASEAN5: insurance markets 3
asset-specific hold-up 222
attitudes: buyers/sellers 235; pro-business 234
Australia 44, 112, 113, 152–3, 173, 223, 245; appeal 51–2; Closer Economic Relations Trade Agreement (CERTA) 245; Competition and Consumer Commission (ACCC) 41; competition policy principles 49–52; corporatisation/privatisation utilities 45; economic objectives **47**; economic regulation 46–9; executive agencies 45; internal agency objectives 48; market structure 46; stakeholders 45; sunk costs 48; Telstra 255n; transparency 52, 59; universal service obligations (USOs) 47
Australian Competition and Consumer Commission (ACCC) 150

Bank Negara Malaysia 198, 199
Bank of Thailand 204
Beijing 28
bid rigging 63–4
bilateral relationships: regulated industry 56

Birdsall, N.: and Lawrence, R.Z. 74
Bolton, P.: and Aghion, P. 220
bottleneck facilities 60n
Bowen, J.T. Jr.: and Leinbach, T.R. 156
Branson, R. 153
Brazil 64
businesses and governments: association 236

Camacho, J. 101
Canada 112, 173
Cancun Ministerial (2004) 62, 80
cartels 21, 22, 67–8, 82n; hardcore 184n
Carty, D. 146, 166n
Cathay Pacific 148, 154
Caves, R.E.: and Uekusa, M. 39
chaebols (Korea) 35, 242
Chen, E.: and Lin, P. 233
Chen, K.Y.: and Lin, P. 33
Chile 127
China 15, 112, 151, 153–4, 218, 242; administrative monopoly 29; competition cases 29; competition policy 25–31; compulsory associations 29; Law of Public Tendering (2000) 27; Price Law (1998) 25, 27; privatisation 254; Public Tendering Law (1999) 30; regional monopoly 29; sectoral monopoly 29; State Administration for Industry and Commerce (SAIC) 27, 30; State Development and Reform Committee 31; Telecommunications Ordinance (2000) 30; trade with Japan and South Korea *163*; Trademark Law 26–7; Unfair Competition Law (1993) 25, 26–7
Colombia 247
COMESA 245
Commerce Act 1986 (New Zealand) 223, 224, 227n
competition: allocative efficiency 4; technical efficiency 4

competition agencies: advocacy function 66–7
competition authority 13
competition and consumer protection: globalisation 232; harmonised approach 232; laissez-faire 232
competition culture 234–6
competition law 3, 15–40, 73, 223; abuse of market power 16; contracts and vertical restraints 219–21; East Asia *17*; effectiveness 16–18; mergers and acquisitions 16; restrictive arrangements 16; violation 17
competition policy: functions 9; multilateral framework 76–80
Conference Pacific Area Forum on Trade and Development (2002) *xiii*, 1
consumer protection 232
contract enforceability: theory/history 215–18
contract enforcement institutions 213
contracts: competition law 3; and enforcement 214–15; forward integration strategies 221; long-term 221–3, 226; minimum retail prices 215; spot market 217; spot markets and vertical integration 218–19; vertical integration 219
cooperation: regional 231–56
courts: doctrine of payment 227n

Datuk Tajudin Ramli 156
depression cartels 21, 22
developing countries: dynamic efficiency 70–2; policy space 70–2; technology transfer 65
developing economies 63–7
Doha Declaration 13, 77, 78, 158–60, 182–3, 243
duopolies (Hong Kong) 242

Eastern Europe 64
economic regulation 41–2, *57*, *58*

Economist 21, 22
education: regulation 12; tuition fees 12
electricity industry: early reforms 86–92
electricity markets 86–110
Enronisation 52
entry barriers 234
Estoppel 228n
European Union (EU) 76, 160
Evans, L.T.: and Quigley, N.C. 3, 223
exclusionary abuse 6
exploitive abuse 6

Federal Trade Commission Act (1947) 35
Findlay, C. *et al* 2
Finks, C. *et al* 113
flexibility 53–4, 252
fraud 254n

General Agreement on Tariffs and Trade (GATT) 82n
General Agreement on Trade in Services (GATS) 2, 112, 113–14
globalisation 232, 249–51
globalising firms: regulation 251
Goddard, D. 221
government policy 7
governments and businesses: association 236
Guangdong 28

Hong Kong 15, 31–4, 112, 113, 154–5, 233, 242; Broadcasting Authority Ordinance 32; competition cases (telecommunications) *33*; government regulatory agencies 33; sector specific policy framework 31; Telecommunications Authority 32, 39n
Hong Kong Telecom CSI Ltd 33, 34
horizontal mergers: monopoly 18
Huenemann, R. 3

imperfect information 8
implementing change 42–3
India 64, 71
Indonesia 16, 34, 112, 113; Central Bank Act (1999) 197; insurance industry 196–8; Insurance Law (1992) 197; Pakjun/Pakto 196–7
industrial policy: Japan 22
industry: citric acid 67; graphite electrodes 67; seamless steel pipes 67; vitamins 67
information: asymmetry 8; imperfect 8
insurance companies: foreign controlled 188; joint ventures 188; national private 188; state-owned 188; type of business ASEAN5 *187, 188*
insurance density/penetration in US and Asia *193*
insurance industry 186–212; ASEAN5 186; commercial banks 194; competition policy 206–10; density/penetration 190, **191**, *192*; financial sector ASEAN5 *195*; foreign participation in ASEAN5 *189*; insurance regulation ASEAN5 *208, 209*; market structure/performance 187–94; solvency oversight 206
insurance markets: ASEAN5 3
insurance premium volumes in ASEAN5: life/nonlife **193**
international anticompetitive practices 67–70
international cartels 67, 68, 69
international cooperation 73–4, 129
international trading regime 14
invisible hand (Smith) 4

Japan 112, 113, 155, 173, 242; Antimonopoly Act *19*–25, 34; Antimonopoly Law 15; antitrust system changes 22–4; competition policy 19–25; competition policy evaluation 24–5; court cases JFTC (1995–2000) *24*; Deregulation

Promotion Plan (1995) 23–4; industrial policy 22; Ministry of Economy; Trade and Industry (METI) 18; Ministry of International Trade and Industry (MITI) 16; 'miracle economy' 35; Omnibus Act (1999) 37n; share ownership 21; surcharge system 24
Japan Fair Trade Commission (JFTC) 16, 20
Jenny, F. 2

Kahn, A. 147
Kamal, Y. 81n
Kapuni gas case (New Zealand) 224
keiretsu (Japan) 242
Kenya 64, 71
Korea 35, 64, 112, 113, 242; *chaebols* 35
Korean Air 158

laissez-faire 232, 233
Lawrence, R.Z.: and Birdsall, N. 74
lawyers 55
Leinbach, T.R.: and Bowen, J.T. Jr. 156
Lin, P. 2; and Chen, E. 233; and Chen, K.Y. 33, 34
litigation management 54–5

Malaysia 112, 113, 156, 198–200
market failures 5, 251
market power in industry **7**
markets 14n
Mathewson, F.: and Winter, R. 220
Mexico 64, 247
Milo, M. 3
Ministry of Economy: Trade and Industry (METI); Japan 18
Model Law on Competition (UNCTAD) 16
monopoly 5, 6, 12, 14n; horizontal mergers 18
most favoured nation (MFN) 159
Mrongowius, D.: and Pangestu, M. 130

multilateral framework: competition policy 76–80
Munich Group 76, 78
Murdoch, R. 152

national/regional cultures for competition 233–6
New Zealand 11, 42, 112, 152–3, 173, 223, 224–6, 245; Closer Economic Relations Trade Agreement (CERTA) 245
Nikomborirak, D. 3
North American Free Trade Agreement (NAFTA) 243

Okimoto, D.I. 22
open skies bloc (Northeast Asia) 162
Organisation for Economic Cooperation and Development (OECD) 57
organisational skills and culture 54–6

Pacific Area Forum on Trade and Development (PAFTAD) *xiii*, 1
Pacific Economic Development Council (PECC) 207, 235, 244, 256n
Pakistan 64, 71
Pangestu, M.: and Mrongowius, D. 130
path finding 43
peer review mechanism 75
People's Daily 31
Perez, V. 101
perfect competition 4
Philippine Daily Inquirer 102
Philippine National Oil Company (PNOC) 91
Philippines 15, 86–110, 112, 113, 156–7, 200–2; Anti-Pilferage Act (1994) 92; average rates of Asian utilities *107*; Build-Operate-Transfer Laws (1991/94) 93, 96; cross-ownership 99; Department of Energy (DOE) 89; electricity industry reform **87**; electricity

industry reforms *88–9*; electricity sector 2; electricity industry problems 96–106; Energy Regulation Board 91; Executive Order 215 (1987) 90; financial liberalisation 200; independent power producers (IPPs) 87, 95, *96*; inefficient energy distribution 101–6; insurance industry 200–2; Luzon-Visayas grid 103; Manila Electric Company (Meralco) 103; National Electrification Administration (NEA) 89; national energy generation mix *102*; National Power Corporation (NPC) 87; National Power Corporation (NPC) privatisation 97–101; Power Sector Assets and Liabilities Management Corporation (PSALM) 100; private sector participation 92–6; private utilities *104*; Republic Act 6957 (1991) 90; Republic Act (9136) 97, **98**; systems electric loss 105, *106*; transmission/distribution losses *107*
poverty alleviation 61
predatory pricing 27
predictability 53
price fixing 12, 18
principal-agent relationship 228n
privatisation 13, 97–101; China 254; telecommunications 112
problem solving 43

Qantas 150, 153, 154, 155
Quigley, N.C.: and Evans, L.T. 3, 223

Ramos, F. 92–6
regional consensus 240–2; local controls 241
regional cooperation 231–56; practical detail 242–56; regulatory agency 249
regional philosophy 238–40; flexibility 240

regional trade agreements (RTAs) 73, 243
regulated industry: bilateral relationships 56
regulation: education 12; globalising firms 251; sovereign risk 248
regulatory agency: regional cooperation 249
Round, D.K. 3, 243
Russia 151

Schumpeter, J.A. 249
sector-specific regulation 231, 255n
sector-specific supranational regulators 249
September 11 (2001) 151–2
share ownership: Japan 21
Sherman Act (US) 17, 18
shipping industry 170–85; cartels WTO 180–1; conditions on foreign liners ASEAN5 *179*; consortiums 173; corporate taxation 176; Doha Declaration 182–3; GATTs negotiations 181; liner operators *175*; Shipping Act (1916) 171; Shipping Conferences Exemption Act (1987) 171; shipping registry 177; stabilisation agreements 173; tax exemptions ASEAN5 *178*
Shogo, I. 24
Shogren, R. 2
Singapore 112, 113, 167n, 171; insurance industry 202–4; Policy-owners' Protection Fund (1987) 203
Singapore International Airlines 152
Singapore issues 1
Smith, A. 4
Soros, G. 153
South Africa 64, 71
South China Morning Post 155
South Korea 158
sovereign risk: regulation 248
Sri Lanka 64, 71
state-owned enterprises 242
structural barriers 6, 7, 234

Swiss challenge system 12
synergy 56–9

Taiwan 16, 34, 112, 113, 158–9, 242
Tanzania 64, 71
technical efficiency 4
technology transfer: developing countries 65
Telecom New Zealand vs Clear 225–6
telecommunications 2, 111–30; broadband internet services 125; fixed lines (China) 127; influence of policy on penetration rates *121*; market liberation 117, **119**; new technology 124–5; policy index 115–19, *117*, **118**, *123*; policy information by economy 131–44; privatisation 112; service quality 126–8; voice over internet protocol (VOIP) 124
Thailand 35, 112, 113, 167n, 170; Competition Commission 35; Financial Services Agreement 205; Frozen Food Association 177; insurance industry 204–6; Maritime Navigation Company (TMNC) 176
trade barriers 6
trade and competition law 237–8
trade liberalisation: supply-side response 65–6
trading regime: international 14
transparency 52, 81n
tuition fees: education 12

Uekesa, M.: and Caves, R.E. 39
Unfair Competition Law (China) 15; (Articles 5–15) 26–7
United States (US) 25, 112, 147, 150, 173; antitrust suits 25; Federal Trade Commission Act (1947) 35
Uruguay Round of GATT 147, 159

Venezuela 247
Vietnam 112, 113
Villamejor-Mendoza, M.F. 2

websites 38n
Winter, R.: and Mathewson, F. 220
World Bank 253
World Trade Organisation (WTO) 1, 61–85; Doha Round 13; Trade Related Aspects of Intellectual Property Rights (TRIPS) 255n

Yamada, A. 23
Young, L.: and Anderson, J.E. 217

Zambia 64, 71
Zhang, A. 3

For Product Safety Concerns and Information please contact our EU
representative GPSR@taylorandfrancis.com
Taylor & Francis Verlag GmbH, Kaufingerstraße 24, 80331 München, Germany

www.ingramcontent.com/pod-product-compliance
Lightning Source LLC
Chambersburg PA
CBHW060557230426
43670CB00011B/1857